EDWARDIAN SCOTLAND

By the same author:
Discovering British Postage Stamps
Discovering Picture Postcards
Scotland in Stamps
Joseph Chamberlain

and, for children,
The Jock and Jonathan Stories

EDWARDIAN SCOTLAND

C. W. HILL

SCOTTISH ACADEMIC PRESS
EDINBURGH & LONDON
1976

Published by
Scottish Academic Press Ltd.
33 Montgomery Street,
Edinburgh EH7 5JX
and distributed by
Chatto & Windus Ltd
40 William IV Street
London W.C.2

First published 1976
SBN 7011 2178 5

© 1976 C. W. Hill

Printed in Great Britain
at the Alden Press, Oxford

For

Clare Hill and Colin Shearer,

whose great-grandparents

were Edwardians

Contents

Illustrations

I

Introduction

According to the calendar the Edwardian period began on 22 January 1901, when Queen Victoria died at Osborne House in the Isle of Wight, and her eldest son, Bertie, succeeded to the throne as King Edward VII. Two other important events coincided so nearly with the accession of the new monarch that together they form a watershed in British history. They were the resignation of the Prime Minister, Lord Salisbury, on 13 July 1902 and the signature on 30 January 1902 of a treaty of alliance between Britain and Japan. Lord Salisbury's resignation marked the end of a long chapter of Conservative rule, for he had headed three administrations covering fourteen of the previous seventeen years. The Japanese alliance marked the end of the 'splendid isolation' which had been Britain's position, if not her deliberate policy, since the Crimean War had taught its expensive lessons.

But economic and social changes can seldom be so clearly dated as political events and many of the problems which beset the Edwardians had their origins in the last years of the Victorian era. The name by which the final decade of the nineteenth century is usually known, the 'Naughty Nineties', is more appropriate to the character and taste of the rakish new King than of the stern old Queen.

Again according to the calendar the Edwardian period ended on 6 May 1910, when King Edward VII died at Buckingham Palace and his eldest surviving son, Georgie, succeeded to the throne as King George V. Many of those who lived through the First World War into the troubled years before the outbreak of the Second looked back with regret and nostalgia to the Edwardian years, which seemed in retrospect to have been ordered, prosperous and sunny. But the period did not seem to them to have ended with the old King's life. For them its passing was marked by the fading of the leaves in the late summer of 1914, as Europe marched to war.

However it is reckoned, the Edwardian period was frighteningly brief. Yet it has left its imprint on British history and when one speaks of Edwardian dress, of Edwardian taste in art, music or drama, of Edwardian opulence or of Edwardian morals, distinctive images spring to mind, their characteristics clear and unmistakable. For Scotland, as for the remainder of the United Kingdom, it was a period of discontent and violence, of bitter extremes of wealth and poverty, of radical change and conservative reaction. Scotland's fortunes were so closely bound to those of England and Wales, and to a lesser extent to those of Ireland, that to ignore the English contribution would be as presbyopic as to minimise the Scottish contribution. The purpose of this book is to show something of Scotland's part in the history of Britain during the Edwardian period and to offer a glimpse of how Scots lived, worked and played in those turbulent days so near to us in time, so far by almost any other measure.

2

The Merry Monarch

On the morning after Queen Victoria's death, the new King travelled from Osborne to St. James's Palace to take the oaths of sovereignty at a Privy Council. During the ceremony he made a brief speech, beginning with a reference to the national loss in the passing of the Queen and expressing his determination 'to be a constitutional sovereign in the strictest sense of the word'. He then announced an unexpected personal decision.

'I have resolved', he said, 'to be known by the name of Edward, which has been borne by six of my ancestors. In doing so I do not undervalue the name of Albert, which I inherit from my ever-lamented great and wise father, who by universal consent is I think deservedly known by the name of Albert the Good, and I desire that his name should stand alone.'

This decision was in direct conflict with the wishes expressed by Queen Victoria in a letter to him nine years before. 'It was beloved Papa's wish as well as mine', she had written, 'that you should be called by *both* (names) when you became King, and it would be *impossible* for you to *drop* your Father's. It would be monstrous.'

The King's choice of name aroused some opposition in Scotland, where no Edward had ever reigned and what little was known of the first three English Edwards, at least, was unlikely to hallow their memory in Scottish hearts. The Scottish Patriotic Association, a Glasgow group of nationalists, protested against the King's decision and at a meeting on the field of Bannockburn in June 1901 began to collect signatures for a petition which eventually filled five large volumes and was exhibited in Glasgow Art Gallery. Even the Church of Scotland omitted the King's ordinal numeral from its loyal address and protests continued on a smaller scale for several years.

After lying in state at Osborne for ten days, the body of Queen Victoria was escorted to Portsmouth by the King in the royal yacht *Victoria and Albert* and by the German Emperor William II, a grandson

3

of the Queen, in his *Hohenzollern*. The next day, under cold grey skies, the funeral cortège passed through London on its way to Windsor, preceded by a procession of troops, blue-jackets, members of the Royal Household and aides-de-camp, and followed by the King, the German Emperor and a galaxy of lesser monarchs, princes, dukes and foreign notables. After the service in St. George's Chapel, Windsor, the body of the Queen Empress was laid in the mausoleum at Frogmore beside that of her beloved and long-lamented husband.

Mourning for the late Queen and for her eldest daughter, the Dowager German Empress, who died on 5 August, precluded a date in 1901 being chosen for the King's Coronation. Besides, there was much to be done. Only the most elderly could recall the previous Coronation, in 1838, and none of those who had played an important part in it were still alive. The late Queen's abhorrence of public ceremonies and state processions had deprived court officials and government departments of more than a rare opportunity to organise such occasions. There was the clutter of sixty years to be cleared from the royal residences, Osborne House, Windsor Castle, Buckingham Palace and Balmoral Castle. For the Victorian bric-à-brac the King substituted his own treasures, taking particular delight in ordering the removal or destruction of the various busts and plaques which had been installed in honour of the late Queen's faithful Highlander, John Brown. Finally, there were distinguished guests to be invited, British, Indian and Colonial troops to be assembled, and spectators to be accommodated. Eventually Thursday, 26 June 1902, was appointed as Coronation Day and the elaborate preparations began.

Guests, troops and spectators were already gathering in London when rumours started to circulate that the King was unwell. During a wet, cold day spent at a military tattoo at Aldershot, he was said to have 'contracted a chill'. To this ailment was next added lumbago but on 23 June, when the King travelled from Windsor to Buckingham Palace to prepare for his part in the Coronation ceremony, it was obvious that he was seriously ill. The following morning came the announcement that the Coronation was 'indefinitely postponed'. The King's medical advisers had diagnosed his illness as perityphlitis and an immediate operation being essential, this had been performed by the King's doctors in a room specially equipped in Buckingham Palace. There followed a fortnight of anxiety. In churches throughout the United Kingdom intercessionary services were held and prayers were said for the King's recovery.

The *Aberdeen Free Press* reported on 30 June that at Lerwick 'a religious service was held in the Parish Church, in which all the ministers of the town took part, the Rev. Mr. Campbell, parish minister, presiding. The Provost, Magistrates, Sheriff (in official robes), Burgh and County Councillors and a number of the inhabitants of the burgh were in attendance. . . . Hope is expressed by one and all that our beloved King may soon be restored to health, and that the interesting ceremony of the Coronation may yet be gone through'. 'It is true', added the Press Association, 'that the invalid is permitted to smoke in strict moderation and His Majesty also continues cheerful, hopeful and patient.' In fact it was untrue that His Majesty was patient, for he had argued fiercely with his harassed and nervous doctors, had ordered them on one occasion to leave his room at once, and had threatened to appear at Westminster Abbey for his Coronation on the appointed day, even if he were to drop dead during the ceremony. But the operation was a complete success. The King emerged from the chloroform to ask for the Prince of Wales, to promise a baronetcy to Sir Frederick Treves, who had performed the operation, and to make a rapid recovery, having lost during his illness two stones in weight and six inches of his forty-eight inch waistline.

After a brief convalescence on board the *Victoria and Albert* in the Solent, the King was crowned on 9 August. Although most of the distinguished foreign guests had already returned home, there was a magnificent procession through gaily decorated streets and a glittering congregation in Westminster Abbey for the service conducted by the aged Archbishop of Canterbury, Dr. Frederick Temple. During the ceremony there was a touching moment when the King, seeing that the kneeling Archbishop was too infirm to rise, leaned forward and helped him to his feet. Characteristically, the incident which the King himself found most impressive, he later confided to Sir Frederick Treves, was the graceful movement of the peeresses as they put on their coronets. 'Their white arms arching over their heads', he recalled, had seemed like 'a scene from a beautiful ballet'.

A week later the King returned to Portsmouth for a naval review and to greet the Shah of Persia, who was paying a state visit to Britain. He then resumed his cruise in the *Victoria and Albert*, this time bound for the west coast of Scotland. Among his party were the Queen, Princess Victoria, the Marquis Luis de Soveral, who was the Portuguese ambassador and a constant companion of the King, and the newly appointed Postmaster-General, Mr. Austen Chamberlain, as minister in attendance. The royal yacht left Cowes on 22 August, escort being provided by the cruiser *Crescent* and the torpedo-boat destroyers *Gipsy* and *Lively*. Calls were made at Weymouth, Milford Haven, Pembroke Dock and Ramsey, Isle of Man, where members of the royal party were entertained by the celebrated Manx novelist, Hall Caine. As the *Victoria and Albert* neared the Scottish coast, Austen Chamberlain was interested to hear the King instruct Meidinger, his Austrian valet, to lay out 'un costume un peu plus écossais' for the following day. Another call was made in Arran, where the King and Queen were the guests of the Duchess of Hamilton at Dougrie Lodge, and on the evening of 29 August the yacht anchored in the bay of Onich, in Loch Leven, so that a deer drive could be arranged for the party at Ballachulish. Another friend on whom the King called was Lord Knutsford, who was staying with his family at Torloisk, in Mull. The yacht left Loch Linnhe at dawn on 1 September and anchored that night in Uig Bay, in the north of Skye. 'Nothing could be simpler or less formal than life on board or our parties ashore', commented Austen Chamberlain in his diary. 'The King and Queen are both in excellent health and spirits, thoroughly enjoying themselves, I think, and making the trip as pleasant as possible for other people. In short, it is a very pleasant, very jolly party on a particularly fine and comfortable yacht.'

The next port of call was Stornoway, which had never before been visited by a British monarch, and the yacht then passed through the Pentland Firth to anchor off the Castle to Dunrobin, the seat of the Duke and Duchess of Sutherland. Here the King and his party spent three days, their entertainment including deer-stalking near Loch Brora, a drive to Skibo Castle, near Dornoch, to call on the Scottish-American steel and railway magnate, Andrew Carnegie, and aquatic sports off Dunrobin pier. 'The King apparently enjoyed the proceedings', reported the *Northern Scot*, 'smoking his cigar, chatting with the competitors and laughing heartily at the ludicrous incidents associated with the natatorial display. In the race for boys under thirteen one of the youthful competitors, apparently nervous at the unparalleled prospect of swimming with the King as spectator, could not be prevailed to take the plunge with the others. His Majesty, however, smilingly reassured the affrighted laddie, patted him on the head and by transferring a coin from his pocket to the little fellow's hand changed tears to smiles.'

On Monday morning, 8 September, the *Victoria and Albert* sailed from Golspie Bay for Invergordon, where the King and his party landed to join the royal train. They passed through Dingwall at ten miles an hour but although the station was densely packed with townsfolk, even the school-children on the platform were too excited to raise a cheer. Outside Millburn Station, Inverness, there was a change of engines for the train, so the King was loudly cheered by the waiting crowd. Another change of engines at Elgin gave the opportunity for an official greeting from the provost and councillors. At Buckie the children from the Public School and the Lady Gordon Cathcart School, wearing their Coronation medals and waving their flags, lined the railway fence on McLaren's Brae and were rewarded by a glimpse of the King and Queen in the fifth coach as the train slowed a little to pass through the station. The route then lay through Cullen, Portsoy and so to Aberdeen and Ballater, where the party left the train to complete their journey to Balmoral by road.

On 11 September the King visited the Braemar Gathering, which had been suspended for two years because of the Boer War and the death of Queen Victoria. The royal carriages arrived shortly before four in the afternoon, driving through a double line of Farquharson, Duff, Deeside and Balmoral Highlanders, the last headed by William Campbell, the King's Piper. With the King, in Royal Stewart tartan, were the Prince of Wales and his two elder sons, Edward and Albert, later to reign as Edward VIII and George VI. Queen Alexandra, an enthusiastic amateur photographer, took snapshots of some of the participants in the various competitions, among them piping, tossing the caber, sprinting and dancing, before the King and Queen departed at about half-past four. One notable visitor to Balmoral during the King's holiday was General Lord Kitchener, who had returned from South Africa in mid-July and was to leave before the end of the year for his new appointment as Commander-in-Chief in India. An unusual compliment was paid to the General when he stepped from the train at Ballater to find the King's guard of honour turned out to receive him. For the rest, the King enjoyed what was for him some strenuous walking and riding, picnics and deer drives. His Scottish holiday ended with two days as the guest of Prince and Princess Edward of Saxe-Weimar at North Berwick. While there he called on the Prime Minister, Arthur J. Balfour, at Whittinghame and then took tea with the Earl of Haddington at Tyninghame, where he planted a memorial oak, 'shovelling in the earth with a full-size silver spade in a workmanlike manner', reported the *Illustrated London News*, and expressing 'hearty good wishes for the tree's growth'. The King performed a like task in the Market Square of North Berwick, in the presence of Provost Macintyre and the town council, before leaving on 11 October by train for King's Cross.

This Scottish holiday epitomised the King's character and his way of life. He was a restless spirit, always in need of entertainment, an extrovert delighting in the company of pretty, vivacious women and quickly bored by academic or intellectual pursuits. He was jovial and courteous in public, though he could be irritable and ill-mannered in private, and he entered the business of kingship with obvious gusto, helped by his prodigious energy, his abiding interest in people and his unashamed enjoyment of the privileges of his position. In matters of etiquette, court precedence and dress, and the minutiae of public ceremonial, the King was fastidious; in political and constitutional matters he was careful and correct; in morals he was markedly less so. The King's year normally began with the state opening of Parliament towards the end of January. He then went to Biarritz for a week or two, breaking both the outward and the homeward journey in Paris. Every spring there was a cruise in the royal yacht, usually in the Mediterranean, and sometimes a visit to the Queen's family in Copenhagen. The King invariably attended the race meetings at Ascot, Epsom and Goodwood during June and July. After the racing season there was yachting at Cowes and then a visit to Marienbad for the cure, with again a day or two in Paris to enliven the journey. In the autumn the King spent a few weeks at Balmoral before returning to Sandringham for Christmas, when his birthday, 9 November, and that of the Queen, 1 December, were also celebrated. In the intervals of this crowded routine he found time to visit the country houses of at least a dozen friends, as well as to perform countless such minor functions as laying foundation stones, opening or inaugurating public works, holding levées, entertaining foreign celebrities, reviewing regiments and going to the theatre.

Of outdoor sports, the King's favourites were shooting and racing. He lacked the placid temperament to make a successful angler and he was too obese and bronchitic to enjoy golf. The King's racing colours were 'purple, gold braid, scarlet sleeves, black velvet cap with gold fringe'. He had begun his career as an owner in 1878 in partnership with Lord Marcus Beresford, an officer in the 7th Hussars. One of his early horses was *The Scot*, by the famous Derby winner *Blair Athol* out of *Columba*. *The Scot* was sent to Baden-Baden in 1883 for the great steeplechase there, but finished third to *Lady of the Lake*. The following year *The Scot* ran in the Grand National but fell after Becher's Brook and lost to *Voluptuary*, which had at one time belonged to Lord Rosebery. The King's only classic steeplechase victory was in 1900, when his *Ambush II* won the Grand National. The horse came near to another victory in the same race in 1903 but fell at the last fence while in a clear lead. *Ambush II* ran again in the 1904 Grand National but shortly before the 1905 race broke a blood vessel while training and died instantaneously.

The King was more successful in flat racing. Although he lost his first match, when his *Alep* was beaten at Newmarket in 1877 by Lord Strathnairn's *Avowal*, he went on to achieve some notable successes. In 1896 his *Persimmon* won the Derby and the St. Leger, and in 1900 his *Diamond Jubilee* won the five classic races, the Newmarket Stakes, the Derby, the Two Thousand Guineas, the Eclipse Stakes and the St. Leger, whose prize money totalled £27,985. Another classic victory came in the last racing season of the King's life, when his *Minoru* won the 1909 Derby. His enthusiasm for racing was vividly illustrated only a few hours before his death. His *Witch of the Air* was running in the Spring Two-Year-Old Plate at Kempton Park on 6 May 1910, and in an exciting finish which delighted the crowd the filly won by half a length. When the Prince of Wales gave the news to his father, then gravely ill in Buckingham Palace, the King's reply was: 'Yes, I have heard of it. I am very glad.'

By the time he was fifty, the King had given up fox-hunting and deer-stalking, and turned to the less strenuous sports of shooting and deer-driving. His estate at Sandringham was well stocked with partridge, pheasant and wild duck, while woodcock, grouse, hares and rabbits were available in smaller numbers. Windsor Park also provided excellent sport and the bags were characteristically opulent. On three days in November 1909 the King, the Prince of Wales, the King of Portugal, the Duke of Connaught and Prince Arthur of Connaught were able to account for 2,555 pheasants. On four days in January 1910 the same five guns accounted for 3,534 pheasants, 466 wild duck and a few partridges and rabbits. Impressive as these figures may seem, they are modest in comparison with the tally of creatures once shot by the Hon. Harry Stonor, one of the King's favourite shooting companions. During a four-week visit to the estate of a Hungarian nobleman in 1894, Stonor and five or six other sportsmen recorded a bag which included 22,996 partridges, 2,912 pheasants and 11,346 hares. Even in the teeming coverts of Windsor and Sandringham such slaughter would have been remarkable.

In Scotland the King's education as a sportsman had begun at the age of seven when, recorded Queen Victoria on 18 September 1848, she, the Prince Consort and young Bertie set off from Balmoral House in a post-chaise and drove 'beyond the house of Mr. Farquharson's keeper in the Balloch Buie'. They then mounted ponies and, accompanied by gillies, eventually turned along a glen immediately below Craig Daign, where they dismounted and 'scrambled up an almost perpendicular place to where was a little box made of hurdles and interwoven with branches of fir and heather, about five feet in height'. Here the Queen sat and sketched a landscape while Albert drew a portrait of one of the gillies, Macdonald, and Bertie waited beside them. Almost an hour later Macdonald reported that he could see stags approaching. As they came within range, Albert fired at one. 'He ran up to the keepers', wrote the Queen, 'and at that moment they called from below that they had got him, and Albert ran on to see. I waited for a bit, but soon scrambled on with Bertie and Macdonald's help. Albert joined me directly, and we all went down and saw a magnificent stag, a Royal, which had dropped soon after Albert had hit him.' The exhilaration of that day must have stayed long in Bertie's memory, for he remained until the end of his life a devotee of deer-stalking and driving.

The queen had laid the foundation stone of Balmoral Castle, which was to replace the old Balmoral House, at a ceremony on 28 September 1853, and when she arrived for her autumn holiday in 1856 the new building was complete. She later took a long lease of Abergeldie Castle, an old Gordon stronghold on the south bank of the Dee, about two miles east of Crathie. The first royal tenant was the Queen's mother, the Duchess of Kent, but after her death in 1861 the Prince of Wales used the castle for his autumn shooting parties. He shot his first stag as a youth of seventeen in September 1858 on Conachcraig, in Glen Gelder, and eight years later killed seven stags in a single day's stalking on Craig-na-gall and in the corrie of Baultchach. When stalking became too strenuous for him, he took to driving in the wooded foot-hills and on 10 September 1902 killed six stags during a drive in Balmoral forest.

With forty thousand acres of deer forest, a dozen miles of salmon-fishing in the Dee, and one of the finest grouse moors in Scotland, the King had ample opportunity for Scottish sport but he preferred the less demanding grouse-drives and covert shooting of driven pheasants at Sandringham and Windsor, and at other English estates where he was a regular guest. Among these were Hall Barn, the Buckinghamshire home of Lord Burnham, owner of the *Daily Telegraph*; Castle Rising, Norfolk, the home of Lord Farquhar, Master of the King's Household until 1907; and Chatsworth House, Derbyshire, the seat of the Duke of Devonshire. In Scotland the King liked particularly to shoot grouse with Arthur Sassoon at Tulchan Lodge, Advie, near Grantown-on-Spey. While staying there he would motor to call on the Duke of Richmond at Gordon Castle, Fochabers, and to visit Cawdor Castle, Cullen House and Castle Grant. He enjoyed shooting, too, at Invercauld, the Aberdeenshire estate of Sigismund Neumann, a London merchant banker who also owned a large estate at Raynham, near Sandringham. There, while spending the 1910 New Year holiday at Sandringham, the King and other guns accounted for over a thousand pheasants and almost as many wild duck in a single day's sport.

As indoor pastimes the King preferred eating, playing cards, lively conversation and the pursuit of attractive women. His excessive smoking, a daily average of twenty cigarettes and a dozen large cigars, aggravated his chronic bronchitis but he drank only in comparative moderation and it was to the consumption of massive quantities of rich and elaborately prepared food that he devoted much of his time. At home he habitually ate six lavish meals each day. They began with a hearty breakfast of haddock, poached eggs, bacon, sausages and kidneys, chicken and woodcock. At eleven there was a substantial cold snack which might include a lobster salad and cold game or chicken. Luncheon was a meal of eight or ten courses, more if there were important guests. Among the King's favourite dishes were game of all kinds, duck, chicken, York ham, chops and steaks, though he would often add a plate of homely roast beef and Yorkshire pudding as a relief from richer fare. Tea was a cold meal with a vast array of scones, crumpets, muffins, tarts, cakes and gateaux, the royal chefs vying with one another to concoct fancy pastries which would please the King's palate. Dinner was the most elaborate meal of the day, stretching to twelve or fourteen courses. Game again figured largely in the menu, one favourite dish consisting of a pheasant or partridge stuffed with snipe or woodcock, the latter being stuffed with truffles and the dish then garnished with a rich sauce. When the King's long day ended and he retired to his suite to read state papers, write letters and smoke his last cigars, a cold tray of cutlets, ham and tongue or quails would ensure that the pangs of hunger did not assail him before breakfast.

The King's gluttony, which the slim, abstemious Queen Alexandra found remarkable and repulsive, was typical of the upper class opulence of his time. A large part of the day in the servants' quarters of a wealthy household was occupied with the preparation and serving of meals. Although Isabella Beeton had died in childbirth in 1865, her *Book of Household Management*, popularly known as *Mrs. Beeton's Cookery Book*, was still the bible of the Edwardian home. It contained, according to its sub-title: 'Information for the mistress, housekeeper, cook, kitchen-maid, butler, footman, coachman, valet, upper- and under-housemaids, lady's maid, maid-of-all-work, laundry maid, monthly, wet, and sick nurses, etc., etc., also sanitary, medical and legal memoranda; with a history of the origin, properties, and uses of all things connected with home life and comfort.' The 1906 edition included a suggested menu for a 'simple summer breakfast'. With tea or coffee and cream or milk, the menu offered 'wholemeal porridge, ham omelet, poached eggs on toast, fried cod, grilled ham, potted game, stewed prunes and cream, scones, rolls, toast and bread, with butter and marmalade or jam'. The portly King, wheezing his way through his customary twelve-course dinner, would certainly have endorsed Mrs. Beeton's maxim, 'Dine we must, and we may as well dine elegantly as well as wholesomely'.

The King's love of playing cards had led to his involvement, while Prince of Wales, in a serious scandal which had a Scottish officer, Sir William Gordon-Cumming, of the Scots Guards, at its centre. During Doncaster race week in early September 1890, the Prince of Wales and Sir William were members of a house-party staying with Arthur Wilson, a wealthy Hull ship-owner, at his Yorkshire home, Tranby Croft. The Prince was at that time passionately fond of baccarat, an illegal game in Britain if played for money stakes, and he had his own counters, marked with the Prince of Wales's feathers and face-values of up to £10. After dinner on the first evening, the guests settled to play baccarat for what were later said to have been modest stakes, a comparative term since Sir William Gordon-Cumming was able to win £20 at one coup. The game had not long been in progress when the host's son, Arthur S. Wilson, noticed that Sir William appeared to be cheating. Instead of making his stake before the cards were dealt, he was concealing counters in the palm of his hand so that he could either stake them or withhold them when he had seen how the cards fell.

After the game young Wilson described what he had seen to his mother, his sister and her husband, and to another guest, Berkeley Levett, who was a subaltern in Sir William's regiment. They agreed to watch Sir William closely when baccarat was played again the following evening. Although Berkeley Levett's nerve failed and he shrank from the possibility of a confrontation with his senior officer, the other four were convinced as they watched Sir William that he was cheating again. The following day three more guests were told of Sir William's conduct and eventually the Prince of Wales was informed. On the advice of two of the older guests, General Owen Williams and the Earl of Coventry, the Prince interviewed Sir William and insisted that he should sign a declaration pledging that, in return for the signed promise of the other guests to preserve silence on the matter, he would never again play cards as long as he lived. Under protest Sir William put his signature to what was tantamount to a confession of guilt, the Prince filed the paper in his archives, and the Wilsons' house-party broke up in disarray. Within a few months, however, the secret was leaking and London society was buzzing with rumours of dark deeds at Tranby Croft. After receiving an anonymous letter warning him that the secret had become common knowledge, Sir William took the only course which offered any hope of clearing his name: he brought a suit for slander against the five people who had first accused him of cheating.

The Prince of Wales and his advisers immediately began frantic efforts to forestall a public court case which would break the Prince's prudent rule of never allowing dirty linen to be washed in the Press. They urged the Adjutant-General to hold a military court of inquiry in private. When this scheme failed, they asked the Guards' Club, of which Sir William had been a member, to institute a private investigation into the matter. Both the Adjutant-General and the Guards' Club having refused to be bullied into furtive accommodations to save the Prince from unfavourable publicity, the case opened on 1 June 1891 before the Lord Chief Justice. The Prince was subpoenaed as a witness and attended court for the greater part of the trial. He had little confidence in the jury, which was, he wrote to his sister, the Dowager German Empress, 'composed of a peculiar class of society and do not shine in intelligence or refinement of feeling'. In the event, the jury endorsed the Prince's verdict on Sir William Gordon-Cumming's conduct. After an absence of less than a quarter of an hour they found for the five defendants.

Dismissed from the Army, expelled from his clubs and apparently disgraced for ever, Sir William returned to his 38,000-acre estate at Altyre, near Forres, to be received by the Provost of Forres with an official address of welcome, by the town band and by cordial greetings for his American bride, Florence Garner, who had defied her family to marry him in earnest of her belief in his innocence.

It was for the Prince of Wales that the severest strictures were reserved. Queen Victoria expressed her fear that his habits were endangering the monarchy, and the German Kaiser was appalled at the impropriety of an honorary colonel in the Prussian Hussars becoming embroiled in a squalid gambling quarrel with men young enough to be his sons. Nonconformists all over the country held meetings to denounce the Prince's way of life and *The Times* wished that he would follow the example of Sir William Gordon-Cumming and pledge himself never to play cards again. William T. Stead, editor of the influential monthly *Review of Reviews*, calculated that since the Prince's birth no fewer than 880,000,000 prayers had been offered for him in British churches, obviously with little effect, and in the House of Commons the breach of No. 41 of *Queen's Regulations*, enjoining that cases of dishonourable conduct on the part of an officer must be reported to the commanding officer of his regiment, brought an admission from the Secretary for War that Field Marshal the Prince of Wales had been guilty of 'an error of judgement'.

The Prince claimed, in a letter to the Archbishop of Canterbury on 13 August 1891, that he had 'a horror of gambling' and considered it, 'like intemperance', to be 'one of the greatest curses which a country can be afflicted with'. But despite these pious sentiments his mode of behaviour changed little, except that by the time he became King he found bridge a more interesting and enjoyable game than baccarat. Among the friends with whom he liked to play was the German-born Duchess of Devonshire, who had two nicknames, 'Double Duchess' because she had previously been the wife of the Duke of Manchester, and 'Ponte Vecchio' because of her age and her fondness for bridge. Another, much younger and more beautiful bridge partner was the Hon. Mrs. George Keppel. She was playing with the King one evening when he put her into an impossible no-trump contract. A succession of poor hands had not improved his temper and Mrs. Keppel was dismayed to see, when he laid down his cards as dummy, that there was hardly a trick among them. Equal to the occasion, she remarked dolefully: 'All I can say, Sire, is—God Save the King and preserve Mrs. Keppel!'

Alice Keppel was the last in the long line of women with whom the King had formed liaisons. The first of whom there is record was a young actress named Nellie Clifden, whom he met a few months before his twentieth birthday, when he was temporarily attached to the Grenadier Guards for training at the Curragh Camp. Some of his brother officers introduced the girl into the Prince's quarters but she proved indiscreet and rumours of the affair soon reached the London clubs and eventually the ears of the Queen and the Prince Consort. They were horrified and heart-broken. The Prince Consort made a special journey to Cambridge to reproach his wayward son but they parted amicably, the Prince of Wales dutifully contrite and his father generously forgiving. A few days later, by an unfortunate coincidence, the Prince Consort developed typhoid and within a fortnight he was dead. Shocked and emotional in her grief, Queen Victoria laid the blame for the loss of her beloved Albert firmly on the shoulders of the Prince of Wales. In reply to an appeal on his behalf from her eldest daughter's husband, the Crown Prince of Prussia, she wrote to her daughter: 'Tell him that Bertie (oh, that Boy—much as I pity, I never can or shall look at him without a shudder, as you may imagine) does not know that I know all—Beloved Papa told him that I could not be told all the disgusting details—that I try to employ and use him, but I am not hopeful.'

The Queen's anxiety was justified. Despite the Prince's marriage on 10 March 1863 to the charming, poor and virtuous Danish Princess Alexandra, the popular London journals were frequently able to publish scurrilous accounts of his amours, not all of them with respectable ladies of noble birth. His conduct displeased others besides the Queen and he was snubbed by the Earl of Rosebery, certainly no prude, when he suggested that he and his brother, the Duke of Edinburgh, should be allowed to use the Earl's London house to entertain what were euphemistically termed 'actress friends'. Lord Rosebery replied curtly that his house was too small for such a purpose and he hoped that the request would not be repeated.

In 1870, when the Prince already had five children by his wife, he was involved in an unsavoury divorce case. One of his childhood

Scottish friends, Harriet Moncrieffe, whose family owned an estate near Balmoral, was married to a wealthy young baronet, Sir Charles Mordaunt. They were ill-suited, for Harriet was pretty, vivacious and promiscuous while her husband was staid, possessive and jealous. After two miscarriages Lady Harriet gave birth prematurely to a baby girl who appeared to be blind. In distress at this misfortune, she confessed to her husband that she had committed adultery 'often and in open day' with several of her friends, among them the Prince of Wales. Sir Charles sued for divorce, citing Lord Cole and Sir Frederick Johnstone as co-respondents, but Lady Harriet's father, Sir Thomas Moncrieffe, filed a counter-petition declaring that she was insane. The case was heard in February 1870 and the Prince was subpoenaed to give evidence of his association with Lady Harriet. He denied that there had been any 'improper familiarity or criminal act' between them, though there was evidence from servants that his frequent visits to her, weekly during 1868, had been prudently made while her husband was out, that he had usually stayed for an hour or two, and that instead of his private carriage he had used an anonymous hansom cab. After complicated and contradictory evidence, Sir Charles Mordaunt's petition for divorce was dismissed on the ground of his wife's insanity and it was five years before he was successful, at a second attempt, naming Lord Cole as co-respondent. For the Prince of Wales there were unpleasant repercussions in the form of admonitory letters from the Lord Chancellor and the Prime Minister, Gladstone, and hisses from crowds when he visited the Crystal Palace and went to a theatre, while *The Times* urged him to model his conduct more closely on that of his father.

Another of the many ladies to whom the Prince temporarily lost his heart was Lillie Langtry, the daughter of the Dean of Jersey. She was twenty-three and already married to a plump and lugubrious widower when she met the Prince of Wales in 1877. Princess Alexandra accepted her as the Prince's mistress and every hostess entertaining him to dinner or for week-ends in the country took care that 'the Jersey Lily' was also invited. When she gave birth to a daughter, there was considerable speculation over the identity of the father and she later described how the Prince light-heartedly tossed a sovereign to decide whether he himself or his nephew, Prince Louis of Battenberg, was responsible. Golden-haired, pale-skinned and shapely, with heavy, sensual features, Lillie Langtry was one of the first of the 'professional beauties' whose photographs were sold as picture postcards in almost every stationer's in the kingdom. Her nickname was popularised in a portrait painted by Sir John Millais in which she was holding a Channel Islands lily, *Nerine sarniensis*. It was by posing for Millais and other leading artists that Lillie Langtry came to the notice of Prince Leopold, Queen Victoria's youngest son, and then of the Prince of Wales. She seems to have been the only one of the royal mistresses to express any warm feelings for Scotland. Her first visit was to Glen Tanar Lodge, in Aberdeenshire, as the guest of Sir William Cunliffe-Brooks, whose daughter Amy was the wife of the Marquis of Huntly.

There was a large house-party, the men, as Lillie Langtry recorded in her autobiography *The Days I Knew*, 'eager for the massacre of grouse and the stalking of deer. They, no doubt, enjoyed themselves hugely killing things, but there is nothing much for women to do, unless they also shoulder a weapon.' Finding time hang heavy on her hands on wet days, Lillie Langtry invented a game for the ladies to play—tobogganning on large tea-trays from top to bottom of the stairs. Cunliffe-Brooks prudently ordered his butler to lock up all the silver trays until his guests had departed.

Evenings, however, were ample compensation for dull days. There was dancing in the ball-room, with schottisches, Highland reels and a solo sword-dance usually performed by the Marquis of Huntly or one of his brothers, Esmé Gordon and Granville Gordon, of the Scots Guards. Lillie Langtry was much impressed by the three brothers, commenting enthusiastically: 'Oh, but they were handsome in their Highland garb, and a man has to be handsome to wear it! And the Gordons knew how! Their tartan is a beautifully blended one of green and blue which, of course, is only worn as full dress with the black velvet jacket, bejewelled sporran, black pumps with immense cairngorm buckles, tartan stockings, and with jewelled dirks and brooches galore. Truly, these three tall, handsome, blue-eyed Northmen were reminiscent of more romantic times.'

Among the guests at Glen Tanar were General Lord Strathnairn and one of Queen Victoria's Scottish ladies-in-waiting, Lady Erroll, so members of the party drove one afternoon to Balmoral to enter their names in the Queen's visiting-book. Lillie Langtry was not impressed by the appearance of Balmoral Castle, thinking it bleak and uninteresting and much preferring the Aboyne of the handsome Gordons. After her stay at Glen Tanar, Lillie Langtry paid visits to other friends in places as far north as Inverness and then joined Sir Allen Young, the Arctic explorer, for a cruise in his yacht. They passed through the Caledonian Canal, which Lillie thought chiefly remarkable for the large number of beautiful country houses which lined its banks, rounded 'the dreadfull Mull of Cantyre', and entered Loch Fyne to steam 'through the Kyles of Bute, studded with lovely villas, and up the picturesque Clyde to smoky, historic Glasgow'.

At the suggestion of the Prince of Wales, Lillie Langtry became an actress and after the death of her first husband in a Chester asylum, she married Sir Hugo de Bathe, a Devonshire baronet eighteen years her junior. One of her first successful theatrical ventures was a tour of ten British cities in the role of Rosalind in *As You Like It*. 'A week of hectic excitement at Edinburgh', she recorded, 'culminated on "Student's Night", when the University attended en masse, and objected to any portion of the play proceeding without my personal assistance on the stage, whether I had anything to say or not, raising clamorous shouts for my immediate return while I was temporarily absent.' A torchlight procession of students escorted Lillie's carriage to the Caledonian Station when she left for an equally successful week in Glasgow, in the course of which she was painted as a Bacchante by John Lavery. Although her interpretation of Rosalind smacked more than a little of sentimental whimsicality, the sight of Lillie's slender legs in stockings cross-gartered like Malvolio's and daringly displayed in a fur-trimmed tunic reaching only to mid-thigh certainly evoked the admiration of Edwardian undergraduates. Lillie Langtry remained the Prince's mistress for only about five years but he retained his affection for her and in December 1902 took Queen Alexandra and his son, the Prince of Wales, to see her in a play at the Imperial Theatre, where he welcomed her to the royal box to offer his best wishes for a forthcoming American tour.

Lillie Langtry's successor in the Prince's affections was Lady Brooke, later Countess of Warwick. She was twenty when she joined the cricle of friends known, from the Prince's London home, as the 'Marlborough House set', and she frequently accompanied him on lively jaunts to Paris. She, too, was strikingly beautiful, with small, fine features and a full bosom, and she was a popular subject for picture postcard photographs. The Prince's affection for her began to cool when she became a Socialist as a result of a conversation with Robert Blatchford, the editor of a left-wing journal, *The Clarion*, in which he had attacked the extravagance of a fancy dress ball she had held at Warwick Castle. Stung by Blatchford's criticism, she called on him at his tiny London office, argued with him and was converted to his views.

A year or two later the Prince met Alice Keppel, the wife of the Hon. George Keppel, an officer in the Gordon Highlanders and younger son of the Earl of Albermarle. Intelligent and witty as well as beautiful and vivacious, Mrs. Keppel remained the King's constant companion throughout his reign. She habitually spent Easter each year with him in Biarritz and was a frequent guest at Windsor and Sandringham, and at country houses where he stayed. She was one of the last of his friends to take leave of him as he lay dying in Buckingham Palace on 6 May 1910.

It is not easy to assess the Scottish view of the King's character and conduct. As in all things, the judgement varied according to the criteria upon which it was based. At one level the King was seen to be a paternal, jovial, energetic monarch whose patriotism, respect for the constitution and zest for living seemed wholly commendable. At another level he seemed to be a gluttonous and lecherous old man of limited intelligence, self-indulgent, pompous and irritable. Between these two extremes lay the general opinion that he was an industrious and affable ruler who, despite occasional falls from grace, had revitalised the institution of monarchy and fitted it for its role in the government of a world-wide Empire and Commonwealth at the beginning of a restless new century. There were plenty of traditionalists in Scotland who looked back with nostalgia to the old Queen's sombre and strait-laced regime yet who regarded with kindlier eyes the faults and foibles of the man called by birth to be King than they would regard similar failings in a footman or a farm-servant.

3

Fine Feathers

When Lillie Langtry was making her debut in London society, Lord Randolph Churchill met her at a friend's house. 'I dined with Lord Wharncliffe last night', he wrote to his wife, who was in Ireland, 'and took in to dinner a Mrs. Langtry, a most beautiful creature—quite unknown, very poor, and they say has but one black dress.' The black dress also has a niche in Lillie Langtry's own memoirs. 'Through all this procession of opera, dinners and balls', she confessed in *The Days I Knew*, 'I wore, extraordinary as it may sound to members of my sex, my one black evening gown, the creation of ,Madame Nicolle, the fashionable dressmaker of St. Helier, Jersey; still, the meagreness of my wardrobe did not seem to be noticed by others, and it was not even realised by me. The gown, needless to say, had grown considerably the worse for wear as the season wore on, and my maid, I am sure, disapproved of it heartily. It had its end like all things earthly.'

Black had become a fashionable colour because Queen Victoria wore little else after the death of the Prince Consort in 1861. But by the 1890s the Queen and her entourage were considered hopelessly old-fashioned in dress as in so much else. The ladies of the Marlborough House set, the wives of the Prince of Wales's wealthy Jewish friends, the *nouveaux riches* and the professional beauties were fond of bright, sometimes garish and discordant colours, many of them reds, blues and purples made from the aniline dyes which had been developed by a young English chemist, William Perkin, with the encouragement of the famous Scottish firm of dyers, Pullars of Perth. As well as bright colours, a characteristic of women's dress during the first years of the Edwardian period was its lavish adornment. Lace was particularly popular not only to decorate the corsage, collar and cuffs but also as trimming for sleeves and skirt.

'Simplicity in sleeves is a thing of the past', announced the *Northern Scot* in its 'Our Ladies' Column' on 16 January 1904. 'It's the sleeve this year that stamps the gown a new creation or a last year's model. . . . They must widen below the elbow, whether in a bag-like puff or a long, flowing drapery. They must be trimmed but in no set way. . . . Elaboration, too, must be the keynote of their fashioning. Frills and furbelows distinguish more than half the new sleeves. A fashionable sleeve for a cloth gown is entirely a mass of lace frills from wrist to near elbow, the frills widening as they go up the arm. At the head of the lace frills is a narrow turn-back cuff of velvet, trimmed with appliqués of lace.' Eight years later, on 10 February 1912, the same column was still asserting that 'beautiful laces, in many cases metallic, are used upon some of the sumptuous evening wraps and coats of the moment, and daring effects are produced with velvet and peltry'.

Although lace or its cheap substitute, Irish crochet-work, remained popular throughout the period, the general outline of women's clothes and indeed, to the superficial eye, the shape of women's bodies underwent several metamorphoses. The fondness of the King for mature women of ample figure encouraged an emphasis on bust and hips. This was achieved by corsets which held the body rigidly straight in front while throwing the bosom forward and tilting the pelvis to form the fashionable S-shaped stance. The waist was held firm in the corset and its slenderness was enhanced by a bell-shaped skirt flaring out and reaching to the ground. From the blouse, usually of silk, satin, chiffon or crêpe de Chine, cascaded frill upon frill of lace, each overlapping the one below and reaching to the waist.

Towards the end of the King's reign the S-line fell out of favour and the exaggeration of bust, waist and hips gave way to a slimmer silhouette emphasised by perpendicular lines and narrow skirts. Beneath these was a longer corset exemplified in the 1912 advertisement of an Elgin draper offering 'Warner's Rust Proof Corset, style 536, for average, well-developed figures. An original model that gives extraordinary length over the side hips but not in the front. The back is very long but the last three inches are unboned. Long waist, very low bust, white courtille, same in white batiste, price 8s. 11d.'.

Hats, which during the 1880s and 1890s had been small and neat, became larger, with elaborate decorations of feathers and artificial flowers. 'A prophecy which is very welcome', said the *Northern Scot* on 17 February 1912, 'is that of the return of the flower-trimmed hat this spring. Feathers, wings, plumes and "fantasies' of all kinds have reigned for so long that there is no doubt a warm welcome will be accorded to the large picture hat covered with spring flowers. Hats made of taffetta promise to be very much in evidence and these will be decorated with swathings of the same material or with tiny wreaths of flowers.'

Finally, as the Edwardian period was ending, another radical change brought absurdly narrow skirts to hobble the fashionable woman. Sometimes she had to wear, just below the knees, a pair of garters linked together by a short strip of braid so that she could not absent-mindedly take a long stride and split her skirt. A daring innovation, seen only seldom even in the stylish streets of large towns, was the tight skirt gathered or looped in folds to the knee, exposing a pair of harem trousers reaching to the ankles. Considered almost as daring, but eventually accepted by younger women, was the blouse with a V-neck, ineffably modest by modern standards but outrageous to eyes used to seeing women's outdoor coats and dresses buttoned or collared to the chin.

Younger women, especially those who were playing golf, croquet or tennis, or who went boating, cycling or motoring, favoured simpler, tailor-made suits with long, full skirts, a small waist-band and a short jacket. Corsets were adapted to fit the young Edwardian. 'The new Golfing and Sports Model' offered in 1912 by another Elgin draper was 'especially designed for those leading an athletic life, giving ample support together with perfect freedom of movement. Four hose supports. Price 8s. 11d.' Since lace would have been unsuitable on a sporting costume and since some decoration was considered essential, popular choice fell upon braid trimmings and buttons. The fashions introduced for sports wear were adopted by older women for more conventional occasions. 'There is a decided touch of the picturesque in the fashionable coat and skirt of today', recorded the *Northern Scot* on 6 January 1912. 'The severely plain costume, free of all decoration, is now reserved for country wear, and smart models plentifully braided and buttoned are preferred for all ordinary occasions. Quite a number of the new models are made of two materials, one plain and the other a plaid, check or stripe. For visiting, nothing really equals the velvet costume, but both velvet and the cut must be of the best. Exceedingly effective was a velvet coat and skirt in olive green velvet trimmed with black silk braid and large mother-of-pearl buttons. The short skirt was cut up the front and the space filled in with a piece of chinchillo. The coat was fastened with five mother-of-pearl buttons and more of these buttons decorated the collar, cuffs and trimmed the skirt.'

The keynote of Edwardian women's fashions was thus ornate decoration, except where this conflicted with the younger generation's increasing participation in outdoor sports. Men's fashions also generally became less restrictive. Although the long frock-coat and tall silk hat were invariably worn on Sundays and on formal occasions by any man with pretensions to be well dressed, the rounded bowler hat, once considered suitable only for week-ends in the country, and a shorter coat, colloquially known as a 'bum-freezer', were increasingly favoured. The King's preference for one of the new soft felt hats for sporting events and country pursuits brought into favour the homburg and the trilby. For bank holidays at the seaside or on the river the young middle-class male chose a tweed or flannel suit with a square-cut jacket and narrow, tight-fitting trousers. His straw boater was linked to his lapel by a black cord and a spring clip, so that he could retrieve it if it blew off his head. Even the King was happy to wear equally flamboyant attire when he was satisfied that the occasion permitted it. While staying in Marienbad in 1903 he appeared one day in a green cloth cap, pink tie, white gloves, knee-breeches, grey shoes and an overcoat with a large brown check. 'Loyal subjects must sincerely hope', commented *The Tailor and Cutter* anxiously, 'that His Majesty has not brought this outfit home.'

Despite the touch of unconventionality about his dress on informal occasions, the King was adamant on the necessity for correct uniform or court dress for formal occasions and ceremonies. Stories about his attention to the smallest details of dress were legion. His assistant private secretary was intending to wear a frock-coat one morning when he accompanied the King to an exhibition of paintings. 'I thought everyone must know', said the King icily, 'that a *short* jacket is always worn with a silk hat at a private view in the *morning*.' On another occasion he was heard to remark irritably to the German Emperor, who was wearing the uniform of one of the British regiments of which he was an honorary officer, 'Willy, you're wearing the wrong trousers!'

'But, Uncle', remonstrated the Emperor, 'these are the trousers Grandmamma sent me.'

'We've changed the width of the stripe since then!' was Uncle Bertie's curt reply.

Highland dress remained as popular as it had been in the golden days when Queen Victoria and her beloved Prince Consort had discovered the delights of Scottish life and culture. Soon after the King's accession he found at Windsor Castle a Highland dress which had been made for the late German Emperor Frederick III, husband of the King's eldest sister, Victoria. The King had the dress despatched as a Christmas gift to his nephew, Frederick's son and successor.

'Dearest Uncle', wrote the delighted Willy, 'I hasten to offer you my sincere and warmest thanks for the kind letter by Sir Frank (Lascelles), the kind message, and the most touching and splendid gift of dear Papa's Highland dress. It was a most kind thought and has given me great pleasure. I well remember having often stood as a boy in Papa's dressing-room and enviously admiring the precious and glittering contents. How well it suited him and what a fine figure he made in it! I always wondered where the things had gone to, as dear Mamma never said anything about them, and I had quite lost sight of them. The last time I wore Highland dress at Balmoral was in 1878 in September, when I visited dear Grandmamma and was able to go out deer-stalking on Lochnagar. Dear Grandpapa's gigantic old jager was still waiting on Grandmamma and looked after my rifles, whilst a very nice old, but fine Head-keeper, with a good Highland name and a splendid face, stalked with me. All these memories came back to me when I saw the suit again, and made me think how the time flies fast, but I am deeply sensitive to the kind thoughts that prompted you to send the things back to me.'

Much of the day in a wealthy household was occupied in changing into clothes appropriate for the activity of the moment. Tweed costumes for the ladies and tweed suits or sporting jackets and jodhpurs for the men could be worn for breakfast and the morning ride or walk, but something a little more formal was needed for lunch. During the afternoon the ladies changed into tea-gowns and soon after seven were having their hair dressed, choosing their jewellery, and being encased in their tight corsets and elaborate evening gowns, ready for dinner at eight or nine. Sundays enforced at least one extra change, the formal velvet suit or costume needed for breakfast and for morning service before tweeds could be donned for the pre-luncheon walk or drive.

Cloths and fabrics were among the household commodities whose merits members of the aristocracy were happy to advertise in the fashionable magazines. In the *Illustrated London News* for 6 September 1902, a portrait of the Earl of Rosebery adorned an advertisement reading: 'Lord Rosebery says of Harris Tweeds "I mean to buy as much as I can afford, both to wear myself, and in which to clothe those nearest and dearest to me". Pettigrew and Stephens, Sauchiehall Street, Glasgow—Harris Tweeds and Highland Homespuns, price 1s. 11d. to 5s. 6d. per yard. Scotch white wincey for Babies' Frocks, Summer Dresses, for Blouses for Tennis, for Boating, for Underwear, for Nightgowns, from 1s. 3d. to 3s. 6d. per yard.'

Such advertisements were not confined to clothing. Lord Methuen, Colonel of the Scots Guards and a divisional commander during the Boer War, lent his name and portrait to an *Illustrated London News* advertisement for tooth-powder. 'Lord Methuen, the gallant soldier', it announced, 'has undoubtedly won the affection and confidence of the men who served under him in the trying hardships of war, and is surely one of the most chivalrous and at the same time popular figures among the generals who have fought the country's battles. Lord Methuen writes: "I find Odol an 'excellent' mixture for the teeth".' Most remarkable of all, perhaps, were the advertisements which showed His Majesty King Edward VII, resplendent in the full-dress uniform of a British field-marshal, with decorations and medals glittering on his chest and the rich blue sash of the Most Noble Order of the Garter encircling his ample form. Daintily held in his right hand is a steaming white china tea-cup and above his head are the portentous words: 'A Right Royal Drink—Horniman's Pure Tea.'

The time-honoured Scottish ritual of the January Sale provided the ordinary family with an opportunity to replenish its wardrobe at bargain prices. In January 1912, Isaac Benzies, of George Street, Aberdeen, was advertising a wide range of clothing and household furnishings, among them:

Ladies' tweed coats in smart styles   6s. 11d. and 8s. 11d.
Girls' tweed coats   3s. 6d. to 8s. 11d.
Ladies' serge costumes, correct in style and cut   12s. 11d.
Girls' serge and cloth dresses suitable for school wear   3s. 11d. and 4s. 11d.
Girls' hats (fit 3 to 8 years) 1s.
Ladies' white cotton camisoles, lace trimmed   1s.
Ladies' grey fleecy-lined bodices, long sleeves $10\frac{1}{2}$d.
Ladies' tan lace hose $3\frac{1}{2}$d. per pair
Costume tweed, double width, extra value $7\frac{1}{2}$d. per yard
Coloured bath towels, large size $8\frac{1}{2}$d. each

At about the same time, Scott Adie Ltd., 'the Scotch Royal

Warehouse', in Regent Street, London W, was advertising:

Cawdor Capes, Scotch Cheviots and Tweeds from 42s.

Reversible Cheviots and Saxonys from 52s. 6d. to 84s.

Hand-Knit Stockings, Heather Mixture, from 3s. 9d. per pair
With Fancy Top 5s. 6d. to 7s. 6d. per pair

Rugs and Plaids—the best selection in London—

Rugs from 18s. 6d. to 100s.

Plaids from 25s.

Shawls from 15s. 6d. to 84s.

Reversible Tartan Travelling Rugs in any Family or Clan Tartan from 21s.

'Illustrated Catalogues and Patterns Post Free—Prices Same as in Scotland.'

4

Medicines and Murders

Although Edwardian newspapers and magazines had no rivalry to endure from radio, television or the embryonic cinema, they were so numerous—about 4,500 were being published by 1910—that they could hope to survive only by competing fiercely with one another. Britain's imperial role was prompting a wider interest in politics and international affairs but in the popular journals the treatment of these had to be leavened with entertaining snippets, light fiction, brightly informative features, lively advertising and gift schemes to attract readers.

Details of sizes, qualities and prices were an essential part of almost all advertisements, and there was little of the lavish prestige advertising, devoid of detail and innocent of guarantee, which later became customary. Advertisements for food and patent medicines, especially, quoted case-histories at great length, adding the names, full addresses and, if space permitted, even sketches or photographs of sufferers for whom the remedies had proved miraculously effective. During 1903 several family journals carried a series of illustrated advertisements for the 'ready-to-serve cereal', Force. Cartoons depicting 'Sunny Jim', the personification of the satisfied consumer, were supported by testimonials. 'My little boy was very ill and would not take any nourishment', wrote Mrs. J. Lindley Keene in one of them. 'I got a package of Force and fed him on it, and am pleased to say he is thriving. I will now put him beside any boy of his age, as he is big and healthy. All I feed him on is Force.' Mr. E. McKinnon, of Alloa, recommended 'Professor Keith-Harvey's self-applied method' as a cure for deafness. 'I was as deaf as a stone wall', he announced, 'and attended hospital for twelve months without benefit. I then applied your System for three weeks and my hearing was completely restored.' 'Doctor Williams' Pink Pills for Pale People' were widely claimed to cure dozens of diseases, among them St. Vitus' Dance, locomotor ataxy and 'decline'. 'Don't sneeze! but get rid of the Cold by using Doctor Mackenzie's Catarrh-cure smelling bottle, price one shilling' and 'Was told he had consumption—Scott's Emulsion brought back his strength and restored health!' were among the advertisements familiar to readers of the Sunday newspapers.

The large format and compact lay-out of the newspaper page enabled the editor to indulge his readers' taste for detail even in the minor crime reports. On 17 March 1902 the *Aberdeen Free Press* recorded the arrest of an old man at Cupar on suspicion of having murdered his wife with an axe in their cottage at Comerton. 'The woman's body presented a fearful appearance', ran the account, 'the brain protruding and the head having been battered into a shapeless and almost unrecognisable mass.' The same issue also reported that a lodger at a house in Cowlan Road, Glasgow, had been attacked by a fellow-lodger and 'stabbed in four places, in the stomach, on the right arm, on the left thigh and on the right thigh'. As well as reporting such fracas as these in Fife and Glasgow, of little significance in Aberdeen, the newspaper would give considerably more space to crimes in the North-east and copious column-inches to local and national social and political news.

Sure of a generous allotment of space was an action for damages for breach of promise, still the customary consolation for a young woman who had been jilted, even when she had not the extra burden of a child to rear. One such action which set Edwardian Aberdeen by the ears was heard in April 1909. The plaintiff was a Welsh girl, Mary Ann Morgan, a music-hall singer and dancer from Cardiff, and the defendant was Dr. Hubert Dornhurst, medical officer at the Aberdare Cottage Hospital, Glamorgan. They had met six years earlier in Aberdeen, where the defendant was a medical student. He had proposed marriage to her within three months of their meeting but Miss Morgan had at first refused to accept his proposal because she felt herself too young. At Christmas 1903, when Miss Morgan and her sister were appearing in pantomime at Newcastle-upon-Tyne, her suitor followed her there and presented bouquets every night to her and her sister. Then began what plaintiff's counsel, with a fitting sense of historic occasion, described as 'a voluminous correspondence —probably the most voluminous correspondence that has ever appeared in a case of this kind or, indeed, that has ever passed between any two lovers in the world'. The letters soon filled three portmanteaux which, at her suitor's request, Miss Morgan took with her whenever she was on tour.

Early in 1904, while Miss Morgan was appearing in Dundee, young Dornhurst renewed his proposal of marriage. He gave Miss Morgan a ring and in July they finally became engaged. The correspondence increased in volume until Miss Morgan was receiving two or three letters daily from her fiancé, as well as an occasional telegram for good measure. At the end of 1906 she went to South Africa for a theatrical tour lasting five months, during which the literary avalanche continued by registered post, but soon after her return to Britain she received what her counsel described as 'the most callous and brutal letter which a man could ever write to a girl'. Without any warning, said counsel, the defendant announced: 'This is a mock hypocrisy of love, and I don't want anything more to do with you', adding significantly that he had no money.

Then came the moment in the proceedings for which Press and public were always agog, the appearance of the jilted plaintiff in the witness box. She was, reported the *Northern Scot* on 24 April 1909, 'a tall, attractive-looking brunette in a blue costume with a large hat and veil'. She gave a blushing account of the letters she had received. They usually began: 'My very own, fond darling sweetheart' and while she was in South Africa the defendant had written that although he had had many opportunities of kissing girls under the mistletoe, he loved her so much that he felt he could never kiss any other girl as long as he lived. His love, he had assured her, 'would easily withstand the onslaught of flattering women's tongues, should the occasion offer itself'. A wiser woman might have been a little wary of such over-protestation but Miss Morgan came of a respectable Welsh family circle, where Sigmund Freud's newly published theories of sex and the sub-conscious were unlikely to have penetrated, and she was deceived. The defendant's counsel pleaded that Dr. Dornhurst had been a young and indiscreet student when he met Miss Morgan. As a medical officer he was earning only £11 per month and that was the basis upon which the jury should assess his means. The jury, however, found for the plaintiff and her damages were assessed at £300.

In contrast to such breach of promise cases, a crime passionel in New York brought vicarious excitement of a cruder quality to Scottish readers of the popular newspapers. On 25 June 1906 a young American millionaire, Harry K. Thaw, was having a quiet dinner with his beautiful wife Evelyn in the restaurant of Madison Square Roof Gardens. At a table near them was the most celebrated

American architect of his time, Stanford White, who had designed the Gardens themselves, the Washington Arch at the end of Fifth Avenue, and other notable buildings. As the Thaws left the restaurant, Harry Thaw drew a revolver and fired three shots into Stanford White, killing him instantly. Thaw's motive was apparently revenge for Stanford White's seduction of Mrs. Thaw several years before her marriage. Seven months later began the interminable trial of Harry Thaw. It lasted almost twelve weeks and ended with 47 hours of deliberation by the jury, who failed to agree on a verdict. A second trial, in January 1908, ended with Thaw's acquittal on the grounds that he was insane but his relief proved short-lived when the judge, instead of allowing him to be released, ordered him to be detained in a state mental asylum. After repeated but unsuccessful appeals against his detention, Thaw escaped in 1913 to Canada, only to be extradited and returned to the asylum. His saga ended in 1915 when his appeal for release was finally upheld.

Scottish interest in the Thaw case centred on the widely reported belief that Mrs. Thaw was none other than Evelyn Nesbit, youngest daughter of a Caledonian Railway plate-layer, David Nesbit, of Granton. Born in 1883, either at Loanhead, Lanarkshire, or in the Queensferry Road, Edinburgh, (reports differed), Evelyn had been taken to the United States as a girl of twelve by her mother, who was deserting her husband. There were graphic descriptions of the plate-layer's neat little one-roomed cottage near the railway line and of the photographs, letters and needlework his wife had left behind. There was added interest in the more certain knowledge that among the members of the Thaw family attending the trial was Harry's sister Alice, wife of the Earl of Yarmouth, a former subaltern in the Black Watch.

The evidence at the first trial was sensational enough to keep the case in the headlines of many American and British newspapers. There were allegations that on one occasion Stanford White had drugged Evelyn Nesbit, then a seventeen-year-old dancer in the chorus of *Floradora*, and that she had awakened to find him beside her in a room with mirrors on the walls and ceiling. Her marriage to Thaw three years later had not been a bed of roses, for she signed an affidavit that he was a drug addict and a sadist who had repeatedly thrashed her with a whip while they were touring as man and wife in Britain and Austria. Evelyn's appearance in the witness-box created a pleasant impression of dewy freshness and the girlish charm. She wore a short blue frock scarcely reaching the tops of her boots, a white lace collar and a black hat trimmed with artificial violets. The youthful innocence suggested by her dress was a little belied by her admission that she had been cited as a co-respondent in a divorce case, had been receiving twenty-five dollars a week from Stanford White during her association with him, and had read the Bible only 'slightly' and Sir Walter Scott not at all. It was soon possible to buy picture-postcard photographs of Mrs. Thaw at almost every stationer's shop in Britain. They showed her as a plump, dark-eyed beauty with pale, heavy features and a broad brow. Despite his eight years in prison or asylum and the million dollars he spent in lawyers' fees, Harry Thaw failed to retain the affections of his young wife. By the time he had gained his freedom she had divorced him, returned to the stage and married her English dancing-partner.

An even longer struggle against conviction characterised another Edwardian *cause célèbre* which also linked Scotland and the United States. On a cold, wet evening in December 1908, a wealthy spinster, Miss Marion Gilchrist, who lived in a first-floor flat in West Princes Street, Glasgow, sent her young maid out to buy a newspaper. When the girl, Helen Lambie, returned she found the occupant of the downstairs flat, Arthur Adams, waiting in a state of agitation at Miss Gilchrist's door. 'There's something dreadful going on in there', he said. 'There have been bumps and bangs—I thought the ceiling was going to crack!'

As they cautiously opened the door and made their way into the flat, a man in a fawn overcoat suddenly walked past them, hurried down the stairs and disappeared into the dark street. In the dining-room Helen Lambie found Miss Gilchrist lying on the floor, covered by a rug. She had been ferociously battered to death. A light in the bedroom suggested robbery as the motive for the crime but Helen Lambie discovered that a diamond brooch seemed to be the only object missing. A wooden box containing private papers had been wrenched open and rifled but a gold watch, a gold bracelet, a diamond and two rings, even a half-sovereign on the dining-room floor, all lay untouched. With these slender clues and the additional evidence of a fourteen-year-old girl, Mary Barrowman, who had caught a glimpse of a man in a fawn overcoat running along West Princes Street at about the time of the murder, the police began their investigations. Largely as a result of information from a cycle dealer who frequented a sleazy gambling club, they fastened suspicion on a

German immigrant known as Oscar Slater, a member of the same club, who had recently been trying to sell a pawn ticket issued for a valuable diamond brooch. Tracking Slater to his lodgings, they found that he and a young woman companion had sailed from Liverpool for New York in the liner *Lusitania*.

The Glasgow police immediately cabled the New York police asking for Slater to be arrested. Passages to New York were then booked for Helen Lambie, Arthur Adams and Mary Barrowman. There, in the Tombs prison, the three witnesses were brought face to face with Slater and identified him, somewhat uncertainly, as the man they had seen leaving Miss Gilchrist's flat. On the basis of this identification Slater was charged with murder. His trial began on 3 May 1909 at the High Court in Edinburgh. The judge, Lord Guthrie, Senator of the College of Justice in Scotland, was an intensely religious man who had been legal adviser to the Free Church of Scotland and later to the United Free Church. The son of an Edinburgh divine who had been the first editor of the *Sunday Magazine*, Guthrie had himself written a biography of John Knox and other religious works. In his eyes Oscar Slater was an unprepossessing character. His German–Jewish origins, his dark, foreign appearance, his thick, guttural accent, his shady career as a professional gambler and free-lance dealer in jewellery, and above all, perhaps, his separation from his wife and his long liaison with an attractive young French woman must all have weighed heavily against Slater in the judge's mind.

There was astonishing gaps and contradictions in the evidence. The diamond brooch stolen from Miss Gilchrist was never found. That owned by Slater had been pawned weeks before her death and his passage to New York in the *Lusitania* had also been booked weeks previously. Although blood was spattered on a chair, on the rug and high across the fireplace of the room in which Miss Gilchrist was murdered, there was no trace of blood on any of Slater's clothing nor on a small hammer found in his luggage and alleged by the police to be the murder weapon. The evidence of identification was patently unreliable where it was not downright contradictory. Lord Guthrie was undeterred by the flimsy nature of the case against Slater. He was at pains to show in his summing-up that Slater was a villain of the deepest dye. 'Up to yesterday afternoon', said his Lordship, "I should have thought that there was one serious difficulty which confronted you—the difficulty of conceiving that there was in existence a human being capable of such a dastardly deed. Gentlemen, that difficulty was, I think, removed when we heard . . . that he, Slater, had followed a life which descends to the lowest depths of human degradation. . . . I say without hesitation', continued Lord Guthrie, 'that the man in the dock is capable of having committed this dastardly outrage.' There was much more on the same theme. 'He has', reiterated the judge, 'maintained himself by the ruin of men and the ruin of women, and he has lived in a way that many blackguards would scorn to live.'

Conducting himself in a calm and dignified manner, and protesting his innocence to the last, Slater was found guilty by a majority verdict. He was sentenced to be hanged on 27 May 1909. But public opinion in Scotland was becoming disturbed by the prosecution and its outcome. 'The first emotion caused by news of this verdict in the case of nine out of every ten who read the evidence closely', said the *Glasgow Herald* cautiously, 'must have been one of intense surprise.' The *Edinburgh Evening Despatch* echoed the same sentiment in stronger terms. 'It is notorious that the verdict in the Slater trial came as an intense surprise to the public. The universal impression was that the whole case hung on one single slender thread, that the identification of the prisoner by persons who had only a passing glance of his features and in circumstances upon the whole where a sure and trustworthy impression of his personality was far from certain. Jurymen are only human after all, and it is inconceivable that the unfolding of Slater's monstrous crimes against society did not affect the views of the jury. To expect otherwise is to expect too much of human nature.' Doubts were not allayed when the police released from their files the full details of Slater's criminal record in Scotland. In November 1899 he had been convicted of disorderly conduct and had been fined twenty shillings or seven days in default.

While Slater waited in Duke Street Prison for his execution, a petition for his reprieve was launched by his solicitor, Ewing Speirs, and a Glasgow rabbi, E. P. Phillips. Signed by twenty thousand people, it was presented on 17 May to the Secretary for Scotland, Lord Pentland. Thirty-six hours before his execution was due, Slater was informed that His Majesty the King had granted him a reprieve, commuting his sentence to life imprisonment. The matter did not rest there. In April 1910, William Hodge and Co. published an addition to their celebrated series of *Notable Scottish Trials*. Edited by William Roughead and dedicated, not without irony, to Lord Guthrie, it was

The Trial of Oscar Slater. Its careful assessment of the evidence stimulated a greater interest in the case among prominent public men, including Andrew Lang, the Scottish author, and Sir Arthur Conan Doyle, the Edinburgh doctor who had turned author and had twice stood as a parliamentary candidate in Scottish constituencies. Sir Arthur fastened on to the Slater affair and refused to let go. In 1912 he wrote a booklet, *The Case of Oscar Slater*, which had a wide circulation, and after two more years of pressure the Secretary for Scotland finally appointed the Sheriff of Lanarkshire, James G. Millar, K.C., to hold a secret inquiry into the case. But again the verdict went against Slater and a few weeks later the outbreak of war brought other preoccupations for Scottish minds and other headlines for Scottish newspapers.

In 1925 a fellow-convict being released from Peterhead Prison agreed to smuggle out a tiny pellet of paper containing a brief appeal from Slater to Sir Arthur Conan Doyle to make one last attempt to secure his release. The campaign began again and again it was unsuccessful. Eventually, in November 1927, the Scottish Secretary intimated that Slater had been sufficiently punished and would be released on licence. The following July Slater's appeal against conviction was upheld in the High Court, Edinburgh, on the grounds of the judge's misdirection in law, and he was awarded £6,000 in compensation. The long saga was over.

Such cases as those of Harry K. Thaw and Oscar Slater were manna from heaven for the new, cheap national daily newspapers which, with their blaring headlines and brash, breathless prose, were so prominent a feature of the Edwardian scene, but they were also carefully reported in the solid weekly or daily journals to which most Scots remained faithful. With its copious news of national and international events, its articles on local history and topography, its reports from local places of worship, its accounts of sporting events and social occasions, its column for ladies, its short story and its ponderous leader, the Scottish Edwardian newspaper provided its readers with so wide a view of the world that they had little need of any other source of news. Deeply rooted in its locality, such a newspaper seemed as firm and forthright as a good dominie. It had time and space to dignify even the farm animals with their own identities.

In the displenish sale at Rettie Farm, Banff, reported in the *Aberdeen Free Press* on 16 May 1902, *Corinne* was bought by Mr.

McWilliam, of Stoneytown, for 25 guineas, and her bull calf by Mr. Bruce, of Langcot, Forres, for seven. Mr. Campbell came from Ireland to buy *Juno* for 25 guineas, while Mr. McHattie, of Keith, paid 19 guineas for *Dufftown Daisy*. In the sale of Aberdeen-Angus bulls at Perth on 13 and 14 February 1912, reported the *Northern Scot*, Sir J. Macpherson-Grant, of Ballindalloch, sold *Radium* for 45 guineas, *Prince Burnish* for 70 guineas and *Prince Forder* for 170 guineas. Among the other bulls who found new owners at the sale were some with topical names, *Balfour, Gatacre, Black Sambo, Proud Ecosse* and *Tartan Mack.*

5

Crisis in the Kirk

Outwith the industrial towns of the Lowlands, and for the middle class even within them, Scottish family life at the beginning of the twentieth century still centred largely round the church. The ecclesiastical scene in Victorian Scotland had been dominated by the Disruption of 1843, when almost five hundred ministers had left the established Church of Scotland because they insisted on the right of a presbytery to veto the appointment of a minister whom it considered unsuitable. The dissidents formed the Free Church of Scotland and within a few years had raised over a million pounds and built some 650 churches for their services. The United Presbyterian Church, formed by an earlier secession from the Church of Scotland, had been much influenced by the revivalist meetings of the American evangelists Dwight L. Moody and Ira D. Sankey, and began to introduce instrumental music into its services. The Free Church was less progressive, its ministers referring contemptuously to the organ as a 'kist o' whistles', and there was also controversy over the Westminster Confession of Faith, which the United Presbyterian Church was prepared to accept only in a modified form. Despite these differences, and mainly owing to the unremitting efforts of Dr. Robert Rainy, principal of New College, Edinburgh, a large majority of the Free Church was ready by the end of the nineteenth century to amalgamate with the United Presbyterian Church.

The amalgamation took place in 1900, the new organisation, the United Free Church, being composed of over 1,100 Free Church congregations and over 600 United Presbyterian congregations. About thirty ministers of the Free Church, most of them in the Highlands and Islands, refused to accept the union. Popularly known as the 'Wee Frees', they launched a vehement campaign against it and laid claim to the church buildings and funds which, they said, those agreeing to the union had forfeited. The dispute provoked violent scenes and at one stage a warship had to be sent to calm tempers in

Lewis, but eventually the Scottish courts decided in favour of the United Free Church. On appeal, the House of Lords in 1904 reversed this decision, asserting that the majority had modified the doctrine of the Westminster Confession, had abandoned the principle of an established church and had therefore ceased to represent the true Free Church of Scotland. The Wee Frees, by remaining faithful to the historic doctrines of the Church thus fell heirs to its property and funds. Whatever the theological merits of the Law Lords' decision, its practical implications were awkward. Not only had they apparently taken the view that a church was simply a trust for the propagation of a rigid doctrine, unable to alter or amend its beliefs or its constitution to suit changing circumstances, but they had also placed hundreds of church buildings and considerable funds at the disposal of a handful of disgruntled ministers.

The Conservative government decided to overthrow the decision and in 1905 the Scottish Churches Act restored ownership of the disputed property and funds to the United Free Church. The Act also empowered the Established Church of Scotland to alter, without recourse to Parliament, its form of subscription to the Westminster Confession. This clause, described by the Leader of the Opposition, Sir Henry Campbell-Bannerman, as an 'undesirable alien', was defended by the Prime Minister, Arthur J. Balfour, as being 'no intruder'. It paved the way for discussions between the United Free Church and the Church of Scotland on the possibility of amalgamation and in 1909 the two churches appointed committees to report on the proposal. By 1912 a plan had been agreed but the First World War delayed consummation of the union until 1929.

In spite of these controversies over doctrine and organisation, the church in Scotland at the beginning of the twentieth century retained a greater hold over the Scottish people than did the Church of England and the Nonconformist churches over people south of the Border. There were two principal causes for this difference. The Scottish church was presbyterian and therefore less authoritarian in concept than the established Church of England, and Scotland had also been able to avoid the disputes over control of education which were for so long a divisive feature of the English system. In London in 1902 only about two in every ten people attended a place of worship. In Scotland communicants of the Church of Scotland numbered about 15% of the people, those of the United Free Church numbered about 10%, and there was a Roman Catholic community numbering about 10% of the population.

The minister, in burgh or village, was a man of consequence and his advice was constantly sought in matters both spiritual and temporal. He was marriage guidance counsellor, children's welfare officer, community service organiser, social security adviser, burial-ground director and part-time teacher as well as shepherd of his flock. In *The Nor' East*, his reminiscences of clerical life along the Moray Firth before the First World War, Dr. W. S. Bruce tells a story of three parish worthies who were talking by the village pump when a courting couple sauntered by, oblivious of their surroundings, the girl's eyes fixed in rapt attention on her lover's face.

'That reminds me', said the smith, his eyes following the couple.

'Ay', interrupted the hen-pecked shoemaker, 'but it winna be lang like that wi' *her.*'

'Hoo d'ye ken?' said the tailor, himself a bachelor. The two benedicts exchanged looks full of meaning. This suggested to the last speaker to propound the question: 'Why should girls change so much after marriage?'

'Maybe', said the smith, smiling, 'they fin' oot we're nae sae gude as they thocht.'

'Ma ain belief is, it's a' pretence wi' the hizzies at the beginnin'', said the souter, with lively recollections of his wife's sharp tongue.

'Weel, weel, I canna say masel'', said the man of no experience, 'but it looks gey like as if the minister spiles them a'.'

Although in England the Lord's Day Observance Society feared the imminent arrival of what was called ominously 'the Continental Sunday', in Scotland the Sabbath was generally a day of strict ritual. Father, mother, bairns and such servants as could be spared from domestic tasks made their way in solemn platoons to church. Most of the men wore black frock coats and tile hats and the women were in black or dark grey suits with long, heavy skirts and wide-brimmed hats trimmed with intricate specimens of the milliner's art, secured by large hat-pins and covered with black veils. The children were equally decorous in dress and behaviour, with long skirts for the girls and knicker-bocker suits for the youths. The only knees to be seen were those of the smallest boys who might be wearing the kilt.

Dr. Bruce tells two stories to illustrate the character and importance of the Sabbath in the lives of Moray Firth folk during the Edwardian period. A minister in Banff had announced that his church the following Sunday would have a show of flowers at the morning service and that a well-known local tenor would sing a solo at the evening service. A venerable elder absented himself from both the services and when the minister chanced to meet him a little later, the elder was very emphatic.

'I didna gang tae the kirk on Sunday', he said in strong tones.

'Were you not feeling well?' asked the minister.

'Na, it wisna that. It was juist that I was thinkin' that a floo'r show in the mornin' an' a concert at nicht's nae my idea o' the Sawbath!'

When the Duke of Fife, the husband of Princess Louise, the eldest daughter of King Edward VII, used to stay at Banff, the beadle of the Free Church was employed to take the Duke's letters from the post office to the ducal mansion, Duff House. But the beadle was reluctant to perform this task on the Sabbath. 'I aften thocht', he told Dr. Bruce, 'o' King Dauvid's words to Abimelech, "The King's business requireth haste". For, ye see, the Duke was the King's son-in-law, and some o' the letters micht be frae the palace o' Windsor. But I just thocht on Sunday, weel, this is the King's wark tee, and it's mair to be beadle to the kirk than post-runner tae his Grace the Duke.'

6

Council and Classroom

Another figure of importance in Edwardian Scotland was the local councillor. The administration of the burghs had been modernised in 1833 by the Scottish Municipal Reform Act, and the Burgh Police Act of 1892 had consolidated the previous legislation. County councils had been set up under the terms of the Local Government (Scotland) Act of 1889 and the pattern had been completed by the Local Government (Scotland) Act of 1894, which enjoined that parish councils should be elected to replace the parochial boards which had administered the Poor Law, fixing the amount of relief and assessing the rate to be levied. The new parish councils, elected every three years by ratepayers, including single and married women, were normally empowered to levy only a 3d. rate. Their preoccupation with parochial affairs laid them open to a charge of indulging in parish-pump politics but they provided, with the burgh and county councils, a network of democratic government at grass roots level throughout Scotland. The councillor, whether skilled craftsman, retired army or naval officer, dominie, tradesman or manufacturer, was able to make a significant contribution to the life of the community in which he lived. In many ways he was beginning to shoulder responsibilities which had once been those of the laird and the minister.

In his nomination address to the ratepayers of the Royal Burgh of Banff in a council election towards the turn of the century, Charles Innes Shearer, a local draper, spoke of some of the urgent financial problems which beset the burgh, where the excess of expenditure over income during the previous year had been no less than £30 sterling.

'I do not wish to pose as a financier', he said, 'but I venture to suggest one or two things which, if acted upon, would undoubtedly relieve and do away with the financial strain under which the Burgh has laboured and is still labouring. This can be effected without further burdening the already over-burdened ratepayers. . . .

'I venture to suggest that there are two ways out of the difficulty. Before coming to touch on them, I would say that if a business is lossing £50 annually it would be a most unbusinesslike procedure not to attempt a readjustment of affairs so as to drop the adverse balance. This, I hold, exactly describes the condition of the finances of the Burgh, and consequently a readjustment of financial affairs is called for forthwith. As already stated, this can be accomplished in two ways, either by increasing the revenue or by decreasing the expenditure. I am of the opinion that the annual revenue of the Burgh may be increased provided the properties of the town are rented at their full value. I do not speak without data, for on perusing the abstract of the accounts of the Burgh, I noticed one property to my certain knowledge rented under its true value, if I am allowed to judge by comparison. Very well, there may be others in a similar position and if so, then a very substantial increase could be brought about to the revenue by having the properties let at their proper worth.

'There may be a difficulty here, however, owing to lack of competitors and in that case there is another way out of the financial difficulty, the way of decrease of expenditure. What can be done in this direction? I hold that a considerable saving may be effected. As you are aware, the council have the combined services of a town clerk and a clerk to the Police Commissioners. The town clerk or his depute have to be in attendance at every meeting of the council. It would therefore be an easy matter for him to undertake his own work and that performed by the clerk to the police commissioners, and that too without a very great deal of extra labour or inconvenience. . . .

'Another question is that of the cleaning of the streets. Under the present system the cleaning of the town is accomplished by contract labour as far as regards the horse and cart. This work, I believe, is carried out to the satisfaction of the greater portion of the community. Still there is one exception, if not more, and the question arises would the town be better served if it owned a horse and cart? A saving can be effected thus of from 2s. to 2s. 6d. weekly, say £5 to £6 annually, and there is no reason why the work should not be more efficiently performed. This idea I should support.

'There is a part of the town well known to us all. That is the Strait Path, and those of failing breath and feeble limbs find it a difficult pathway and no joke to tackle. There is a decided improvement in the state of the Path but there is still room for improvement. Such, of course, would cost money but then the ratepayers would reap the benefit of this expenditure and perhaps save themselves the pain and inconvenience of a broken limb, for in winter the place is exceptionally dangerous. . . . I would favour its improvement and would suggest that it should take the shape of a terraced centre. This would certainly break the back of the Path and save the backs of its climbers.

'A Town Hall has often been spoken of. That is all or little more than all that has been done in the matter. I am aware it is within the power of the Police Commissioners to levy a tax on the ratepayers for a public hall, but this would not be supported by me. If, however, an effort could be made to raise a substantial sum by voluntary contributions, that would receive my approval and as an adjunct to this, I would do my utmost to promote an Art and Science exhibition along with a series of concerts, the funds derived from same to go to the purpose named. Then if exhibitors were agreeable, they could sell their own work and this would fetch a considerable sum.

'There is one more question I wish to touch before sitting down. I refer to the need of a night watchman. You will agree with me that one would be a great acquisition, and if the council petitioned the Chief Constable, doubtless he would see his way to place one of his men at the service of the town for this purpose or duty, free of extra cash. I do not think I have touched on any questions that can be styled new, but you will perhaps think that some of those considered are by no means unimportant.'

A stone's throw from the steep little Strait Path which Charles Shearer thought should be terraced for the benefit of pedestrians stood Banff Academy. Built in 1838 and extended in 1911, it was a handsome neo-classical edifice typifying the academic education for which Scotland had long been renowned. In the Education (Scotland) Act of 1872, as in its English counterpart of 1870, the state for the first time accepted direct responsibility for educating its children. But the unit of administration remained the parish or the burgh, whose ratepayers were enjoined to elect a school board of between five and fifteen members. Control of parish and burgh schools, whether academies, grammar schools or high schools, was transferred to these school boards, of which there were some 980 in Scotland, except that if any proprietors did not wish to relinquish control of their schools, these could be retained provided that the proprietors, such as the

Roman Catholic and Episcopalian Churches, would maintain them at their own expense.

The immediate task of the school boards was to build extra schools where these were needed and to enforce attendance as far as possible. In 1872 there were places in Scottish schools for about 280,000 pupils but by 1902 the number of places had risen to almost 950,000, and 85% of Scottish children were attending school regularly. In the Highlands attendance was less regular, mainly because of the long distances children had to walk to school and the need of crofters to employ their children for herding cattle, sheep-shearing, harvesting, peat-cutting, 'tattie-picking' and other seasonal tasks. Although the provision of adequate buildings and ensuring regular attendance were the main duties of the school boards, the Act also required them to appoint teachers and pay their salaries, levy a local rate, and fix the amount of school fees that children's parents should pay. If a parent was unable to pay the fee, he was to make application to the parochial board for poor relief for this purpose. The usual fee was twopence or threepence per week, but an Act in 1890 made more government funds available and elementary education then became virtually free, although fees continued to be charged for secondary education.

The next important landmark in Scottish education came in 1908, when another Education (Scotland) Act gave much wider powers to the school boards. They were now permitted to provide for the medical examination and supervision of children at school, to employ medical officers and nurses, and to take legal action against parents whose children were dirty, verminous or unable to profit fully from their education because of lack of food or clothing. Medical treatment had not been specifically provided for in the Act but this was plainly necessary to remedy defects likely to handicap a child in school. Accordingly the Scottish Education Department intimated in 1912 that grants would be made from government funds and the following year another education act legalised the provision of medical and dental treatment. Dunfermline had been the first Scottish burgh to provide free medical treatment, with help from the College of Hygiene and Physical Education founded there in 1905 by the Carnegie Trust. The first Glasgow school clinic was opened in 1912 and its investigations illustrated the need for a comprehensive school medical service. Over 80% of Glasgow's elementary school-children had defective teeth, about 30% were verminous and nearly 10% were suffering from rickets. Small wonder that when the Boer War broke

43

out in 1899, two out of every three volunteers for the Army had to be rejected as unfit because they failed to pass the rudimentary medical tests for enlistment. The Education (Scotland) Act of 1908 also provided for school boards to compel the attendance of children between the ages of five and fourteen, and to establish compulsory continuation classes for children up to seventeen, thus correlating the three grades of education, elementary, intermediate and secondary. Other changes were made in administration and the Education (Scotland) Fund became the central financing account into which the government grant and the local taxation revenue were paid.

For children too young to be placed in the state system, the pioneering work of a Scottish educationist was of great importance throughout the United Kingdom. She was Margaret McMillan, who was born in New York of Scottish parents in 1861. Her father died when she was four and her mother returned, with Margaret and her elder sister, Rachel, to live in Inverness. After being educated at Inverness High School, Margaret went to Bradford, where she joined the newly formed Independent Labour Party and in 1894 was elected as a member of the Bradford School Board. This afforded her the opportunity to introduce a medical inspection of children in the city's schools, but in 1902 Margaret left Yorkshire to join her sister in social work in London. There she continued to campaign for measures to improve the health of school-children and after several unsuccessful ventures she opened a nursery school in Deptford for children under five. This was organised on the pattern of the nursery in an upper-class family, beginning the day at eight o'clock with a bath and a breakfast of porridge, milk and brown bread, followed by a morning of play in the garden. After dinner the children had a short sleep, in the open air if possible, and then took part in organised games, dancing, music and speech-training until tea-time. Their mothers fetched them from school at about five o'clock.

Despite the obvious value of the innovation, the nursery school movement made only slow progress. The first such school in Scotland was opened in 1906 in the Canongate, Edinburgh, and was known as St. Saviour's child-garden. Not until after the First World War, with the foundation of the Nursery Schools Association in 1923, did the movement gather momentum but nursery education has remained the Cinderella of the system.

The Edwardian period saw the development in Scottish education of many features which still characterise it; its centralised financing authority, its unified progression from infant to senior grades, its broad concern for every aspect of a child's welfare, and its special care for the handicapped and needy. Less easy to assess is the change in the status of the dominie. Like the minister, he had once been a central figure in burgh or village life, traditionally learned, humane and wise in the ways of loons and quinies if a little unversed in the ways of the world. Even after the Education Act of 1872 the dominie usually worked closely with the minister, for the latter was often a member of the new school board, but by the turn of the century more farmers, tradesmen and shop-keepers were being elected to the school boards and they tended to have less regard for academic qualifications and more regard for practical teaching ability, so that the dominie himself became less of a preacher and more of a practitioner. He was envied by the less fortunate for the comparative security of his employment, for his steady if unspectacular salary and for the length of his holidays, with their frequent bonus of an extra half-day for some event of national or local importance. The school day normally lasted from nine till four on five days a week, but the half-time system still persisted in some industrial areas such as Dundee and Arbroath, where children could be exempted from full-time attendance. Instead they attended school either on alternate days or for mornings or afternoons only in alternate weeks. This pernicious arrangement, due mainly to the need for cheap unskilled labour in the jute mills, lingered on until the end of the First World War.

Despite its defects the education system in Edwardian Scotland, judged in the context of the time, was competent and progressive. It earned for Scots the reputation of belonging to one of the best educated nations in the world. The two men whose work contributed most to this achievement were Sir Henry Craik and Sir John Struthers. Craik was appointed as the first Permanent Secretary to the Scottish Office under the Act prepared by Gladstone and passed by Lord Salisbury's government in 1885. He was responsible for many educational reforms, introducing history, geography, drawing and science into the curriculum and advocating the abolition of fees in public elementary schools. He instituted the Leaving Certificate Examination, which became widely accepted as the qualification for entrance to the professions; in 1906 he promoted the raising of the statutory school leaving age to fourteen; and he tackled the problem of the training and certification of teachers. When Craik resigned in December 1905 to become the Conservative Member of Parliament for Aberdeen and Glasgow Universities, he was succeeded by John Struthers, who concentrated on the expansion of secondary education. Struthers was determined to free it from the handicaps, most manifest in rural areas, of inadequate buildings, equipment and staff. He moved secondary pupils into selected schools in each county, where adequate provision could be made for them, but ensured that there was still a clear road for the 'lad o' pairts' to proceed from parish school to secondary school and university, from a bleak but-and-ben on a stony Highland croft or a grey tenement in a Lowland city to a chair of medicine, the bridge of a Clyde-built steamer or the board-room of a London company.

7

Street Scenes

Out of school the city child had the teeming streets to educate him. Early morning brought the baker's man with his tray of butteries, baps, softies, scones and pancakes still warm from the oven. He might be followed by an onion johnnie, whose swarthy face, dark hair and brown eyes matched the hazel skins of his onions. The knife-grinder was as entertaining as a fair-ground side-show, for his treadle and grinding-wheel, his strops for razors and his oil-stone for pen-knives held a hint of danger, especially when he tested the gleaming blades across the back of a broad thumb. The music of the barrel-organ or the hurdy-gurdy was a familiar sound. Often the organ-grinder was Italian and his aide was a tiny monkey whose gay velvet jacket and jaunty pill-box hat were belied by his listless shamble and mournful eyes. Winter evenings brought the muffin-man, ringing his bell to fetch the children scurrying with their coppers, or leerie, the lamp-lighter, immortalised in Robert Louis Stevenson's poem.

An alarming sight in Edwardian city streets was a runaway horse. If it was frightened by a sudden noise, a powerful animal harnessed to a light dray or an empty cart was difficult to stop. Even if a plucky passer-by was agile enough to grab the loose reins, he had to run fast enough to keep his feet on the rough or cobbled surface of the roadway and to be strong enough to bring the quivering horse to a standstill before it had bowled over people and vehicles in its path. Horse traffic was noisy and in quiet residential streets a layer of straw was often scattered across the roadway to deaden the sound of cart-wheels and horses' hooves in front of houses where someone was ill.

By the beginning of the Edwardian period the internal combustion engine was firmly established as the ideal means of propelling the new 'horseless carriage'. In Britain progress had been retarded by the notorious 'Red Flag Act', which imposed a strict speed limit and enjoined that every horseless carriage travelling on a public highway should be preceded by a pedestrian to warn other

47

road users of its approach. In 1896 this act was replaced by the Locomotives and Highways Act, which dispensed with the pedestrian and raised the speed limit to fourteen miles per hour. The first British motor-show had been held the previous year at Tunbridge Wells and by the end of the century the English Daimler Company had been formed in Coventry, Herbert Austin had constructed his first motor vehicle in Birmingham, and the Prince of Wales had made his first trip in a motor-car, a twelve horse-power Daimler belonging to Mr. W. E. Scott Montagu, M.P., a pioneer motorist who was a grandson of the Duke of Buccleuch and who afterwards became Lord Montagu of Beaulieu. The Prince quickly became an enthusiast and ordered several motor-cars, among them a Daimler, a Renault and two Mercedes, for himself. There was even speculation that he might ride in a motor-coach in his Coronation procession, but the proposal was abandoned because of the impossibility of providing a vehicle innocent of vibration, noise and exhaust fumes. But after his accession the King had garages built at Windsor, Sandringham and Buckingham Palace, and appointed a motor engineer, Mr. C. W. Stamper, to be his chief mechanic, sitting beside the chauffeur in order to deal with any emergencies.

The King was immensely proud of having driven at more than sixty miles per hour on the Brighton road as early as 1906, and even after a short and uneventful journey he would always step down from the car remarking, 'A very good r-run, Stamper, a very good r-run indeed!' He acted as patron to the 1905 Automobile Exhibition at the Crystal Palace and in 1907 granted the dignity of 'Royal' to the Automobile Club.

Another early motoring enthusiast was Mr. Arthur J. Balfour. After the general election of 1900 Lord Salisbury travelled by train to Balmoral to discuss with the Queen the formation of his new ministry. As he was passing through Edinburgh, Balfour, who was his nephew, planned to meet him there. Balfour set out from his home at Whittinghame on a dark, windy October evening to drive the twenty-six miles to Edinburgh. Every few minutes the car head-lights blew out, not surprisingly, since they were only candle-ends in small glass-sided lamps. Balfour had to stop in Musselburgh to buy a stable lantern and this he waved from his seat beside the chauffeur until they reached the lighted streets of Edinburgh.

Despite the King's enthusiasm for motoring, the horseless carriages were not universally popular and even inn-keepers were apt to shake their heads at the foolhardiness of making long journeys in such noisy, malodorous and unreliable contraptions. One of the earliest motorists in Scotland was Mr. J. H. Turner, agent to the Duke of Portland. In September 1901 Turner, with three companions, drove from Paisley to Langwell, in Caithness, a distance of almost three hundred miles, in three days. Their car was a ten horse-power Arrol Johnston with a tiller instead of a steering-wheel, wooden wheels with solid tyres, and 'open to a' the airts the wind could blaw'. Throughout the journey the party saw no other motor vehicle of any kind and when they reached Helmsdale the inn-keeper there begged them not to take their car over the Ord of Caithness to Berriedale, for if they did, he was sure, they would live to regret it. Despite his pleas they succeeded in covering the twelve miles from Helmsdale without mishap in an hour.

The 1906 edition of Black's *Shilling Guide to Scotland* gave warning of some of the hazards of motoring in Edwardian Scotland. 'Owners of large cars fitted with costly pneumatic tyres', it advised, 'would do well to avoid certain of the rougher roads, such as that between Tyndrum and Ballachulish, and still more the one leading from Tyndrum to Oban through Glencoe. Whatever the rugged grandeurs of the scenery, they scarcely compensate for the ruining of tyres worth £20 apiece.' Care was also necessary when crossing hump-backed bridges at the bottom of steep inclines. 'Some of them are overhung by trees', warned the *Guide*, 'and therefore greasy after rain, thus adding the possibility of side-slip to the awkward conformation of the turn. If the motor-car in use be of the dog-cart type, it is essential that the rear passengers should be on the watch, or fore-warned by the driver, in the case of any of the sharply crowned bridges referred to; otherwise there is a strong probability of their being jerked out as the front wheels clear the rise.'

The *Guide* obligingly provided a complete list of the Scottish towns where petrol could be bought. They were Edinburgh, Glasgow, Dundee, Aberdeen, Stirling, Perth, Banchory, Greenock, Annan, Ayr, Kirkcaldy, Paisley, Hamilton, Keith, Helensburgh, Kilmarnock, Callander and Castle Douglas. Although an ordinary six horse-power car could carry sufficient petrol in its tank for a distance of up to 400 miles, and might also carry extra in tins, motorists touring in remote areas, and especially north of Aberdeen, were advised to arrange for supplies to petrol to be sent by rail to accessible points on their route. In case of breakdown or accident, spare parts could also be obtained quickly by rail but the motorist venturing into Scotland was obviously expected to carry out most of the running repairs himself, while 'such an eventuality as a broken spring might be put right by any blacksmith'.

Although the Automobile Club of Great Britain had been founded in 1897, there were probably no more than a hundred motor-cars in the whole of Scotland, including about a dozen taxi-cabs in Edinburgh. By the time the compulsory registration of motor vehicles was introduced from 1 January 1904, together with the raising of the speed limit to twenty miles an hour, there were some 8,500 motor-cars in the whole of the United Kingdom, about a third of them in London. By 1910 the total had reached 100,000 and by 1914 there were about 132,000 private motor-cars in Britain. By this time, too, a feature later to become even more sadly familiar, the road accident report, was beginning to appear regularly in Scottish local newspapers. 'Motoring Fatality near Buckie', ran a headline in the *Northern Scot* on 11 July 1914. 'A distressing motor cycling fatality occurred yesterday (Friday) afternoon on the turnpike road between Cullen and Buckie, by which Mr. John Allan, tailor and clothier, Buckie, lost his life, while Mr. Alexander Miller, cycle agent, Buckie, had an extremely narrow escape. Mr. Allan, who was a recent accession to the ranks of motor cyclists, had just got a finely-fitted side car to run with his Triumph cycle, and he was on a trial to Cullen with Mr. Miller in the side car. Going through the wood near Rannas farm, Mr. Allan lost control of the motor, which executed a sudden swerve into a grass ditch. Mr. Allan was thrown violently over the handle-bars and alighted on his head against a stone wall, with the result that death was instantaneous. Mr. Miller was thrown over the wall and escaped with a severe shaking. The body was put upon a door and conveyed to Buckie by a spring cart.'

The following week the *Northern Scot* had another road accident to record. 'Motor accident at Elgin—Boy run over', ran the headlines. 'Yesterday about noon a distressing accident occurred on the High Street, Elgin, a small boy, Harry Petrie Burns, seven years of age, son of John Burns, plumber, having been run over by a motor car. The accident occurred opposite the shop of Mr. Bissett, grocer. It appears that Harry had been sent on an errand to one of the shops on the High Street, and while crossing the street he was knocked down by a large Daimler car belonging to Mr. Christie of Newton. The car was driving slowly but as the boy appeared suddenly from behind a hurley he was not observed in time to avert an accident. The front wheel passed over the boy's body but the car was stopped before the rear wheel touched him. He was carried into a neighbouring shop, where he was seen by Dr. Taylor, who conveyed him to Dr. Gray's Hospital in his motor car. He was afterwards examined by both Dr. Taylor and Dr. Alexander, when it was found that he was suffering from internal injuries. On inquiry at Dr. Gray's Hospital at a late hour last night, the boy's condition was considered to be somewhat serious.'

Doctors, indeed, were among the first professional men to use motor-cars and most of the other private motor vehicles belonged either to those who could afford to employ a chauffeur or to prosperous tradesmen with an engineering bent who were capable of supervising or carrying out repairs to their own vehicles.

Also becoming familiar in local newspapers were the reports of court proceedings against motorists who exceeded the speed limit. 'Prosecution of Scorchers', announced the *Perthshire Courier* on 6 September 1910. 'A bag of four was the result of the County Police setting a trap for scorchers in Auchterarder parish on the 10th of August, and the delinquents subsequently were cited to appear at the Perth Sheriff Court on Friday but only two of the men made their appearance, the others being tried in absence, the fines imposed by Sheriff Sym in the four cases ranging from one guinea to £5.

'Henry Clark, motor engineer, Leamington, was charged in absence with travelling at a speed of over 20 miles per hour through Auchterarder, where the ten mile limit is in existence. In the course of the evidence one of the constables stated that on Clark being stopped by Sergeant Reid and told that if he had been exceeding the speed limit he would be charged, he had shoved a half-sovereign into the Sergeant's hand. The Sergeant refused to be bribed, however, and Clark put the money back into his pocket, at the same time exclaiming, "Well, I don't care a d - - -." Mr. Forrest, solicitor, Perth, said on accused's behalf that he did not have a speedometer on the car, and in passing sentence of £5 or fourteen days imprisonment on Clark, Sheriff Sym said he had better have spent his half-sovereign in getting one.

'Thomas C. Dunlop, Caigowan, Ayr, who was also charged with travelling nearly 20 miles per hour, pleaded not guilty and in the evidence one of the constables said that he thought there was a lady in the car with accused, but it turned out to be a dog. The Fiscal explained that there had been an error in the accused's citation and he had been advised not to appear but he had considered it more honourable to do so. Mr. Jamison asked His Lordship to keep that fact in mind in passing sentence. One guinea of a fine was imposed.

'A fine of one guinea was imposed upon George Stein Smith, engineer, Flemington, Motherwell, who pleaded guilty to travelling over 14 miles per hour on a motor cycle on the same road. Another motor cyclist, Peter Rothnie, of Longside, Aberdeenshire, was tried in absence with travelling nearly 19 miles per hour and a fine of two guineas was imposed.'

For the ordinary folk of Edwardian times the most popular means of road transport was the bicycle. In its quiet, uncomplicated way this produced a social revolution. It brought the countryside, the lanes, the lochs and mountains for the first time within easy reach of the working classes of the big industrial towns. It enabled a man to live farther from his place of work and so to enjoy a measure of choice in his employment. It led to a change in young women's clothing, for those who had once been content to walk in skirts which swept the ground, even to skate and play tennis or golf in them, now found that such skirts were a handicap if not a positive danger when cycling. The female ankle at last made its appearance in public. The bicycle led also to a greater freedom in courtship, for young men and women could join a cycling club or even go for cycle rides together, away from the inquisitive eyes and clacking tongues of their own neighbourhood.

For a brief period before motor-cars became readily available for those who could afford them, the bicycle enjoyed a certain popularity even among the wealthy. Arthur Balfour chose a Sunday afternoon in March 1895 for his first cycle ride through the streets of London because, he wrote to Lady Elcho, 'the traffic was small, and I hoped that I might escape being run over by hansom or omnibus, even though my skill should be somewhat in default. I got on pretty well; in fact the streets were so empty that I found no difficulty at all except on one occasion when a hansom immediately in front of me turned the wrong way in order to get to its stand. The driver apologised, which is a rare exercise of politeness on the part of his kind.' The following year, when he was invited to stay with Gladstone at Hawarden, Balfour shocked the elderly statesman by riding up from the station on his bicycle.

Indirectly, the bicycle was also to some extent responsible for that ubiquitous symbol of the Edwardian scene, the picture postcard.

Although picture postcards had been popular for years in other countries, their production in Britain was retarded by the insistence of the Post Office that only the official plain postcards could pass through the posts for a halfpenny. Privately printed postcards were charged postage at the letter rate of one penny. In September 1894 the Post Office removed this restriction by fixing the postage on all types of postcards at the same halfpenny rate.

The first commercially produced postcards to show views of Scotland were placed on sale a few weeks later by an Edinburgh firm of printers, George Stewart and Co., and during the early years of the new century many other firms, including Valentine and Sons Ltd., of Dundee, and Millar and Lang Ltd., of Glasgow, were publishing picture postcard views. These made cheap and appropriate souvenirs of cycle rides as well as of railway day-excursions and summer holidays. Soon almost every stationer, newsagent and tobacconist in the kingdom was offering a selection of local views, and almost every middle-class home had its picture-postcard album sharing, with the Bible and the aspidistra, the table in the front-room window. Estimates place the number of picture postcards then being sold in Britain at about ten million every week, and it was not until the First World War brought disruption of social life and an increase in postage rates that the flood began to subside. The impression of Scotland left by the picture postcards in an Edwardian album is of a pleasant, peaceful land. The photographer seldom made his studies in the slums of Scottish cities and his camera best recorded the sunlit countryside, the lochs, mountains and tranquil villages on summer afternoons.

8

On the Stage

'The P. of W. has *never* been fond of reading', wrote the Queen to Mr. Gladstone in November 1872, adding that 'from his earliest years it was *impossible* to get him to do so. Newspapers and, *very rarely*, a novel, are all he ever reads.' Mr. Gladstone was anxious that the Prince, then thirty-one years old, should try 'to master many of the able and valuable works which bear upon Royal and Public duty'. The Queen's reply was not encouraging.

Twenty years later one of the pillars of Victorian literature, Lord Tennyson, the Poet Laureate, died and was buried in Westminster Abbey. There were caustic comments because the Prince of Wales was not at the ceremony; he was at Newmarket for the racing. The apparent slight was almost certainly unintentional. In the Prince's scale of values racing ranked high and literature very low.

If Lord Tennyson had been an eminent playwright or a comic opera librettist, the Prince might have been moved to make some valedictory gesture, for he had a life-long love of the theatre, his taste ranging from grand opera through Shakespeare and French farce to music-hall. When Lillie Langtry appeared at the Haymarket Theatre in a comedy about the Crimean War he attended three performances in the space of seven weeks. His enthusiasm both for the Jersey Lily and for the theatre was shared by many of his subjects. There were more than three hundred theatres in the United Kingdom, hundreds of music-halls and variety palaces, and countless concert halls, pier pavilions and agricultural halls or corn exchanges with facilities and licences for stage productions.

The music-hall had long been a popular feature of Scottish city life when the Naughty Nineties dawned, but it reached the height of its fame during the Edwardian period. Perhaps its zenith came on 1 July 1912, when the first Royal Command Variety Performance was staged at the Palace Theatre, London, in the presence of King George V and Queen Mary, with a party including princes, princesses, dukes

Their Majesties King Edward and Queen Alexandra.

Four sons of King George V, c. 1910:
George (later Duke of Kent), Albert (later
King George VI), Henry (later Duke of Gloucester)
and David (later King Edward VIII and Duke of Windsor).

Bleriot monoplane (pilot J. A. Drexel)
at Lanark, c. 1910.

The Arrol Johnston 18 h.p. motor car,
built about 1905 at Bluevale Works, Camlachie,
Glasgow.

and duchesses and even a Russian grand duchess. At one point in the proceedings the ladies in the royal party were advised, at Queen Mary's express wish, not to direct their gaze at the stage. Those who stole a glance might have seen the dapper little figure of Vesta Tilley, the celebrated comedienne, immaculately dressed as 'Piccadilly Johnny' and wearing—no sight for aristocratic ladies' eyes—a pair of trousers. Other famous performers included George Robey, the 'Prime Minister of Mirth', and Harry Tate, the Scotsman whose sketch of a motorist whose car would not move was amusingly topical. One notable absentee from the cast was Marie Lloyd, the Cockney star whose unorthodox private life and suggestive style of singing even the most innocuous songs would have made her a hazardous choice for a Royal Command performance. In retaliation Marie played to packed houses at the London Pavilion with a billing that scathingly declared 'Every performance given by Marie Lloyd is by command of the British public'.

But for a tragic accident in Edinburgh, the first Royal Command Variety Performance might have been staged there while the Court was in Scotland. The principal organiser of the performance was Sir Edward Moss, the theatre proprietor and impresario, who lived at Middleton Hall, Gorebridge, in Midlothian. Born in 1862, Horace Edward Moss had begun his theatrical career by playing the piano to accompany the scenes on a travelling diorama owned by his father. Moss senior then became proprietor of the Lorne Music Hall, in Greenock, where Edward learned the art of management before striking out on his own in 1877 to acquire the Gaiety Music Hall in Chambers Street, Edinburgh. A few years later he also bought a wooden hall in Leith and when this was burned down in 1888 he took over an old Presbyterian chapel in Kirkgate and transformed it into the Princess Theatre, opening at Christmas 1889. This later became a new Gaiety Music Hall to replace that in Edinburgh. Meanwhile Moss had acquired several English theatres, beginning with the Theatre Royal, Sunderland, which became the Royal Music Hall, and a concert hall in Newcastle-upon-Tyne which became the Gaiety Variety Theatre. The latter was outstandingly successful and formed the basis for the network of Moss Empires which eventually embraced more than thirty British theatres. Those in Scotland included the Gaiety Music Hall in Sauchiehall Street, Glasgow, and the Scotia, in the Gorbals. The most stately and sumptuous of all the Moss theatres was probably the Empire Palace, Edinburgh, which was richly decorated and lit by electricity. The inaugural performance, on 7 November 1892, was a memorable occasion enlivened by the massed bands of the Argyll and Sutherland Highlanders and the Carabineers, and by a troupe of performing dogs, Professor Maud's Canine Wonders.

Edward Moss, who had been knighted in 1906, hoped that the first Royal Command Variety Performance might be presented at the Empire Palace, which held an audience of three thousand. A tragedy prevented this. On the evening of 9 May 1911 the Great Lafayette was topping the bill at the Empire Palace. He was an illusionist who staged the most elaborate performances. In order to safeguard his secrets, he toured with his own stage-manager, scene-shifters and electricians, allowing none of the theatre staff to handle his equipment or props. The programme that evening included a dramatic illusion entitled *The Lion's Bride*, in which the Great Lafayette was arrayed in yellow silk robes as a Sultan selecting new stock for his harem. Among other luxurious accoutrements on the stage was a lively African lion who prowled and snarled in a large cage.

The action began when a beautiful Christian maiden was brought before the Sultan and offered the alternatives of joining his harem or of being thrown to the lion. As befitted a well-bred Christian virgin, she preferred the lion and to crashing crescendos from the orchestra the cage door was opened, the maiden was flung inside and the lion immediately leapt upon her. The illusion lay in the fact that by this point in the proceedings the real lion had been shut in a separate part of the stage, out of sight of the audience. An arrangement of mirrors gave the impression that the animal still had a free run of the cage but the creature which leapt upon the maiden was none other than the Great Lafayette himself, attired in a lion-skin while an understudy played the part of the Sultan.

Tragedy came when a lamp on stage burst into flames and set the drop curtains alight. The fire spread rapidly to the scenery but the fire-proof safety curtain was lowered and the large audience shuffled calmly out of the theatre as the orchestra played *God Save the King*. But on stage there was panic. The pass-doors leading from the stage to the auditorium had been locked as part of the Great Lafayette's secrecy measures and the stage exits were blocked by his extra scenery. Despite valiant efforts by the Edinburgh fire brigade, the Great Lafayette and nine members of his company were trapped on the stage and burned to death. Even then the mysteries did not end.

The Great Lafayette's body had been identifiable only by the fragments of charred yellow silk still clinging to it but there was no sign of two valuable diamond rings he was known to be wearing. The body was taken to Glasgow for cremation and the ashes returned to Edinburgh for burial at Piershill cemetery. Meanwhile the two rings had been found on another body in a scorched lion-skin on the debris-littered stage. This discovery positively identified the second body as that of the Great Lafayette. The first was that of his understudy as the Sultan, a stage-hand named Richards. Sir Edward Moss never fully recovered from the shock of this holocaust at the Empire Palace and he died less than five months after the Royal Command Variety Performance which he had spent so long in planning.

Other Scottish cities had their favourite music-halls, popularly known as 'penny gaffs' because the admission fee was usually one penny. Where it was as much as twopence or threepence, the ticket was in the form of a brass token which could be exchanged inside the music-hall for liquid refreshment or a cigar. In Dundee there was the People's Palace in Lochee Road, which was opened by the Livermore Brothers in 1891 and transferred two years later to a new site in the Nethergate. In 1910 it became a picture-house, or cinema, being replaced by the King's Theatre. Aberdeen was famous for its Alhambra Music Hall, opened in Market Street in 1875 by William McFarland, who also built Her Majesty's Theatre. The latter became the Tivoli Music Hall when the new His Majesty's was opened in 1906. Aberdeen also had its Alhambra Music Hall, opened in Bridge Street in 1898 by the Livermore Brothers.

One controversial Scottish performer at music-halls and theatres was Sam Bodie, billed as Doctor Walford Bodie. Born in 1871, he had been apprenticed as a boy to the National Telegraph Company, in Aberdeen, and there acquired a knowledge of electricity which he later put to good use. He began entertaining at Saturday evening concerts in Aberdeen but when his sister married the proprietor of a Norwich music-hall, Bodie decided to make the stage his career. He was at first a conjurer and ventriloquist but soon, with the help of his wife, who was billed as Princess Rubie, his sister, billed as Mystic Marie, and another girl known as La Belle Electra, he was presenting a dramatic entertainment which incorporated electrical experiments, hypnotism and mesmerism. From these Bodie developed a highly successful act in which, by what he called 'electrical wizardry', he appeared to cure invalids of their ailments and cripples of their deformities. The crutches said to have been discarded by people he had cured were used to publicise Dr. Bodie's act. 'His cures of paralysis by means of massage, electricity and hypnotic suggestions', recorded the *Variety Theatre Annual* in 1906, 'have been the wonder of the world, and he has been patronised by clergy, medical men and the élite of society in every part of the kingdom. Moreover, he has been the means of drawing to our music-halls a class of people who have never before entered their portals, and who, in all probability, would never have done so had it not been for the fame of his miracles—beg pardon—the Doctor emphatically rejects the idea of anything miraculous. Everything he does, he says, can be explained by natural scientific means.'

A striking figure in his silk hat and morning coat, with black moustache neatly waxed and spiked at each end, Dr. Bodie would drive to the theatre through the main streets of the town, in an open carriage with a smartly liveried coachman, much as if he had been a minor Royal personage. His visits were marred only by the vociferous antagonism of medical students, who disapproved of his use of hypnotism, of his 'natural cures', and of his use of the title 'Doctor'. He would jocularly counter that the initials 'M.D.' after his name stood simply for 'Merry Devil'.

Glasgow was the centre of a galaxy of music-halls and theatres. In the 1905 pantomime, *Aladdin*, at the Theatre Royal, Harry Lauder introduced a new song. Earlier that year he had been leaving a London theatre when the stage door keeper handed him a letter in a pink envelope. 'That's sure from a lady, Mr. Lauder', remarked the door keeper. 'I suppose you love a lassie?' The question gave Lauder the theme for a song which he was to make famous, *I Love a Lassie*. His singing of it at the Theatre Royal every night for thirteen weeks brought him fame and a triumphant tour of the United States.

Lauder had been born at Portobello on 4 August 1870, one of the seven children of a potter employed at Musselburgh. When Lauder was eleven his father was tempted by a promise of higher wages to move to a pottery near Chesterfield, in Derbyshire, but within a few weeks of arriving there he died suddenly of pneumonia. Fortunately his life had been insured for fifteen pounds and this sum was sufficient to pay for his funeral and for the return of the family to Scotland, where they settled near Mrs. Lauder's relatives in Arbroath. There Harry Lauder began work as a 'half-timer' in a local flax mill for a weekly wage of 2s. 1d. (10½p). He made his first public appearance as a singer at a Band of Hope temperance meeting where he stood, barefoot and ragged, to intone with unconscious irony a melancholy ballad entitled *I'm a Gentleman still.*

The Lauder family's next move was to Hamilton, where Harry became a miner at ten shillings a week. By the time of his marriage in 1890 to the daughter of a colliery underground manager he already enjoyed local fame as a singer at Saturday evening concerts, street-corner singing contests and church bazaars. His earnings as a butty miner, working on contract, reached three pounds a week and in his autobiography, *Roamin' in the Gloamin'*, he later gave an amusing account of how he and his bride, Annie Vallance, were able to furnish a miner's but-and-ben cottage, rented at 3s. 6d. per week, for less than fifteen pounds.

Soon afterwards Lauder answered an advertisement in the *Evening Citizen* asking for a comedian to join a Glasgow concert party at a weekly salary of 35s. for a fourteen-week tour starting at Beith. Despite a temporary set-back when he was forced to return to his work as a Hamilton miner, Harry Lauder was thenceforth determined to make a career as a professional comedian. By studying the technique of such recognised performers as Dan Leno and Gus Elen when they played at the Glasgow Empire, he gained enough confidence to take a third-class single ticket to Euston on 19 March 1900. His venture was successful. He began as a stand-in at Gatti's Music Hall in Westminster Bridge Road, where he made instant hits with his *Tobermory*, *The Lass o' Killiecrankie*, and *Calligan, Call Again*. He was soon appearing at the renowned Tivoli Music Hall, in the Strand, known to every young London man-about-town as the 'Tiv', where whisky cost threepence a glass, beer twopence, and cigarettes were threepence for ten. The 1905 pantomime and the success of *I Love a Lassie* led to a contract for a tour of the United States in the autumn of 1907. Harry Lauder's only son, John, then a boy of sixteen, went with his father as accompanist. Another memorable Glasgow pantomime for Lauder was that of 1910, when he sang for the first time his *Roamin' in the Gloamin'*, a song inspired by the sight of two lovers whom Lauder had noticed one summer evening while strolling along the road from Innellan to Dunoon.

The image of Scotland which Harry Lauder so assiduously propagated during the Edwardian period was irritatingly trite and trivial where it was not downright spurious. The 'ower thrifty wee mannie' with his crooked stick, his cackling voice and his pawky humour, was a superficial caricature, and his jokes, like the words of his sentimental songs, lie leaden on the printed page. But he combined a masterly stage technique with a popular appeal which made him the idol of the Scottish music-halls. Behind the caricature Lauder was a warm-hearted, generous and homely Scot who never ceased to rejoice in the combination of talent and good fortune which had brought him wealth and fame, and who, despite his disservice to it, dearly loved his native land.

The noisy, vulgar, smoke-laden music-halls provided entertainment mainly for working-class men and women, and for young men of the middle class who were engaged in the characteristic Edwardian pastime of sowing their wild oats. For the soberer and more genteel families there were church and school concerts, choral recitals, musical evenings and, in the more enterprising communities, amateur performances of musical comedies and Gilbert and Sullivan operas. These entertainments were supplemented in provincial towns by the professional companies who toured with productions of the musical plays which were so popular with middle- and upper-class Edwardian audiences. These stylish plays gave greater scope than the Gilbert and Sullivan operas for actors and actresses to parade their individual talents, the trifling plot being usually no more than a vehicle for a series of catchy tunes, a succession of topical jokes and a display of colourful costumes, pretty faces and fashionable hour-glass figures.

'This is supremely the day of musical comedies', declared the *Perthshire Courier* on January 1910 in its review of *The Cingalee*, which was being staged that week at the Perth Theatre, 'and it will not do to be in this respect "rank outsiders", so that those to whom the term was applied should hasten to remove the stigma and see *The Cingalee*, in which there are no fewer than 26 musical numbers. A devilish fire dance connected with the rites of the Bhuddist religion is a striking item, but its comedy is its greatest feature, roars of laughter following the piece from start to finish.'

The leading Scottish classical actor of the Edwardian period was Johnston Forbes-Robertson, who was born in London on 16 January 1853, the sone of an Aberdeen art critic. He seemed destined to become an artist and his handsome face and fine bearing led Rossetti to choose him as the model for Dante in the painting *Love Kissing Beatrice*, but he turned instead to the theatre. He toured at first in minor parts with Samuel Phelps, Ellen Terry, Squire Bancroft and Mary Anderson, the Scottish–American actress, before playing Romeo at the Lyceum Theatre, with Mrs. Patrick Campbell as Juliet. In September 1897 Forbes-Robertson achieved his greatest success in *Hamlet* at the Lyceum. His golden voice and commanding appearance invested two of his other productions, *The Passing of the Third Floor Back* and *Mice and Men*, with an authority which neither of those mediocre plays merited, and it was appropriate that for his farewell London performance at Drury Lane on 6 June 1913 he again played Hamlet. He was knighted at the end of the 1913 season and toured in England, Scotland and the United States before retiring in 1916.

In the realm of serious music one of the most notable events of the period was the building of the Usher Hall, Edinburgh. Its donor, Andrew Usher, had intimated to the Lord Provost in June 1896 that he wished to make a gift of £100,000 to the city to build a hall which 'should remain a centre of attraction to musical artistes and performers, and to the citizens of Edinburgh and others who may desire to hear good music, instrumental and vocal'. Usher's death in November 1898 was followed by a long controversy over a suitable site for the hall but in July 1911 King George V and Queen Mary were able to lay memorial foundation stones, one at either side of the Cambridge Street entrance, and on 6 March 1914 the hall was officially opened by Mrs. Usher. The City Fathers were present in force and an audience of 2,500 heard the dedicatory performance, an organ recital and a choral-orchestral concert which included an *Imperial March* by Sir Edward Elgar, an improvisation on Scottish airs, and a Rachmaninoff prelude as well as works by Grieg, Wagner, Mendelssohn and Meyerbeer.

9

Kailyard and Comics

If music and drama of all kinds, sacred and profane, sentimental and serious, flourished during the Edwardian period, Scottish literature presented a paradox. It was widely popular, especially among the mass of new readers provided by the new schemes of universal education. Yet it suffered from excesses of coy whimsicality and sugary sentimentality. Such qualities were particularly characteristic of what was known as the 'Kailyard School'. This had its origins in 1894, when an English-born minister of Highland descent, John Watson, produced, under the pen-name 'Ian Maclaren', a collection of sketches of Scottish characters entitled *Beside the Bonnie Briar Bush*. The title was taken from an anonymous popular song of the mid-eighteenth century, which contained two lines quoted in Watson's book:

'There grows a bonnie briar bush in our kailyard
And white are the blossoms on't in our kailyard'

In the same genre and equally successful was his next book, *The Days of Auld Lang Syne*, published in 1895. Another member of the Kailyard School was Samuel R. Crockett, who was born at Balmaghie, in Galloway, on 24 September 1860. He took a degree at Edinburgh University and was a private tutor before returning to Edinburgh to study at New College for the ministry. His early books, *The Stickit Minister and Some Common Men*, published in 1893, and *The Lilac Sun-Bonnet*, published in 1894, were examples of Kailyardism at its worst but some of his later historical novels, in which Crockett had less scope to depict contemporary Scottish life as he believed he knew it, were of better quality. Two, *The Raiders*, published in 1894, and *The Black Douglas*, published in 1899, were competent stories, but his later work was again mediocre and by the time he died in 1914 his sentimental romances were mannered and superficial.

But the Kailyard cult found its arch-priest—arch, indeed—in James Matthew Barrie. Born in Brechin Road, Kirriemuir, on 9 May

1860, Barrie was the son of a hand-loom weaver and his wife Margaret Ogilvy, an uncompromisingly religious woman who had belonged before her marriage to the puritanical Protestant sect known as the Auld Lichts. There were ten children, of whom two died in infancy, and although the family was poor the parents were industrious and careful of their children's education. The eldest boy won a bursary at Aberdeen University, three of the daughters became pupil teachers, and James, after spells at Glasgow Academy, Forfar Academy and Dumfries Academy, went up to Edinburgh University. His first post was as a leader-writer on the *Nottingham Journal*, but in 1885 he decided to seek his fortune as a free-lance journalist in London. His second book, *Auld Licht Idylls*, published in 1888, was moderately successful and he followed it in 1889 with *A Window in Thrums*. He was meanwhile contributing regularly to the *British Weekly*, a 'journal of social and Christian progress' edited by William Robertson Nicoll, another Scottish ex-minister who had sought literary fame and fortune in London. Nicoll had been born in 1851 at Lumsden, near Huntly, and after Free Church charges at Dufftown and Kelso he turned to journalism as a career, writing a life of 'Ian Maclaren' in 1908.

The Kailyard School of writers, of which these four were the leading proponents, was notable for its technical skill and lively imagination and notorious for its sentimental whimsy and the narrowness of its range. Kailyard literature was peopled by shallow caricatures which many readers took to be genuine Scottish characters. There were saintly ministers, beautiful gypsy girls, dedicated doctors and poverty-stricken dominies surrounded by a gaggle of half-witted villagers, some virtuous and therefore duly rewarded either here or in the hereafter, others less so and earning redemption only by timely repentance, but most of them mawkish misrepresentations of the true Scottish people. To the comfortable English middle-class reader, the Kailyard stories were gently humorous and complacently reassuring. They were exposed as half-truths when another Scottish literary exile in London, the Ayrshire-born George Douglas Brown, wrote his *House with the Green Shutters* in 1901. In this, 'George Douglas' presented the harsher aspects of Scottish life, with its hard drinking, coarse language and grinding poverty as well as its piety, patriotism and nobility.

Four years before his death in 1937, Barrie opened a baazar in Kirriemuir to raise funds for the town band. He spoke whimsically of his pet canary, sentimentally of the baby Princess Margaret, and nostalgically of 'this town of memories', the 'Thrums' of his early sketches. 'How strange to find it is now a town of motor-cars', he said. 'You step into one at a door, and before you have time to sit down you step out at another door in one of the glens. It is also to me, naturally, a town of ghosts. I see them running about terrified through the square, through the wynds, and I guess they are running away in fear of the electric light.'

Barrie spent his life running away from the electric light of reality. His early books, like the Kirriemuir town band, survived the First World War but foundered before the Second. A few of his plays, notably *The Admirable Crichton*, *Dear Brutus* and *Mary Rose*, remained favourites with the repertory companies of provincial theatres but only his *Peter Pan* has stood the sternest tests of time, a perennial delight to audiences composed mainly of the very young or the very elderly and a source of income for the Great Ormond Street Hospital for Sick Children, to which Barrie gave the copyright.

By the turn of the century the Education Acts had brought into existence a huge new reading public. It consisted of two general categories: those who sought merely to be amused and entertained through the medium of the printed word; and those who, although by no means academic in inclination, sought as an extension of their elementary schooling some form of instruction, whether in classical literature, a foreign language, an indoor hobby, a domestic craft or an outdoor pastime. The newspapers of the time began to reflect this demand for both entertainment and instruction. Periodicals such as *Tit-Bits*, founded in 1881 by George Newnes, *Answers*, founded in 1888 by Alfred Harmsworth, and *Pearson's Weekly*, founded in 1890 by Arthur Pearson, were readable, sprightly and amusing. Their success led Harmsworth to launch, on 4 May 1896, a new halfpenny newspaper, the *Daily Mail*. Brisk, hard-hitting, exciting and above all profitable, the *Mail* was soon joined by other newspapers of a similar type. Among these were the *Daily Dispatch*, first published in Manchester in 1900, the *Daily Express*, launched by Arthur Pearson, also in 1900, the *Daily Mirror*, founded in 1903 as a penny paper for women but unsuccessful until Harmsworth took control of it, the *Daily Sketch*, founded in Manchester by Edward Hulton in 1909, and the *Daily Herald*, the first Labour daily newspaper, founded in 1912. The solid, closely printed columns of the traditional daily press were now enlivened by headlines, cross-heads, chatty space-fillers and pictures. During the years between 1901 and 1910, an average of one new newspaper made its appearance somewhere in the United Kingdom every fortnight. Most of the newcomers were provincial weeklies and they were supplemented by a wide range of new, tabloid, comic papers for children and for semi-literate adults.

Of these comic papers the best known was *Comic Cuts*, launched in May 1890 by Alfred Harmsworth. It was followed two months later by *Chips*, another Harmsworth venture, for which Tom Browne, a Nottingham artist, created the two immortal tramps, Weary Willie and Tired Tim. Colour came to the comic world in two more Harmsworth weeklies, *Puck*, first published in July 1904, and *The Rainbow*, which in February 1914 brought to life Tiger Tim and the Bruin Boys. Also for younger readers there was an annual collection of fairy stories, legends and historical romances under such titles as *The Violet Fairy Book* (1901), *The Book of Romance* (1902), *The Red Book of Romance* (1905) and *Tales of Troy and Greece* (1907). These collections were edited by Andrew Lang, yet another Scot who had migrated to London to devote himself to journalism and belles-lettres. Lang was a Borderer, born in 1844 at Viewfields, Selkirk. He attended Selkirk Grammar School and later Edinburgh Academy, from where he went to the University of St. Andrews and Balliol College, Oxford. He was for seven years a fellow of Merton College and then moved to Kensington to establish himself as a critic, poet, essayist and editor. His output was prodigious and his scholarship deeper than that of most of his Scottish contemporaries in London literary circles. The success of his collections of stories for children enabled him to spend the last years of his life in the study of Scottish history. His *Prince Charles Edward*, published in 1900, and his four-volume *History of Scotland from the Roman Occupation*, published between 1900 and 1907, were his most notable works. Lang died at Banchory on 20 July 1912.

Among the staider magazines, *Blackwood's* and *Chambers's Journal* pursued their stately careers, the former over eighty and the latter almost seventy years old when the new century dawned. They had been joined in January 1891 by a livelier illustrated monthly, the *Strand Magazine*, founded by George Newnes, which reached a sale of 400,000 copies per month during its heyday in the Edwardian era. Many famous authors wrote either fact or fiction for the *Strand*, among them the Edinburgh-trained doctor, Arthur Conan Doyle, whose Sherlock Holmes has his own place in English literature.

A young Scot who during the Edwardian years was embarking upon a varied and distinguished career in journalism, authorship, politics and diplomacy was John Buchan. He was born at Perth in 1875, the son of a Free Church minister of Border descent, and was educated in Glasgow and at Brasenose College, Oxford. His first book, a light historical romance, was published while he was still an undergraduate, but after leaving Oxford he became a barrister and was then appointed private secretary to Lord Milner, the High Commissioner for South Africa. Two years later Buchan returned home and became a partner in the Edinburgh publishing firm of Thomas Nelson and Sons. 'Apart from a few short stories', he wrote later in his autobiography, *Memory Hold the Door*, 'I let fiction alone until 1910, when, being appalled as a publisher by the dullness of most boys' books, I thought I would attempt one of my own, based on my African experience.'

The book was *Prester John* and its opening scenes are set in Kirkcaldy, Fife, where Buchan had spent part of his childhood. The novels recounting the adventures of Richard Hannay, *The Thirty-Nine Steps*, *Greenmantle* and *Mr. Standfast*, were not published until after the outbreak of the First World War, but they have about them an unmistakably Edwardian atmosphere which adds to their interest as period pieces while detracting from their value as studies of the human condition. But taken as forthright adventure stories, which was Buchan's own estimate of them, his books are models of their kind, exciting, aseptic, morally uplifting and superbly written. This, indeed, was true of much of the writing of Scottish Edwardian authors, and particularly of those who emigrated to southern England.

Ill-health and personal tragedy so restricted the output of another Scottish author that his reputation has come to rest almost entirely on a single book for children, *The Wind in the Willows*. Kenneth Grahame was born in Edinburgh in 1859 but when his mother died five years later and his father, a lawyer, took to drink, the child went to live with a grandmother in Berkshire. He entered the Bank of England as a clerk and rose to become its Secretary before he retired in 1908. His book, redolent of summer afternoons in sunny woodlands along the banks of the Thames, was based on stories he told to amuse his small son, Alastair. Its delicate poetry and gentle humour have made it a favourite with children but Alastair died in a level-crossing accident while at Oxford and Kenneth Grahame wrote little in the last years of his life.

At a deeper level *The Wind in the Willows* repays study, for it presents a microcosm of the Edwardian age. Toad is the bombastic *nouveau riche* whose vanity and egotism are intensified beyond all reason as soon as he grasps the steering-wheel of that repulsive new contraption, the motor-car. Ratty has a touch of the poet, a genteel trait, in his nature and comes nearest to nonconformity when he is tempted by the Water Rat, the personification of the seafaring tradition which had brought Edwardian Britain so much wealth and influence. Badger and Mole, on the other hand, are the epitome of solid good sense, and the only threat to the tranquil life of the River Bank comes from the anarchistic lower classes of the Wild Wood, the roistering stoats and weasels.

10

The Liberal Landslide

One fine morning at the turn of the century four Liberal Members of Parliament climbed a hill on a Fife estate, Raith, which belonged to one of them, Sir Ronald Munro-Ferguson, member for the Leith Burghs. The others were Herbert Asquith, Richard Haldane and Augustine Birrell, all later to hold high office in Liberal governments. From the top of the hill they had a wide view of the Firth of Forth and the surrounding countryside. 'What a grateful thought,' said Birrell, 'that there is not an acre in this vast and varied landscape which is not represented at Westminster by a London barrister.'

His remark, although true, was misleading. Asquith's constituency at that time was East Fife, Birrell's was West Fife, and Haldane's was Haddingtonshire, and all three men had been called to the bar; but the implication that Scotland was not only ruled by a parliament which sat in England but was also represented in it by Englishmen ignored the dominating position which Scotsmen had achieved in successive governments and the influence they exercised over Britain's affairs during the Edwardian period. Of the five prime ministers who held office during the twenty-two years between Gladstone's resignation on 3 March 1894 and that of Asquith on 5 December 1916, Rosebery was a Scot, Balfour's family could claim descent from Robert the Bruce, Campbell-Bannerman was a Scot, and although Asquith was a Yorkshireman, he was married to a Scotswoman and he sat for the whole of his thirty-six years in the Commons as a member for Scottish constituencies.

The Scottish contribution to British politics throughout the late nineteenth and early twentieth century was predominantly Liberal in character. The Parliamentary Reform Act introduced by Disraeli in 1867 had allotted seven extra seats to Scotland, making a total of sixty, and the Re-distribution Act of 1885 increased this to seventy-two. Excepts for the 'khaki election' of September 1900, held in the jingoistic atmosphere engendered by the outbreak of the Boer War, the Liberals consistently won a majority of the Scottish seats, whatever the result of the general election as a whole.

When Gladstone resigned office in 1894, six months after the rejection by the House of Lords of his second Irish Home Rule Bill, Queen Victoria pointedly ignored his offer to advise her in the choice of his successor, and made her own decision instead. It was an unexpected one. Disregarding both Earl Spencer, whom Gladstone would have suggested, and Sir William Harcourt, the Chancellor of the Exchequer, she invited the Foreign Secretary, Archibald Philip Primrose, the fifth Earl of Rosebery, to form the new Liberal administration.

Born in London in 1847, the son of Viscount Dalmeny, the new Prime Minister had been educated at Eton and Oxford. While still an undergraduate he succeeded his grandfather to the earldom, and although outstandingly talented he left Oxford without taking a degree because the university authorities objected to his keeping a racehorse. Already immensely rich, he added to his possession by marrying one of the greatest heiresses in England, Hannah de Rothschild, so that he enjoyed an income of towards £150,000 a year at a time when a salary of £150 a year spelled comfort and security for a craftsman or a clerk. His property included a house in Berkeley Square, a mansion at The Durdans, near Epsom Downs, for the racing in which he delighted, a Rothschild palace at Mentmore, near Leighton Buzzard, a villa near Naples, the family seat at Dalmeny, and Barnbougle Castle, on the Firth of Forth.

For all his eloquence and literary talents, his aristocratic charm and easy manner, his mature judgement and sparkling bursts of anger or enthusiasm, Rosebery was not a successful politician on the national scale. He had never fought a parliamentary election campaign, with what Winston Churchill described as 'its disorderly gatherings, its organised oppositions, its hostile little meetings, its jeering throng, its stream of disagreeable and often silly questions'. One of Rosebery's masters at Eton had said of him that 'he sought the palm without the dust'.

Rosebery had entered politics during Gladstone's Midlothian campaign and immediately began his agitation for a separate government department to deal with Scottish affairs. At that time these were the responsibility of the Home Secretary, who was advised by the Lord Advocate. In practice the latter was normally too preoccupied with his work in the law courts to give more than cursory attention to other Scottish matters, much less to initiate new policies. When Gladstone finally yielded in 1880 to pressure for the introduction of a Scottish Under-Secretary for Home Affairs, Rosebery was appropriately the first to be appointed. Five years later the Liberals introduced a bill to provide for a full Secretary for Scotland, independent of the Home Office and with a seat in the Cabinet. Lord Salisbury's 'caretaker' government passed the bill into law and the first Scottish Secretary was the Duke of Richmond, but when Gladstone became Prime Minister again in February 1886, he appointed an Englishman, Sir George Trevelyan, to the Scottish Office. This so incensed some of the Scottish Members of Parliament that the following year they formed the Scottish Home Rule Association, with Dr. G. P. Clark, Liberal member for Caithness, as chairman, and Mr. R. B. Cunninghame Graham, Liberal member for North-West Lanarkshire, as secretary. The same year, with Gladstone's introduction of his first Irish Home Rule Bill on 8 April 1886, the next chapter in the long and bitter struggle over Ireland began. During the succeeding years almost all the Scottish Liberal and Labour members, as well as many English Liberal and Labour members, also favoured some measure of Scottish Home Rule, and a motion advocating a separate Scottish parliament was introduced in the Commons almost every year between 1889 and 1900.

Soon after he took office in March 1894, Rosebery proposed the appointment of a Grand Committee comprising all the Scottish members, with fifteen others to ensure a fair balance of parties, to take the committee stage of bills relating exclusively to Scotland. But the Prime Minister also made clear his agreement with Lord Salisbury's view that before Irish or for that matter Scottish Home Rule could be granted, England, as the dominant partner in the United Kingdom, would have to be convinced of its justice and equity. Rosebery later expressed some regret at his blunt endorsement of Conservative policy over Ireland and there is little doubt that if the thorny Irish problem could have been solved, he would have prosecuted more vigorously the campaign which he had set in motion for a greater measure of Scottish control over Scotland's own affairs. Other members were more determined and the day after the scheme for the Scottish Grand Committee had been introduced, Mr. J. H. Dalziel, Liberal member for the Kirkcaldy Burghs, called for a Scottish legislature to deal with Scottish domestic matters. His proposal was

Countess of Warwick

Duchess of Sutherland and her
daughter

Harry Lauder

Mrs. Evelyn Thaw

Glasgow Cross, with a Springburn tram.

Dutch seamen at Lerwick.

accepted by 180 votes to 170, the first occasion that the Commons had voted in favour of Scottish Home Rule. The young member for the Caernarvon Boroughs, David Lloyd George, had an even wider view of the need for devolution. At one of his Welsh Nationalist meetings in the spring of 1895 there was, records Frank Owen in his biography of Lloyd George, *Tempestuous Journey*, some celebrated backchat.

'Home Rule for Ireland! Home Rule for Wales! Home Rule for Scotland! Yes, and Home Rule for England, too!' declaimed Lloyd George.

'Home Rule for Hell!' shouted a heckler.

Quick as a flash came the Welshman's reply. 'Quite right—let every man speak up for his own country!'

But despite Augustine Birrell's more serious argument that Home Rule for Scotland would be safer and easier to introduce than Home Rule for Ireland, because Scotland had no Fenians or Orangemen, the proposal was not accepted by the government. Not for the first time or the last the quarrels of Irishmen spilled across the narrow seas to bedevil Scottish aspirations.

Rosebery's term of office, from March 1894 to June 1895, was difficult. He had a majority of fewer than fifty in the Commons, he was surrounded by a hostile majority in the Lords, and his Chancellor of the Exchequer, Sir William Harcourt, was still jealous and resentful at having been passed over for the premiership. The ministry's most solid success lay in Harcourt's 1894 budget, which introduced a comprehensive scale of death duties, ranging from 1% on estates valued at between £100 and £500 to 15% on estates of over a million pounds sterling. The Prime Minister's most spectacular achievement was to win the Derby twice in successive years, in 1894 with *Ladas* and in 1895 with *Sir Visto*. Even this unique success was not unalloyed, for the Liberal Party was strong in Nonconformists who believed that racing, and the gambling which accompanied it, were inappropriate activities for the successor of Mr. Gladstone. For the rest, in Asquith's telling phrase, the government was 'ploughing the sands'. In June 1895, during a debate on the Army Estimates, a snap division on the supply of cordite was carried against the government and Rosebery resigned. The Conservatives won the following month's general election and Lord Salisbury again settled quietly into office.

Two years later Rosebery resigned his leadership of the Liberal Party and was succeeded in the Lords by Earl Spencer and in the

Commons by Sir William Harcourt, who resigned in December 1898 and was replaced by Sir Henry Campbell-Bannerman. Meanwhile the quarrel with the Boers was splitting the Liberal Party into three groups. On the left of the party were the Pro-Boers or Little Englanders, who represented the Gladstonian tradition in distrust of imperialism. Their leader was John Morley, member for the Montrose Burghs. Another active spokesman for the twenty or thirty Pro-Boers in the Commons was Lloyd George, who narrowly escaped with his life when he spoke against the war on 18 December 1901 in Birmingham Town Hall. The supporters of Joseph Chamberlain, the Liberal Unionist and arch-imperialist, would almost certainly have torn the fiery little Welshman limb from limb had he not been smuggled out of the Town Hall in a policeman's uniform.

At the other extreme of the party were the Liberal Imperialists, whose fifty members in the Commons included Herbert Asquith, Edward Grey and Richard Haldane. Their leader was Rosebery himself, who in 1902 launched a new organisation, the Liberal League, to attack the government for its incompetent conduct of the war, to oppose the introduction of Home Rule for Ireland, and to promote the concept of the British Empire as, in Rosebery's own perceptive phrase, 'a Commonwealth of Nations'.

Between these two extremes lay the great bulk of the Liberal Party, led by Sir Henry Campbell-Bannerman, M.P. for Stirling. They supported the Boer War in principle but attacked the methods by which it was being fought and urged the necessity of a negotiated settlement instead of the unconditional surrender of the Boers which the government was demanding as a pre-condition to peace. In a speech at Edinburgh on 31 May 1901 Campbell-Bannerman castigated as folly the 'most unworthy policy of enforcing unconditional surrender upon those who were to be their legal and contented subjects in the new colonies'. In London a fortnight later he declared that the war was being 'carried on by methods of barbarism'. Over Home Rule for Ireland the divisions were blurred. Asquith had for years been convinced of its necessity while Campbell-Bannerman believed that it might best be achieved by prudent instalments rather than in one fell swoop. Such divergent views even within the rival factions served only to emphasise the apparent disintegration of the Liberal Party.

Meanwhile the Conservative Party was beginning to suffer divisions as deep as those which were rending its opponents, with the significant difference that although the end of the Boer War was likely to heal some of the wounds which the Liberals were inflicting on one another, those which were afflicting the Conservatives were likely to be aggravated when peace in South Africa brought other problems to the fore. On 11 July 1902 Lord Salisbury resigned the premiership he had held, except for two brief periods, since 1885. Just as Rosebery seemed to be the last of the great Whig aristocrats, with roots deep in the eighteenth century, so Salisbury was the last exponent of the old aristocratic Conservatism. He had been born when there was still a Bourbon on the throne of France and had lived to see transatlantic wireless telegraphy, the *Daily Mail*, the *Daily Express* and girls on bicycles. He had been an opponent of the Parliamentary Reform Act of 1867, of an eight-hour working day for coal-miners, and of Irish Home Rule. He was criticised for nepotism and his Cabinet was nicknamed the 'Hotel Cecil' because three of its portfolios were held by members of his family and his eldest son was Under-Secretary for Foreign Affairs. Yet his policies in overseas affairs had seemed firm and wise, he was pious and intellectual, sincere and patriotic. Inevitably his successor was the Scottish nephew who had become his Parliamentary Private Secretary in 1878 and had served him faithfully in defeat and victory for almost a quarter of a century.

Arthur James Balfour was born at Whittinghame, East Lothian, in July 1848, the son of James Maitland Balfour and his wife, Lady Blanche Gascoyne Cecil, sister of the Lord Robert Cecil who afterwards became Marquis of Salisbury and Prime Minister. The eldest boy in a family of nine, Arthur was only eight when his father died, so that his relations with his mother were particularly close. Her death in 1872 was followed three years later by the death of an English girl, May Lyttelton, whom Balfour had hoped to marry. The two bereavements left an indelible mark on his temperament, and although he was far from being the dour, taciturn Scot of the stereotype, he came to be regarded as cold and unemotional, with the sybarite's enjoyment of human companionship and the cynic's contempt for it. He had many close acquaintances but few deep friends. 'It is just possible', wrote Lord Beaverbrook of him in later years, 'that he didn't believe in anything or anybody.'

Balfour entered Parliament in 1874 and when Lord Salisbury formed his second ministry in 1886, he appointed his nephew to the Scottish Office. That summer in Skye and Tiree there was a crofters' rent strike which threatened to become violent. Balfour handled the affair so firmly and wisely that when it was settled Salisbury promoted the Secretary for Scotland to Cabinet rank. Balfour did not enjoy the promotion for long. In March 1887 he succeeded Sir Michael Hicks-Beach as Chief Secretary for Ireland, an office he held for over four and a half turbulent years, during which he pacified Ireland by turning it into an armed camp and ruthlessly suppressing every outbreak of disorder.

In 1891 Balfour left the Irish Office to become First Lord of the Treasury and Leader of the House of Commons. He held the same posts in Salisbury's next administration, from 1895 to 1900. By this time the Prime Minister's health was beginning to fail, so that after the 'khaki' election' of 1900 his doctors prevailed upon him to give up the Foreign Office, which was taken by the Marquess of Lansdowne. To Balfour fell increasingly the responsibility of acting as a deputy Prime Minister. At Hogmanay 1900, celebrated as the end of the nineteenth century, the Balfour family gathered at Whittinghame and Blanche Dugdale, Balfour's niece, later described in her biography, *Arthur James Balfour*, how on New Year's Eve Uncle Arthur insisted that all the children should be awakened to join the older members of the family. There came a procession of little figures in pig-tails and scarlet dressing-gowns, and with another niece, Alison, on his knee, Uncle Arthur dispensed the traditional mulled claret to young and old. Then the front door was opened and the twentieth century was admitted.

At the beginning of June 1902 news reached London that peace terms between the British and the Boers had been agreed at Vereeniging and the following month Balfour succeeded his uncle as Prime Minister. His Chancellor of the Exchequer was Dundee-born Charles T. Ritchie and his Home Secretary was A. Akers Douglas. The Balfour ministry was notable in foreign affairs for the *Entente Cordiale*, the convention negotiated with France in 1904 to settle outstanding differences between the two countries, and for the renewal of the Japanese alliance. It ran into a storm of criticism over the employment of Chinese labourers in the South African gold mines. This was categorised as 'Chinese slavery' because the Chinese, of whom there were about 47,000 by the end of 1905, were brought to South Africa without their womenfolk, forced to live in compounds, worked long hours for very low wages and were subject to corporal punishment. The arrangement aroused criticism from trade unionists on economic grounds and from Nonconformists on moral grounds, although Churchill was later to admit that the epithet 'Chinese slavery' was, in his memorable euphemism, a 'terminological inexactitude'.

At home the government's record was mediocre. An Education Bill for England and Wales, introduced in the previous session, became law in December 1902. It replaced the school boards by education committees of the county or county borough councils and provided scholarships at fee-charging secondary schools so that the 'lad o' pairts' had at least a small chance to progress from elementary school to university, a chance he had enjoyed in Scotland for centuries. But the bitter opposition of many Nonconformists was aroused by the Act's Provision that Church of England and Roman Catholic voluntary schools should receive financial aid from the new education committees while continuing to give denominational religious instruction and to retain a measure of private management, especially in regard to the appointment of teachers. A less controversial Licensing Act in 1904 provided that public-house licences which the justices at Quarter Sessions decided to be unnecessary should be withdrawn and that compensation should be paid to dispossessed licensees from a fund to be raised by the brewing trade. Meanwhile the large Conservative majority which had been gained at the 'khaki election' was being steadily whittled away as the war fever subsided and the wounds of the Liberal Party began to heal. At a by-election in November 1902 the Liberals regained the seat at Orkney and Shetland which they had lost to the Conservatives in 1900. In the seven by-elections fought during 1903, the Conservatives lost six seats, four of them, including Argyllshire and St. Andrews, to the Liberals, and another to Labour. The trend continued throughout 1904 and 1905, when seventeen by-elections resulted in the loss of fifteen Conservative seats, fourteen of them, including Ayr, North-East Lanarkshire, and Bute, to the Liberals.

The principal architect of these misfortunes was Joseph Chamberlain, a Liberal who had split his party by opposing Irish Home Rule and leading 93 Liberals Unionists to vote against Gladstone's first Home Rule Bill. Chamberlain had then moved steadily to the right in politics, finally accepting the office of Colonial Secretary in the government formed by Lord Salisbury in 1895. Under Balfour he retained the office, having transformed it into one of the most important in the Cabinet. His close contacts with the colonies persuaded him to the need for a fiscal policy based on tariff reform and imperial preference. His proposal was that a tariff wall of duties on all imports, including food, should be erected round Britain. By agreement this wall would be lowered at certain points to admit food and manufactured goods from the colonies at reduced rates of duty. In this way Britain would become the centre of a vast customs union covering a quarter of the world's land surface and embracing 400 million people.

To spread the doctrine of protection, Chamberlain and his supporters formed the Tariff Reform League, and in September 1903 he resigned from the government to devote his entire energies to the campaign. He opened it on 6 October 1903 with a speech in St. Andrew's Hall, Glasgow. 'I am in a great city, the second of the Empire,' he began, 'the city which by the enterprise and intelligence which it has always shown is entitled to claim something of a representative character in respect of British industry.' He went on to propose a two-shilling duty on corn and the same on flour; a 5% duty on foreign meat and other food products, except bacon; and reductions in the existing duties on tea, sugar, coffee and cocoa, which came principally from the colonies.

The Liberals were not slow to pour scorn on the apparent inconsistencies in Chamberlain's political career. Campbell-Bannerman, addressing a large meeting in January 1904, also in St. Andrew's Hall, compared Chamberlain to 'an ingenious practitioner whose pockets are full of patent medicines'. 'He has', went on Campbell-Bannermann, 'a prescription for each patient. He strives to keep them separate and all goes well so long as each prescription reaches nobody but the right patient. Unfortunately for Mr. Chamberlain, however, newspaper readers frequently get more than one drug at the same time. Those who swallow all that Mr. Chamberlain says', concluded the Liberal leader, 'must be reduced to a lamentable mental condition.'

In a speech made in Aberdeen the same month, Winston Churchill used a different metaphor. 'We now observe', he said, 'that the brilliant defender of free trade has become the foremost champion of protection. It looks less like a political manoeuvre than like that very novel acrobatic performance which is known as "looping the loop". It is a very dangerous performance. Sometimes it is successful and wins the applause of the spectators. Sometimes it ends in disaster and the principal performer is removed from the arena in a damaged condition.' Churchill was even more scornful of Chamberlain's jingoism. 'We have had from Mr. Chamberlain', he said, 'sentiment by the bucketful and patriotism by the imperial pint.'

Chamberlain's resignation from the government triggered off those of three prominent Scottish free traders, Charles T. Ritchie, the Chancellor of the Exchequer, Lord George Hamilton, Secretary of State for India, and Lord Balfour of Burleigh, Secretary for Scotland. They resigned their offices because the Prime Minister seemed to be keeping his options open, condemning protection, but not too vehemently, and praising free trade, but not too heartily. The split in the Conservative and Unionist ranks, exemplified by these important Scottish resignations, was widening as those in the Liberal ranks were closing. Already unpopular with the Nonconformists because of the Education Act and the Licensing Act, the government stumbled through two years of humiliating defeats in by-elections and finally shuffled to a halt. Balfour resigned on 4 December 1905 and the following day Sir Henry Campbell-Bannerman began to form a Liberal government.

The new Prime Minister has been one of the most under-rated British politicians of modern times. He was not eloquent by the standards of Asquith or Lloyd George, nor witty by the standards of Rosebery or Balfour. He came to be leader of the opposition because there seemed no other suitable, experienced, middle-of-the-road candidate when Sir William Harcourt resigned in December 1898. Yet through the testing years of the Boer War and the bitter controversies over Irish Home Rule, education, the licensing laws and tariff reform he persevered in his quiet, reasonable, rather bumbling manner to preserve the Liberal Party and to prepare it for office. The burly figure and the broad Scottish face, with its bright blue eyes and mutton-chop whiskers, offered clues to the strength of character and steadiness of purpose; they did not reveal the lucid mind and powers of humane leadership which came eventually to impress both supporters and opponents.

The son of Sir James Campbell of Strathcathro, a lord provost of Glasgow, Henry Campbell was born at Kelvinside in 1836. He was educated at Glasgow High School and Glasgow University, and then spent several years at Cambridge before returning to work in his father's warehouses. In 1868 he was elected to the Commons as member for the Stirling Burghs, a seat he held for the rest of his life. He took the additional surname of Bannerman from an uncle who left him a fortune which, with other family legacies, made Campbell-Bannerman a millionaire. His London home was a large mansion in Grosvenor Place but he spent four months of the year in Scotland, at Belmont Castle, where he walked in the grounds each morning and talked to the trees. Every summer Campbell-Bannerman and his wife spent a holiday in Marienbad, one of the King's favourite spas.

There was one obstacle to be overcome before Campbell-Bannerman could be certain of forming a viable government. The three leading Liberal Imperialists, Asquith, Haldane and Sir Edward Grey, M.P. for Berwick-on-Tweed, feared that the elderly leader of the Liberal Party would be unable to shoulder the double burden of the premiership and the leadership of the House of Commons. An opportunity for them to agree on a joint approach to Campbell-Bannerman occurred in September 1905. Sir Edward Grey, who had been Under-Secretary at the Foreign Office for three years during Gladstone's last ministry and that of Rosebery, was an enthusiastic and knowledgeable angler. He had already written one book, *Fly Fishing*, which was to become a minor classic and he liked nothing better than to be casting for trout in the Hampshire Itchen or for salmon in the Spey, the Findhorn or the Divie. For the summer of 1905 Grey and his wife had taken Relugas House, a fishing lodge in Morayshire at the point where the Divie sparkles into the Findhorn. Asquith and his wife had taken a house in Glen of Rothes, about fifteen miles away, and there Haldane joined them.

'After consultation', wrote Haldane later in his *Autobiography*, 'Asquith and I decided to go over to confer with Grey. This was at the beginning of September 1905. We talked the situation over with him. It was decided that it was of great importance that the King, who would soon have to summon a Prime Minister, should be cognizant of the situation. Asquith thought that as I had been much in contact with the King over London University I would be a natural channel of communication. Grey did not dissent but he thought that Asquith should also see Campbell-Bannerman as early as possible and tell him of our difficulties.'

In conversation among themselves the three men used afterwards to refer to their decision as the 'Relugas Compact', for when Asquith and Haldane left Grey to resume his quiet fishing in the Findhorn, they had agreed that they would not accept office under Campbell-Bannerman unless he went to the Lords and allowed Asquith to become leader in the Commons, with Haldane as Lord Chancellor and Grey as Foreign Secretary. The trio would thus effectively control the government and the Prime Minister would be little more than a figurehead. The King, with whom Campbell-Bannerman had spent many hours during their holidays that summer in Marienbad, favoured the course proposed by Asquith, Haldane and Grey because he believed that Campbell-Bannerman, at almost seventy, was too old and ailing to sustain the premiership. Campbell-Bannerman avoided a direct confrontation with the three imperialists. He intimated that he would carefully consider their suggestion, put to him by Asquith, and would also consult his wife when she joined them from Scotland. With this cautious promise Asquith had to be satisfied and he thereupon agreed to accept office as Chancellor of the Exchequer. He later justified his apparent capitulation by explaining that when the agreement with Haldane and Grey had been made they had expected that the Liberal ministry would be formed after, and not before, a general election, and that to risk a serious split in the party before an election would have been disastrous for its prospects.

Haldane's position was more difficult because Campbell-Bannerman intended that his old friend Sir Robert Reid, M.P. for Dumfries, should become Lord Chancellor, with a barony as Lord Loreburn. Haldane accordingly agreed, after some hesitation, to accept instead the War Office. Grey, under severe pressure from Asquith and Haldane, eventually decided to accept the Foreign Office. Within a few days Campbell-Bannerman had completed the remainder of his appointments. As well as Asquith, the new ministry included two other future prime ministers, Lloyd George at the Board of Trade and Winston Churchill as Under-Secretary for the Colonies. The Earl of Crewe, a son-in-law of Lord Rosebery, became Lord President of the Council, the Earl of Elgin became Colonial Secretary, and John Sinclair, later Lord Pentland, was appointed Secretary for Scotland.

Another notable Scottish appointment, outside the Cabinet, was that of the Earl of Aberdeen to be Lord-Lieutenant of Ireland. He had already occupied this storm-wracked outpost for eight months during Gladstone's brief ministry in 1886 but his second term was to last for nine years and to be, by Irish standards, conspicuously successful. Much of Lord Aberdeen's success was due to the talents and personality of his wife, Ishbel Marjoribanks, a lady of ample form and generous heart. She had been president of the Women's Liberal Federation in both Scotland and England, and was, like her husband, an ardent advocate of Irish Home Rule. The Women's National Health Association of Ireland, founded in 1907 with a travelling exhibition and leaflets by the million, and the Irish Industries Association, with a yearly sale of £25,000 worth of hand-made lace and schemes to market tweeds, linen, honey and other rural products, were among the projects pioneered by Lady Aberdeen. Her sincerity and her concern for Ireland made it possible for her and her husband to establish a friendly working relationship with John Redmond, the moderate Irish Nationalist leader.

Campbell-Bannerman's most radical appointment brought into the Cabinet for the first time an ordinary working man. He was John Burns, the London-born son of a Scottish engineer and since 1892 the member for Battersea. His appointment was to be President of the Local Government Board and whatever his faults, the handsome, bearded leader of the London dockers did not lack self-confidence. 'Bravo, Sir 'Enery, bravo!' he said when offered the post. 'This is the most popular thing you have done yet!'

With his Cabinet complete, Campbell-Bannerman appealed to the electors to endorse it and polling began for the new House of Commons on 12 January 1906 in the borough of Ipswich. The result there portended the outcome of the general election, for two Liberals were returned, a gain of one seat from the Conservatives. The first main polling day, 13 January, brought even more remarkable results. In Manchester, the traditional stronghold of free trade, the Conservatives lost all their seats, two to Labour and six to the Liberals, among them Balfour's own constituency of East Manchester, which he had held for over twenty years. Similar results flooded in from all parts of the United Kingdom. In Stirling, Campbell-Bannerman was returned unopposed. In Glasgow, two of the seven seats were held by Unionist free-traders but the others went to Liberals or Labour. Of the 72 Scottish seats, the Liberals took 58 and Labour 2. When the last returns were made, the Liberal gains totalled over two hundred. The new House comprised 157 Conservatives and Unionists, 83 Irish Nationalists, 29 Labour members, and 401 Liberals, including 24 with Labour support, popularly known as 'Lib-Labs'. Even in the unlikely event of Irish Nationalists and Labour members voting with the opposition, the government had an overall majority of 132.

II

Problems and Portents

'Although he is called the leader of the opposition he really leads nobody, never had led anybody and is never likely to lead anybody', asserted *The Times* in 1899, after Sir Henry Campbell-Bannerman had succeeded Sir William Harcourt as leader of the Liberal Party. 'C.-B. is a mere cork, dancing on a torrent which he cannot control', wrote Balfour to Lady Salisbury as the results of the 1906 general election were being announced. Neither estimate of the new Liberal Prime Minister was notable for its prescience, for he rapidly made clear his intention to dominate both his party and the Commons. One of his first instructions to his ministers was that they must surrender any directorships they held in public companies. He allowed exceptions in the cases of two junior ministers, both of whom were chairmen of prosperous firms of grocery and provision merchants. When pressed at question-time to justify the exceptions, the Prime Minister replied that a minister could not be expected to give up a family directorship or a directorship in a philanthropic institution.

'Is the sale of tea a philanthropic business?' demanded a persistent Unionist.

'That', replied Campbell-Bannerman, 'depends on the tea.'

He was not always so pawkily humorous. When the new Parliament met on 20 February 1906, Balfour was not a member but a seat was quickly found for him by the resignation of the Conservative member for the City of London. He took his seat on 12 March and after taking the oath he moved to a place on the opposition front bench. The business of the day was a motion in favour of free trade and Balfour at once seized the opportunity to put a series of complicated fiscal questions to the Prime Minister, hoping to trap him into a diffident or confused reply. But this was a new Campbell-Bannerman, self-confident and incisive.

'The Right Honourable Gentleman', he said, 'is like the Bourbons in the oft-quoted phrase—he has learned nothing and he has forgotten nothing . . . I say "Enough of this foolery". It might have answered very well in the last Parliament, but it is altogether out of place in this Parliament. The tone and temper of this Parliament will not permit it. Move your amendments and let us get to business.'

Sir Henry Campbell-Bannerman had the incidental honour of being the first to be constitutionally recognised as Prime Minister. The chairman of the Cabinet and chief adviser to the monarch had hitherto always held some other office, usually that of First Lord of the Treasury, if only as a formality. He ranked in the court table of precedence according to that office, because the premiership was not an official position and did not figure in the table. King Edward VII, with his passion for the minutiae of court etiquette, decided to remove this anomaly. In December 1905 he issued a warrant recognising the office of Prime Minister and allotting the holder a place in the official order of precedence. In England he was to rank after the Archbishop of Canterbury, the Lord Chancellor and the Archbishop of York, and in Scotland after the Lord Chancellor and the Moderator of the General Assembly of the Church of Scotland. Balfour preferred that the change should take effect on the appointment of his successor, so that Campbell-Bannerman became the first prime minister to enjoy constitutional status in that office.

The first important legislation of the government concerned a trade union matter. One reason for the success of the new Labour Party candidates at the general election had been the bitter dissatisfaction of trade union members over the Taff Vale judgement of 1901. Following a strike in 1900 on the Taff Vale Railway, in South Wales, the railway proprietors sued the trade union involved, the Amalgamated Society of Railway Servants, for damages and loss of profits occasioned by the strike. On appeal, the House of Lords reversed the decision of lower courts and awarded the railway company £23,000 damages and an almost equal sum in costs. This unexpected judgement virtually destroyed the power of trade unions to engage in a strike, since they now appeared liable for crippling damages. The unions accordingly offered support at the general election to Liberal candidates in constituencies where there was no Labour candidate, on the understanding that the Liberals would introduce legislation to reverse the Taff Vale judgement as soon as opportunity occurred. But when the Liberal bill was presented to the Commons in fulfilment of this undertaking, Labour members found it less than satisfactory. Although it went some way towards allowing peaceful picketing and provided that an act performed in combination should not be deemed illegal if it was legal when performed by an individual, the courts were left with wide latitude in the matter of claims for damages. Fortunately, by the luck of the ballot, the Labour Party secured the right to introduce a private member's bill at the beginning of the session. This bill, drawn up after a conference of trade unionists, proposed to remove the possibility of civil claims on union funds as a result of strike action. Campbell-Bannerman, after listening to the debate on the bill and without waiting to consult his Cabinet, announced that the government would drop its own bill and use the Labour proposals as the basis for new legislation.

The remainder of the government's programme ranged over a wide spectrum of economic, social and parliamentary reform. A Workmen's Compensation Act in 1906 consolidated previous legislation and extended to a further six million workers the right to compensation for industrial accident or disease. Even shop assistants and, at Campbell-Bannerman's insistence, domestic servants were brought within the protection of the Act.

An education bill introduced by Augustine Birrell, President of the Board of Education, to provide for fuller public control of state-aided church schools in England and Wales, and for the abolition of denominational religious teaching in public elementary schools, revived all the controversy which had raged round Balfour's Education Act of 1902. Many of the leading participants in the debates were, in a sense, disinterested. Birrell, Balfour and Asquith were agnostics and Campbell-Bannerman was an unenthusiastic Presbyterian who held himself aloof from English theological disputes. Although the bill was passed in the Commons, the Church of England majority in the Lords, buttressed by the bishops, ensured that it was so extensively amended that the Prime Minister decided not to proceed with it. But the manner of the dismemberment angered him and in announcing the government's decision in December 1906, he declared that 'a way must be found, a way will be found, by which the will of the people expressed through their elected representatives in this House will be made to prevail'. These words were the first omens of a coming storm.

Meanwhile legislation of great importance to Scottish education was being initiated. An act in 1906 authorised Scottish school boards to provide for the conveyance to school and the education of epileptic, crippled and handicapped children. Following the disturbing report in 1904 of a committee investigating the physical health of school-children, the Education (Scotland) Act of 1908 gave the school boards considerable permissive powers to deal with this and other problems. Provision was made for the medical examination of children in school, and for the supply of food and clothing to children whose education was suffering because of their parents' poverty. The Act prescribed penalties for child neglect and empowered school boards to issue orders compelling the attendance of children between the ages of five and fourteen. By-laws could also be framed by school boards to establish compulsory continuation classes for children up to seventeen, the curriculum to include instruction relevant to the industries and crafts of the district, the study of English language and literature, and of the Gaelic language and literature in Gaelic-speaking districts, as well as instruction in hygiene and physical training. A superannuation scheme, on a contributory basis, was introduced for both elementary and secondary teachers, and the different sources of income available for higher education were consolidated into a single fund, known as the Education (Scotland) Fund, so placing secondary education for the first time on a sound financial footing.

Among several improvements in parliamentary procedure, Campbell-Bannerman revived the Scottish Grand Committee, which had lapsed under the Conservative administration. Instead of being a select, or sessional, committee, it became a standing, or permanent, committee, though it had still to include English members to maintain the requisite balance of parties, since Scotland returned so many Liberals. The Lords, however, rejected a bill to extend to Lowlanders the benefits already enjoyed by Highland crofters, a measure of control over rents and protection from unjustified eviction. Although a conflict between the Commons and the Lords, between the elected Liberals and the hereditary Conservatives, was thus becoming inevitable, an even more acrimonious parliamentary controversy was claiming public attention during Campbell-Bannerman's ministry. This was the campaign for 'Votes for Women'.

Pressure for women's suffrage had begun after Disraeli's Reform Act of 1867, which had extended the franchise to male householders in the borough constituencies, but it was confined at first to reasoned arguments in favour of granting the vote also to women householders. At a local level they could already vote for and serve as parish overseers of the poor and as members of school boards. Dr. Elizabeth Garrett, later Garrett Anderson, had even headed the poll in the first election for the London School Board. As the Victorian era, with its rigid insistence on the subordinate role of women in society, ebbed away, what had begun as a movement of upper-class women, who regarded the vote as a passport to the learned professions from which they were barred, spread inexorably to the lower classes. 'Opinion in favour of the suffrage is growing very rapidly amongst women', observed Lady Aberdeen, 'especially since they have been admitted to local franchises. You may find thinking women against it in the upper and middle classes; but among the working classes, though many be indifferent, all those who think are for it.' But the attitude of the two main political parties was ambivalent. There was a general belief that enfranchised women, especially if the franchise was limited to householders, would tend to vote Conservative. This possibility was sufficient to gain the support of Conservative leaders, among whom Disraeli, Randolph Churchill, Salisbury and Balfour all favoured women's suffrage, but insufficient to enlist that of Conservative back-benchers, traditionally hostile to innovation. On the other hand radical Liberal and Labour back-benchers supported women's suffrage as a matter of principle while most of their leaders, among them Joseph Chamberlain, Rosebery and Asquith, were prudently unsympathetic in practice if not in principle. Only Keir Hardie seemed willing to subordinate political advantage to the principle of women's rights and, as his adversaries were not slow to observe, his party had neither a Conservative tradition of male superiority nor a Liberal likelihood of electoral success to sacrifice.

By the end of Balfour's unhappy ministry the patience of woman suffragists was wearing thin. A new organisation, the Women's Social and Political Union, was founded in Manchester in 1903 by Mrs. Emmeline Pankhurst, the widow of a radical barrister, and her two eldest daughters, Christabel and Sylvia. They were far more militant and far abler at gaining publicity than the sedate and genteel blue-stockings who had campaigned during the previous forty years, and the *Daily Mail* gave them a new name, 'suffragettes'.

On 21 December 1905 in the Albert Hall, Sir Henry Campbell-Bannerman made his first public speech after forming his government. Although invited by Mrs. Pankhurst in the name of the Women's Social and Political Union to announce his government's intention of giving women the vote, the Prime Minister ignored the subject. At the end of his speech two suffragettes unfurled banners reading 'Will the Liberal government give women the vote?' and 'Will the Liberal government give justice to working women?' Amid angry shouts from the audience and stony silence from the platform, the women were hustled from the hall. Despite Campbell-Bannerman's sympathy with their cause, the suffragettes had to be content with two acts passed simultaneously in 1907 to permit women to sit on county and borough councils in England and in Scotland. A private member's bill in favour of women's suffrage, introduced by a Liberal in November 1907, was supported by the Prime Minister but talked out by back-bench opponents.

The following year, with the formation of the Women's Free-dom League, the suffragette campaign took a more violent turn. The Pankhursts, a sweet-voiced but indomitable Lancashire mill-girl named Annie Kenney, and diminutive Flora Drummond from the Isle of Arran, popularly known as 'the General', were the leaders in a struggle which rapidly grew more desperate and painful until it reached a peak in 1912 and 1913. In March 1912 suffragettes broke almost every window in Regent Street and Oxford Street, adding those of 10 Downing Street for good measure. They poured acid on golf greens, burned the contents of pillar-boxes, slashed pictures in art galleries and set fire to empty houses and churches. On Derby Day in 1913 Emily Davison threw herself under the King's horse and died from her injuries. Mammoth processions and public meetings organised by Flora Drummond ended in violent scenes, and when the agitators were imprisoned they went on hunger strike. Many were forcibly fed, others were released, injured and emaciated, only to be re-arrested under the terms of the Prisoners' Temporary Discharge for Ill-Health Act, popularly known as the 'Cat and Mouse Act', as soon as they were judged to have recovered sufficiently to continue serving their sentences. Much of the virulence with which the suffragettes waged their campaign after 1908 stemmed from the knowledge that the resignation of Campbell-Bannerman had brought to the premiership, in place of a sympathiser, an avowed opponent of women's suffrage, Herbert Henry Asquith. 'A man might as well chain himself to the railings of St. Thomas's Hospital', Asquith had remarked disdainfully, 'and say that he will not move until he has had a baby!'

The suffragettes replied by making Asquith a special target for their attacks. When he drove through Bannockburn to unveil a monument to Sir Henry Campbell-Bannerman, two women lay down in the road to halt his car while others lashed him and his daughter Violet with dog-whips and shook huge pepper-pots in their faces. On another occasion Violet had to rescue him from suffragettes who attacked him on Lossiemouth golf course and tried to tear the clothes from his back.

Campbell-Bannerman did not live to see the fiercest fury of the suffragette campaign. The last months of his ministry were clouded with other troubles. His wife, Charlotte Bruce, was a very stout and nervous woman who had been for many years an invalid. They had no children and were so devoted to each other that Campbell-Bannerman seldom took any important decision, whether personal or political, without first seeking his wife's advice. They shared a love of France and the highlight of their year was their summer holiday in Marienbad. Almost as soon as Campbell-Bannerman became Prime Minister his wife's health broke down completely and he spent hours of each day and night at her bedside, helping to nurse and comfort her. Arthur Ponsonby, his Principal Private Secretary and successor as member for Stirling, later recalled that throughout the early months of his premiership Campbell-Bannerman had hardly a single night of undisturbed rest and he was frequently found dozing over his papers during the day. Finally, in August 1906, Lady Campbell-Bannerman died while on holiday in Marienbad and the Prime Minister brought her body sadly home for burial in Scotland.

Although after the recess he seemed to relish the challenge of renewed involvement in the day-to-day work of the Commons, the loss the Prime Minister had suffered was plainly irreparable. 'It used to be always "we"; now it is "I", which is very different', he said wistfully to his Irish friend T. P. O'Connor, the member for the Scotland division of Liverpool. During 1907 the Prime Minister was granted the freedom of both Glasgow and Edinburgh but in the November of that year he began a day by attending a lunch at the Guildhall, London, in honour of the German Emperor, after which he took a train to Bristol, where he attended a banquet and addressed a public meeting enlivened by the interruptions of the customary contingent of suffragettes. That night, at the home of a Liberal supporter, the Prime Minister had a severe heart attack. He recovered sufficiently to spend a holiday in Biarritz and when he returned to London in January 1908 he at once began preparations for the new parliamentary session. But another heart attack soon after the opening of parliament brought the inevitable consequence. After several weeks of hesitation in the vain hope that he might again make a recovery, Campbell-Bannerman wrote on 1 April to the King, then in Biarritz, tendering his resignation. Two days later the King telegraphed his acceptance and forthwith invited Asquith to form the new administration. Unwilling to interrupt his holiday, the King also intimated that Asquith should go to Biarritz to kiss hands upon his appointment. After a journey of a thousand miles, Asquith waited upon the King in the Hôtel du Palais and thus became the first British prime minister to assume office on foreign soil.

12

Home Rule

Born in 1852, Asquith came of a Yorkshire Nonconformist family. He was called to the bar in 1876 but because, as he said, 'briefs were few and fees were small', he turned to political journalism to supplement his income. Friendship with Richard Haldane led to his decision to stand for Parliament and he was adopted as Liberal candidate for the East Fife constituency in the 1886 general election. In his *Memories and Reflections* Asquith later recalled his experiences as a carpet-bagging Englishman 'unversed in the indigenous Scottish art of heckling', seeking votes among the canny electors of the Kingdom of Fife.

At Auchtermuchty, 'where hand-loom weaving then still survived', wrote Asquith, 'I can well remember standing for more than an hour, after my first speech, while the old weavers in the audience put me mercilessly through every item of their Shorter Catechism of the Radical faith. It was by no means plain sailing, and when with my agent I returned from our nightly quota of village meetings, there was often little enough to encourage us in the survey of our evening's adventures. I can recall our once inducing the local baker—a strong Tory, as it turned out—to take the chair. There were perhaps a dozen men in the room and when I had done my best to light the heather, after a prolonged pause the village doctor rose and in a tone of icy courtesy proceeded to move that "Mr. Asquith is *not* a fit or proper person to represent this constituency". The "flesher", whose mind dwelt exclusively on the impending massacre of the Ulster Protestants, was at last induced to second the resolution, which was then declared by the chairman to be carried unanimously.'

In the early years the constituency was difficult of access, for the Tay Bridge had been blown down and the Forth Bridge was still unfinished. At the end of a week of strenuous campaigning Asquith decided to spend the Sunday in Edinburgh. The only means of crossing the Forth was by the ferry steamer from Burntisland to

Granton but Asquith's agent, an Elie solicitor and banker named Ketchen, was horrified at the prospect. 'My dear sir', he exclaimed, 'I would rather pay down a hundred pounds than that it should be known that you had used the ferry on the Sabbath Day!'

Despite its inauspicious beginnings, Asquith's campaign enjoyed a successful outcome. He was elected with 2,862 votes to his opponent's 2,487 and from that day until the 'coupon election' of December 1918 he was consistently returned as the member for East Fife.

Meanwhile Asquith had made a name for himself as a barrister by his spirited defence of two Scottish radicals, John Burns and R. B. Cunninghame Graham, who were arrested during a huge demonstration organised in Trafalgar Square on 13 November 1887 to protest against the imprisonment of an Irish Nationalist M.P. The demonstration was the climax of a series of processions of unemployed workers, Socialists and radicals, whose numbers had so unnerved Lord Salisbury's government that the Thames bridges were garrisoned by infantrymen, the Life Guards were prepared for action and the Chief Commissioner of Police even planned the deployment of artillery. In the event, Trafalgar Square was not cleared by a Napoleonic whiff of grape-shot but a contingent of marchers from North London came under fierce police attack and its leaders, Burns and Cunningham Graham, were beaten to the ground and arrested. A charge of rioting failed but both men were found guilty of unlawful assault and sent to prison for six weeks.

By the end of 1905 there had been a change in Asquith's personal fortunes. His first wife, the daughter of a Manchester doctor, had died in 1891, leaving him with five young children. In 1894 he married Margot, the youngest daughter of a wealthy Peeblesshire industrialist, Sir Charles Tennant. A beautiful and fashionable woman of glittering talents and remarkable vivacity, she was to give Asquith financial security and an entrée into the most opulent Edwardian high society. The change gradually accentuated his virtues until they eventually became vices. His serenity became indifference, his patience became procrastination, his enjoyment of good living earned him a reputation for intemperance, and his delight in the company of attractive young women came, in the view of his detractors, near to lechery. Yet he was the last of the great Victorian statesmen, calm, lucid, kind and dignified.

Daunting problems faced the new Prime Minister. At the root of many lay the chronic poverty which afflicted the working classes, but there were others which more urgently threatened the stability of the United Kingdom and the existence of the British Empire. Nearest and most intractable was the problem of Ireland. Throughout the hundred years since Ireland had been formally brought into the United Kingdom there had been discontent, and often open conflict, with British rule. The basic cause was less religious than economic. The Irish suffered from absentee landlordism on a massive scale. It was estimated that 750 men between them owned half of Ireland. Almost all the great landowners were Protestant and Conservative, so that the Parliament at Westminster, and particularly the House of Lords, was sympathetic to their cause and antipathetic to any measure likely to curtail their religious freedom or diminish their wealth. Throughout the nineteenth century discontented Irish Catholics had two courses open to them, to emigrate or to stay and struggle for a more equitable economic and social system. Gladstone came eventually to believe that the only effective means of pacifying Ireland was to allow the Irish their own parliament in Dublin; but his two Home Rule bills were rejected, the first in 1886 by the Commons as a result of the revolt of Liberal Unionists led by Joseph Chamberlain, and the second in 1893 by the Lords because they claimed the proposal did not enjoy overwhelming public support. Palliative measures in the form of land acts giving tenants some security of tenure, compensation for improvements and the possibility of raising government-financed mortgages to purchase land, coupled with acts restricting the possession of arms and giving the police wide powers to coerce malcontents, had brought a degree of peace to Ireland by the end of the century. The victory of the Liberals in 1906 seemed to open the way at last to Home Rule, for both Campbell-Bannerman and Asquith were convinced of its necessity.

As his Chief Secretary for Ireland, Campbell-Bannerman had appointed James Bryce, an Ulsterman of Scottish descent who had moved from Belfast to Glasgow as a boy and was educated at Glasgow High School. The member for South Aberdeen, Bryce had held office under Gladstone and Rosebery. He was a man of great erudition, a professor of civil law at Oxford, the author of a wide range of books on history, politics, the law and even on the flora of the Isle of Arran, but he was too closely identified with the Ulster cause to be trusted by the Nationalists. In 1907 he was appointed as ambassador to the United States and Augustine Birrell became Chief Secretary for Ireland. Birrell was another man of letters, an ardent advocate of Irish Home Rule and a firm believer in the old Irish maxim: 'Be aisy, but if you can't be aisy, be as aisy as you can.' But he did not like the Lord-Lieutenant, Lord Aberdeen, or Lady Aberdeen, whose zeal for welfare work, Birrell felt, made her too prone to interfere in administrative matters which were not her concern. Above all, Birrell was to fail because he underestimated the determination of the Ulster Protestants not to be ruled by a Catholic-dominated parliament in Dublin. He also underestimated the lengths to which the Conservative Party was prepared to go in support of the Ulster Protestants in order to destroy the detested Liberal government. He overestimated the strength of British parliamentary democracy, dependent as it is upon the willingness of the minority to accept the decisions of a democratically elected majority. Other members of the government besides Birrell made the same misjudgement. It was not discreditable but it was to prove costly.

Eventually, in April 1912, Asquith introduced the third Irish Home Rule Bill. It provided for an Irish parliament in Dublin, with an elected House of Commons and a nominated House of Lords. Certain powers in defence, foreign affairs, finance and trade were reserved for the Imperial Parliament at Westminster, to which forty-two members representing Ireland were to be elected. Asquith's intention was to introduce similar forms of Home Rule for Scotland and Wales, linking the four constituents of the United Kingdom in a federal union. In June 1910 about twenty Liberal members had formed the Scottish Nationalist Committee to press for self-government in domestic affairs. The following year Sir James Henry Dalziel, member for Kirkcaldy and later Baron Dalziel of Kirkcaldy, was able to secure a majority of 99 for the first reading of a Scottish Home Rule bill, Scottish members voting 31 to 4 in its favour. A similar result was obtained by Dr. W. A. Chapple, member for Stirlingshire, whose bill passed its first reading in 1912 by a majority of 98, with Scottish members voting 43 to 6 in its favour. Members of the Scottish Nationalist Committee were so encouraged by these results and by Asquith's clear, if tardy, move in the direction of federalism that one of their number, Mr. W. H. Cowan, the member for East Aberdeenshire, was then able to secure a majority of 45 for the second reading of a bill he introduced in 1913 proposing that a Scottish parliament should be established forthwith in Edinburgh. This was the nearest Scotland was to get to achieving Home Rule. The measure for Ireland aroused so violent a storm of opposition that

Scottish hopes foundered with it.

In the Commons the Conservatives had a new leader for the attack on Asquith's bill. Balfour had resigned six months previously. He was sixty-three and gave ill-health as the main reason, but there had been for some time a desire within the Conservative Party to replace him by a more vigorous leader who would mount a more forthright campaign against the Liberals. Impatience with his aristocratic aloofness, his courteous cynicism and his equivocation over tariff reform had put him out of tune with the new men on the Conservative back-benches. The slogan 'Balfour must go!', popularly abbreviated to 'B.M.G.', which had been coined in the *National Review* by its editor, Leo Maxse, brought matters to a head. 'I really think I must ask Leo Maxse to dinner tonight', Balfour remarked on the day of his resignation, 'for we are probably the two happiest men in London.'

Balfour's successor as leader seemed likely to be either Walter Long, a wealthy English squire, or Austen Chamberlain, Joseph's eldest son and still nominally a Liberal Unionist. Each was jealous of the other but their supporters were more militant and less genteel. To avoid the antagonism of the two factions causing a split in the party, a compromise was agreed. The new leader was another alumnus of Glasgow High School, a Scottish-Canadian named Andrew Bonar Law. Born in New Brunswick in 1858, he was the son of a Presbyterian minister with Ulster connections. Before entering politics in 1900 as the member for the Blackfriars division of Glasgow, Bonar Law had made a fortune in the city's iron and steel trade; but he lost his seat in the 1906 Liberal landslide and thereafter sat for Dulwich and Bootle. At the opening of the 1912 parliamentary session, Bonar Law and Asquith walked side by side on their way back to the Commons after hearing the King's Speech in the Lords. 'I am afraid I shall have to show myself very vicious, Mr. Asquith, this session', said Bonar Law. 'I hope you will understand.'

The adjective he chose was inaccurate in one sense, accurate in another. Bonar Law had none of the normal human vices. Moreover, he showed no interest in pretty women, in art, literature or even nature; and he seemed to derive little pleasure from the company of his fellows. Yet this shrewd, taciturn ironmaster introduced into British politics a vicious element which bitterly reflected the violence inherent in much of Edwardian society. Few leading British politicians of the twentieth century have been so flinty, so dangerous and so little loved.

In April 1912, at a rally at Balmoral, near Belfast, a huge crowd of Protestant Ulstermen gathered to hear Bonar Law, Sir Edward Carson, the member for Dublin University, and other Unionist leaders pledge themselves to resist the proposals for Irish Home Rule. Three months later, at a Conservative fête held at Blenheim Palace, Bonar Law gave a specific pledge: 'I can imagine no length of resistance to which Ulster will go which I shall not be ready to support.' He reiterated this 'Blenheim Pledge' in the House of Commons: 'In regard to what I said at Blenheim, I am very glad to have the opportunity of repeating it here.' Finally, on 28 September 1912, hundreds of thousands of Ulster Unionists thronged to the City Hall in Belfast and to other centres in Northern Ireland to sign 'Ulster's Solemn League and Covenant', in which they swore to use 'all means which may be found necessary to defeat the present conspiracy to set up a Home Rule Parliament in Ireland'.

As the Home Rule Bill proceeded on its stormy passage through the Commons and Lords, the Ulster Unionists made plans for a provisional government to seize power in Northern Ireland should the bill become law. A para-military force, the Ulster Volunteers, which had been formed in 1911, enlisted a hundred thousand recruits during 1913. They paraded and drilled and prepared for war. The Catholic South was taking parallel steps. Since 1902 Sinn Fein, the republican 'We Ourselves' movement, had been advocating that the Irish people should themselves settle the question of Ireland's future government. Another para-military force, the Irish Volunteers, was formed in October 1913 to counter the threat by the Ulster Volunteers. Both sides looked to Germany for support. In the *Irish Review* Sir Roger Casement, an ex-member of the British diplomatic service and a Nationalist leader, argued for an alliance between Ireland and Germany, while an Ulster M.P., Captain James Craig, later Viscount Craigavon of Stormont, declared that 'Germany and the German Emperor would be preferable to the rule of John Redmond, Pat Ford, and the Molly Maguires'. The Germans were astonished but delighted. Baron von Kühlmann, an official of the German embassy in London, bustled to and from Ulster to offer discreet support. German journalists scurried to Belfast and Dublin to report events for their newspapers.

Meanwhile the Home Rule Bill had made the first of its three statutory journeys through Parliament in successive sessions. It passed its third reading in the Commons on 16 January 1913 by a majority of 110 but eleven days later, without debating its clauses, the Lords rejected it by 326 to 96. The summer brought a general strike in Dublin and a spate of inflammatory speeches from both sides. In an effort to resolve the deadlock Asquith offered, on 9 March 1914, a compromise in the form of an Amending Bill which provided that the Ulster counties should be excluded for six years from the operation of the Home Rule Act, but at the end of that period should be incorporated into a self-governing Ireland. Carson immediately rejected the proposal. 'We do not want a sentence of death', he exclaimed, 'with a stay of execution for six years.'

The Cabinet now began to make contingency plans for a military occupation of Northern Ireland, but clumsy handling by the War Office led to the notorious strike, variously described as an 'incident', an 'affair' or a 'mutiny', according to the speaker's political persuasion, which took place at the Curragh Camp, near Dublin. On 20 March 1914 General Sir Arthur Paget, commanding the British troops in Ireland, held a conference of his senior officers in Dublin, painting a lurid picture of the military measures which were about to be taken in Ulster. He added that he had wrung from the War Office, with great difficulty, the concession that any officers who were domiciled in Ulster and who were unwilling to take part in the Ulster operations would be permitted to 'disappear' until these were completed. Other officers also unwilling would be required to resign their commissions and to leave the Army. General Hubert Gough, commanding the Third Cavalry Brigade, with his three regimental commanders and 57 out of the 70 subordinate officers, declared that they would prefer to be dismissed rather than serve in Ulster to enforce the law.

That officers in the infantry regiments at the Curragh did not make a similar decision was largely due to the integrity of a Scottish general. He was Sir Charles Fergusson, of Ladyburn, Ayrshire, who commanded the Fifth Division, of which the King's Own Scottish Borders were a part. Although a Conservative and opposed to Irish Home Rule, Fergusson appreciated the dangerous precedent of allowing officers to choose whether or not they should obey the legitimate albeit distasteful orders of their government. How, asked Fergusson, could the rank and file be expected to obey orders to disperse strikers, for example, if their officers claimed the right to disobey orders to disperse rebels? The affair was resolved when

Asquith decided to treat it as an unfortunate misunderstanding. General Gough, whose resignation had been proffered, was reinstated in his command, though Colonel Seely and Sir John French, Chief of the Imperial General Staff, resigned.

Asquith thereupon decided to take over the War Office himself. 'The Army', he said, 'will hear nothing of politics from me, and in return I expect to hear nothing of politics from the Army.' Nevertheless the Curragh affair had serious repercussions. It widened the gulf in Ireland by persuading the Ulster Protestants that the government lacked both the will and the means to impose Home Rule on them, while convincing many Catholics that the moderate, constitutional methods of John Redmond and the Irish parliamentary party were ineffectual. It also encouraged the German High Command to think that Britain was less likely to participate in a continental war while she had Ireland in a ferment at her back.

Despite naval patrols, the Ulster Volunteers succeeded in clandestinely shipping a large cargo of rifles and ammunition from Hamburg. These were landed at Larne during the night of 24–25 April 1914 from a small steamer, the *Clyde Valley*, and rapidly distributed by lorries and cars. Not to be outdone, the Irish Volunteers shipped a similar but smaller cargo from Hamburg in a tiny yacht, the *Asgard*, unloading at Howth on 26 July 1914. An unsuccessful attempt was made by the Dublin police and a contingent of the King's Own Scottish Borderers to prevent the distribution of the cargo, but they were outwitted. On the way back to barracks the soldiers were beset by a jeering crowd of Nationalist supporters who flung stones and abuse. The Borderers opened fire, killing three people and wounding more than thirty.

Even before this confrontation, King George V had intervened personally in the crisis. After consultations with the Speaker and the Prime Minister he invited the leaders of the main parties to a conference at Buckingham Palace to find, if possible, a compromise solution. In his speech of welcome on 21 July the King spoke movingly of his fears. 'For months we have watched with deep misgivings the course of events in Ireland', he said. 'The trend has been surely and steadily towards an appeal to force, and today the cry of Civil War is on the lips of the most responsible and sober-minded of my people.'

The eight leaders, two from each of the four parties, Liberal, Conservative, Ulster Unionist and Irish Nationalist, met four times under the Speaker's chairmanship but they could reach no agreement on where Ulster's boundary should be drawn if Asquith's Amending Bill became law. On the morning of 24 July the conference broke up and that afternoon the Cabinet assembled gloomily to discuss what might still be done to avoid the outbreak of civil war. They had, in Churchill's words, 'Toiled for hours around the muddy by-ways of Fermanagh and Tyrone' when they became aware of Sir Edward Grey's quiet voice reading a Foreign Office paper which had just been brought to him. It was the text of the ultimatum, belligerent and unacceptable, which Austria-Hungary had presented the previous day to Serbia.

Ten days later Grey announced in the Commons that Britain could not stand aside while a German invasion violated the neutrality of Belgium. John Redmond then rose to speak. 'I say to the government', he said, 'that they may tomorrow withdraw every one of their troops from Ireland. I say that the coast of Ireland will be defended from foreign invasion by her armed sons, and for this purpose armed Nationalist Catholics in the South will be only too glad to join arms with armed Protestant Ulstermen in the North.'

Many members of the Ulster Volunteers joined two newly formed Irish divisions, the Tenth and the Sixteenth. Then Ulster's own division, the Thirty-Sixth, was formed, with thousands of Volunteers in the ranks of the regiments which composed it, the Royal Irish Rifles and the Royal Inniskilling Fusiliers. Many were to lay down their lives not in the streets of Belfast and Londonderry but on the road to Albert, on the Messines Ridge, in Bourlon Wood and along the mud-soaked valley of the Somme. Already, in September 1914, the third Irish Home Rule Bill had become law under the terms of the Parliament Act, without the consent of the Lords. Asquith accompanied it with an assurance that the Act would not be implemented until the war was over. He was not to know that by then he would no longer be Prime Minister, that his constituents in East Fife would be on the point of rejecting him as their Member of Parliament and that Home Rule would be a lost cause for ever in Ireland and, for the foreseeable future, in Scotland too.

13

In Darkest Scotland

In 1890, after one of his African journeys, H. M. Stanley wrote a book entitled *In Darkest Africa*, setting out his adventures in a continent where life was short and brutish. Soon afterwards William Booth wrote a book entitled *In Darkest England*, recounting the miseries and hardships of the English poor whom his Salvation Army was striving to succour. Nobody wrote a book about Darkest Scotland. It might well have been the most horrifying of the trilogy.

The horror can, to some extent, be quantified. One of Balfour's last actions as Prime Minister in December 1905 was to appoint a Royal Commission on the Poor Law and the Relief of Distress. It was to inquire into the working of the Poor Laws and into the other methods used 'for meeting distress arising from want of employment, particularly during periods of severe industrial depression'. The chairman of the commission was Lord George Hamilton and among its members were Beatrice Webb, later president of the Fabian Society, and William Beveridge, later the Liberal member for Berwick-on-Tweed and author of the Beveridge Report which formed the basis of the modern National Health Insurance scheme. The commission spent more than three years collecting evidence, which occupied nearly fifty volumes and provided a comprehensive picture of conditions among the British working classes during the Edwardian period. Issued in 1909, the report was in two parts. The majority report comprised a series of proposals for minor reforms to improve the existing services but the minority report, inspired by Beatrice Webb and written by her husband Sidney Webb, later Lord Passfield, proposed much more radical measures. Among these were the introduction of old age pensions, an eight-hour working day for certain industries, and the recognition of a national minimum standard of living below which nobody should be allowed to fall.

The evidence gathered by the commission included detailed statistics regarding Scotland. These can be supplemented by the *Report on Housing and Industrial Conditions in Dundee*, published in 1905 by the Dundee Social Union, by a study of the home environment of 1,400 school-children in Edinburgh, published in 1906 by the Edinburgh Charity Organisation Society, and by the 1911 census returns. These sources reveal that half the houses in Edwardian Scotland had only one or two rooms. The meanest houses were to be found in the towns of the central industrial belt. In Armadale in 1911 almost 83% of the population lived in one- or two-roomed houses. Among other towns where more than 70% of the population lived in such houses were Airdrie, Clydebank, Lochgelly and Motherwell, while in Perth only 30%, in Edinburgh 37% and in Aberdeen 38.6% of the population occupied one- or two-roomed houses.

Overcrowding was a concomitant hardship. It existed, in the Registrar-General's definition, where the average number of persons per room (not per bedroom) was more than two. The 1911 census recorded that 56% of one-roomed houses in Scotland had more than two occupants, 47% of two-roomed houses had more than two persons per room, and 24% of three-roomed houses also had more than two persons per room. Glasgow was the most overcrowded city in the United Kingdom, for over half its population lived at a density of more than two persons per room. In Dundee in 1904 almost half the population was similarly overcrowded and a detailed study of nearly 6,000 houses in the city showed that 21% had no sanitary accommodation for women and children, while 10% had none for men. Even where the occupants had access to a water-closet or other sanitary arrangements within or adjacent to the home, these were often shared by many people. Of the 6,000 houses studied in Dundee, almost a thousand had sanitary accommodation shared by more than 25 persons, over two thousand had sanitary accommodation shared by between 13 and 24 persons, and two thousand had sanitary accommodation shared by not more than 12 persons. Most of the remaining thousand had sanitary accommodation for men only.

In 1912 a Royal Commission was appointed to inquire into Scottish urban and rural housing conditions, with special reference to the housing of miners and agricultural labourers, and to report on legislative changes considered desirable to remedy the existing defects. The commission's report was not published until 1917. It revealed that although the number of people in Scotland living at a density of four or more per room had fallen between 1901 and 1911 from 9.6% to 8.6% of the population, the number living at a density of more than two per room, and therefore by official definition 'overcrowded', had barely changed, being 45.7% in 1901 and 45.1% in 1911. The report showed that the reason for the failure to reduce overcrowding by any appreciable amount was simply a sharp decline in house-building. In Glasgow, for example, between 1901 and 1904 a total of 13,080 houses (with an estimated 34,500 rooms) had been built; between 1907 and 1910, 3,488 houses (with an estimated 9,460 rooms); and between 1910 and 1913 only 945 houses (with an estimated 2,750 rooms). A classic case of municipal lethargy in enforcing the powers available under the 1890 Housing of the Working Classes Act occurred in Port Glasgow. In 1901 the medical officer of health reported that a district of the town, where houses were crowded together with insufficient sanitary accommodation and inadequate ventilation, was an insanitary area under the terms of the act. The town council accepted the report but because of local objections a statutory inquiry was necessary. Agreement was finally reached in 1904 and the following year Parliament sanctioned an order for the compulsory purchase of the condemned properties. A council committee was appointed to negotiate the purchases and by the end of 1911, ten years after his initial report, the medical officer was able to record that the scheme was nearing completion.

As well as being overcrowded and insanitary, much of Scotland's housing was badly designed and poor in quality. It is difficult to assess the relative merits of a Fife miner's one-storey terrace cottage, damp, draughty and cramped, and two rooms in a Gorbals tenement, dark, malodorous and infested with vermin. Throughout the Edwardian period rents remained fairly stable. They generally ranged from about 1s. or 1s. 6d. (5p or 7½p) per week for a small one-roomed cottage to 2s. 6d. (12½p) for a large one-roomed house, and from 2s. 6d. to 3s. 6d. (12½p to 17½p) for a two-roomed house in a more spacious locality.

Rents were reasonable in relation to workers' wages, which were usually so low that they left little for anything but food, shelter and shoddy clothing. The dominant industries were coal-mining, iron and steel, ship-building and engineering, and textiles. Of these the textile industry was the worst paid but wages in coal-mining made the least advance during the period. The Dundee Social Union's study, published in 1905, quoted weekly wages in the jute mills, to the nearest shilling (5p) above, as 10s. for women sweepers, 15s. for sack machinists, 19s. for calender workers and 30s. for skilled mechanics.

Skilled workers and craftsmen in other industries and trades earned appreciably more. The Edinburgh study for children's environment, published in 1906, quoted such rates as 27s. for a tailor, 31s. for a joiner, 34s. for a stone-mason, 37s. for a plasterer, and £2 for a shipyard worker. Unskilled and casual workers were the worst paid. A cabman might earn 18s., excluding tips, a porter £1 and a carter 22s. Many a Scottish miner's child, as an adult after the First World War, when paper money had become universal, could recall the awe with which the bairns would gather round the kitchen-table to watch father lay on it his week's wages, a single shining gold sovereign.

Agricultural workers were, in the main, lower paid than industrial workers. Large imports of untaxed wheat and meat from the United States, the Argentine, Australia and New Zealand had caused a severe depression in British agriculture during the last years of the nineteenth century, with a resultant decline in wages and a shift of labour from the countryside to the towns. In 1902 the average weekly wage of a farm-servant in the Scottish central belt was about 22s. but where there was less alternative employment, wages were lower. They averaged 19s. in the Borders, Perthshire and Aberdeenshire, 18s. in Inverness, falling to 17s. in Ross and Cromarty and to below 16s. in Sutherland and Caithness. After 1900 there was a partial recovery in agriculture. The wider acceptance of Robert H. Elliott's system of ley-farming, evolved at Clifton Park, Roxburghshire, during the 1880s, and the development of poultry-keeping, fruit-growing and market gardening were among the factors which led to this improvement. Wages also improved, slowly until 1913, when there was a sharp rise, bringing the average level by 1914 to about 15% above that of 1900. During the same period, according to returns made by the Board of Trade Labour Department, retail prices rose by about 12% and retail clothing prices by 17%.

Most industrial workers were less fortunate. Wages in mining, engineering and textiles rose between 1900 and 1913 only by an almost imperceptible amount, perhaps 1%. Even this was not a reflection of a stable level of wages throughout the period, for there was a serious depression in 1905, which took miners' wages down to 20% below their 1900 level, and after a recovery there was another recession during 1908 and 1909, when they fell by more than 10%.

Despite the importance of the engineering industry to Britain's prosperity, it employed fewer workers than that most characteristic of Edwardian occupations, domestic service. Every middle-class household aspired to at least one maid-of-all-work and as paterfamilias prospered and moved up the social scale, he added more servants to his 'below stairs' staff. First, at £30 or £35 per annum, came a nursemaid or a nanny for the children, then at £40 a gardener or an orra man, a cook at £80 to take charge of the kitchen and a lady's maid at £50 to tend the mater. A between-maid, or 'tweenie', and a page-boy, or 'buttons', could be had for £12 or £15 but a chauffeur for the new Daimler, Humber or Wolseley might cost £40 per annum and for a butler to preside over the administration of the household, the going rate was likely to be as much as £100 per annum. Uniform, food and sleeping accommodation were provided in addition to salary but to set against these there were the long hours and laborious tasks, particularly for the younger servants at the base of the domestic hierarchy. The day began early, with fires to lay, coal-scuttles to fill, gallons of hot water to be carried up flight after flight of stairs, and the daunting prospect of a day's work stretching ahead for fourteen or sixteen hours. One free evening a week, a half-day on Sunday and a whole day each month were considered a generous allowance of leisure; for the remainder of her working hours, the domestic servant was at the mercy of the bell.

The working day in other occupations was generally shorter than that of the domestic servant. Coal-miners underground had achieved their eight-hour day in 1908 but few others were as fortunate. In the building trade the average was a fifty-hour week, shorter in winter, longer in summer. In the textile industry the Factory Act of 1901 had introduced a 55½-hour week but a shop assistant under eighteen years of age was permitted, and was usually expected, to work to a maximum of 74 hours, including meal-times. Employees in the warehouses of a highly respected Glasgow firm of wholesale drapers, Arthur and Company, worked five week-days from 8.45 a.m. to 6 p.m. and on Saturdays until 2 p.m. In addition they worked an extra four hours on three evenings per week for about six months of the year. For this, an average week of about 57 hours, apprentices were paid a salary of £10 in the first year, rising by increments of £5 in each of their four years' indenture. There was a canteen where lunch was served at 4d. or 6d. (1½p to 2½p) but the apprentices did not have to 'live in', as they usually did in London. There was no dearth of applicants for apprenticeships and only those who could provide references confirming that they were trustworthy, hard-working and regular in school attendance, with respectable parents and 'other connections', and without any physical handicap or deformity were likely to be accepted. Other firms were less considerate and a working week of 90 hours was not unknown, so that when Winston Churchill, as Home Secretary, considered introducing legislation to improve the working conditions of adult shop assistants, he hoped that the maximum working week might be fixed at sixty hours.

Another occupation regarded as middle class, but offering salaries little better than those of a skilled working-class craftsman, was teaching. In 1902 there were vacancies for a female teacher in Stornoway at a salary of £45 and in Old Kilpatrick at £60, or £70 'with parchment', rising by yearly increments of £5 to a maximum of £100, and a bonus of £5 for a graduate. A science teacher was needed for Alloa Academy at a salary of £140 and a headmaster for Premnay public school was offered £135 with a house and garden, but a university degree was a necessary qualification for both posts. At the other end of the scale was the headmaster of Dollar Academy, who was required to have special charge of the departments of mathematics and science, at a salary of £350, with house and garden.

Between two-thirds and three-quarters of an ordinary working man's wage was spent on food. Since wages in so many occupations were so low, there was widespread malnutrition in the industrial areas and serious deficiencies in the diet even of agricultural workers, who had better opportunities to supplement it from their gardens or their employers' farms. A report published in 1912 by Glasgow Corporation gave details of a study of the diet of the city's labouring classes and concluded that families earning less than £1 a week could not hope to have a satisfactory diet. Bread and potatoes were the staple foods, with tea to drink. Porridge provided Scottish workers with an extra element of nutrition not usually enjoyed south of the Border, where oatmeal was seldom used.

The Dundee Social Union's study devoted a section to diet. In a typical daily menu, breakfast consisted of porridge and milk, bread and butter, with tea or milk to drink. Dinner might consist of broth made from ½ lb. of boiling beef with a pennyworth of leeks, carrots or turnips and a halfpenny-worth of barley. Sometimes the boiled meat was served with potatoes as a second course and there was occasionally a pudding, usually rice. Tea comprised simply bread and butter spread with jam or syrup, and tea to drink, but a working father might also have fish, meat or ham as an extra. There was no regular supper but hungry children might be given a 'piece' of bread and butter at bed-time. Bread was almost invariably the most expensive single item in the diet because so much of it was eaten. Even at times when the price of bread rose, more of it was consumed because it remained the cheapest means of filling empty stomachs and a rise in price resulted in less money to spend on other foodstuffs. Butter was still more popular in Scotland than margarine and fresh milk than tinned. Fish was plentiful but a working-class family seldom enjoyed a roast joint, which was appreciably dearer than minced or boiling meat. Several factors, among them the new methods of milling wheat to produce a white flour almost free of bran or wheat-germ and therefore deficient in vitamins, iron and calcium, and the marketing of cheap, factory-produced jam, combined to further impoverish the diet of many workers. Local newspapers regularly published lists of current market prices as a guide for shop-keepers and housewives. The following are typical of the food prices quoted in the *Elgin Courant and Courier* during the winter of 1904:

beef	9d. to 1s. 3d. per lb.
mutton	9d. to 11d. per lb.
pork	8d. and 9d. per lb.
rabbits	6d. to 1s. each
chickens	1s. 6d. to 2s. each
fowl	1s. 6d. to 2s. 6d. each
eggs	1s. 5d. to 1s. 9d. per dozen
potatoes	7d. per stone
oatmeal	1s. 7d. per stone
fine loaves	2 lbs. 3d.
	4 lbs. 6d.

(old pence: 240 to the £)

In general the agricultural labourer was likely to have a more nutritious diet than the worker in the Lowland industrial towns. But the county medical officer of health for Argyll reported in 1904 that during the previous eighteen or twenty years there had been changes for the worse in the diet of workers in the northern parts of the mainland and in the islands. Porridge, milk, potatoes and fish, which had provided the staple diet, were being replaced by baker's bread, scones and jam. Similar comments were made in 1906 by the medical officer of health for Harris. Both doctors launched an even more remarkable attack on what, to the layman, seemed an innocuous habit. The root cause of many ailments, including ulceration of the stomach, chronic catarrh, dyspepsia, anaemia, constipation, even neuralgia, disorders of the abdominal organs and headaches, was nothing other than the drinking of strong tea.

Thirst for a more potent beverage than tea was one of the most serious evils of the Edwardian era. Drunkenness was categorised by the Church of Scotland as the principal moral cause of poverty in a report presented in 1910 to the Royal Commission on the Poor Law and the Relief of Distress. Other causes of poverty, affirmed the General Assembly's committee on church interests, were gambling and betting, early marriages, lack of ambition and weakness of will, the desertion of families by parents, the neglect by children of the obligation on them to support their parents in old age, and in the case of illegitimate children the reluctance of their parents to make any contribution to their support.

The accuracy of the Church's assessment of drunkenness may be open to question, for it is possible that people drank to excess because they were poor, not that they were poor because they drank, but there is no question that drunkenness was rife. In terms of per capita consumption of alcohol, Scotland and Ireland compared favourably with England. In 1907 Scots consumed an average of 1.4 gallons of alcohol, the Irish 1.6 gallons, and the English 2.1 gallons, but differences in drinking tastes tended to blur the distinction. Scots and Irish preferred whisky, with its higher alcohol content and power of rapid intoxication, while the English were beer-drinkers, taking longer to reach a state of intoxication and not normally becoming so aggressive in the process. In proportion to its population Glasgow had more convictions for drunkenness than London and most of the large Lowland towns had high rates, although there were exceptions. One was Dundee, which was statistically twice as sober, or half as inebriate, as Greenock, Buckhaven or Queensferry. The soberest areas were Ross and Cromarty, Caithness and Sutherland and the Orkneys, but the unenviable record of convictions at Inverkeithing and Cromarty was in some measure due to the presence there of naval units.

Alcoholic drink was relatively cheap. A pint of mild beer cost $1\frac{1}{2}$d. (a little over $\frac{1}{2}$p) and a pint of strong ale cost 2d. or 3d. (about 1p). Whisky was sold at about 3s. or 3s. 6d. (15p or $17\frac{1}{2}$p) a bottle, or 2d. a nip, and hardened drinkers could buy methylated spirits at less than a quarter the price of whisky. In such circumstances the merits of temperance or total abstinence were widely preached. Since

Gladstone's brave attempt in 1872 to regulate the licensed trade, the brewers had supported the Conservative Party and as much of the strength of the Liberals lay in their Nonconformist support, the Liberal Party had come to be regarded as the champion of temperance reform. This did not prevent Balfour from introducing a bill in 1904 to transfer from local magistrates to Quarter Sessions the power to refuse renewal of a licence, and to impose a levy on the brewing trade to provide a fund for compensating dispossessed licensees. The Liberals complained that Balfour's act did not go far enough towards reducing the number of licensed premises but its effect was gradually to do so.

A few weeks before he resigned office, Cambell-Bannerman made a more radical attempt to regulate the licensed trade. A bill introduced in February 1908 provided that the number of licences should be reduced until they reached a statutory proportion to population, with compensation payable only until the expiry of a fixed period, fourteen years. Large and rowdy meetings, enlivened by the presence not only of suffragettes but also of representatives of bar opinion, were held in support of the bill. One of them gave rise to an anecdote illustrative of Asquith's remarkable ability to make long speeches from the sketchiest of notes, in contrast to Campbell-Bannerman, who painstakingly read almost every word of his speeches, holding his notes near to the end of his nose, with a hiatus from time to time as he turned the page. A gushing lady approached Asquith after he had made a particularly eloquent and detailed speech at a public meeting in support of the Licensing Bill, and asked if he would give her his notes as a souvenir of a memorable occasion. Asquith beamed and reached into a waistcoat pocket, drawing forth a crumpled scrap of paper which he courteously handed to his admirer. Unfolding it, she read the words: 'Too many pubs.' Despite Asquith's eloquence and the approval of most of the Church of England bishops, the bill was unpopular and after a conference of Conservative peers at Lord Lansdowne's house, the Lords rejected it.

Neither Balfour's act nor Asquith's bill affected public-house hours of opening. In urban districts these were generally from early morning to late at night, at the landlord's discretion. There was nothing except poverty or disinclination to prevent a man from calling at a public house on his way to work in a morning or from remaining there to drink all day. Although the signs were not immediately apparent, however, the Edwardian period saw the beginning of a more temperate attitude to drinking. There was a steady fall in the number of licensed premises and in convictions for drinking offences. Among the factors which brought about these changes were the temperance campaign, the serious and sobering reverses suffered by the British Army during the Boer War, and the development of alternative leisure activities for the working classes, among them cycling, day excursions by train to holiday resorts, the cinema and the appearance of cheap popular newspapers. Sheer poverty no doubt played its part, as did the marked differences in character and temperament between King Edward VII and his successor, King George V. Drunkenness remained a chronic social disease of the Edwardian era but one which, unlike many others, was showing signs of cure.

It was not surprising that in the overcrowded and insanitary slums of the Lowland cities serious diseases were endemic, but over the period there was a gradual improvement in the nation's health. The average rate of infant mortality in Scotland between 1895 and 1901 was 130 per thousand, compared with 96 in Norway, 105 in Ireland and 156 in England and Wales. During the next seven years the average rate fell in Scotland to 116, in Ireland to 96 and in England and Wales to 130. About one in ten of all the deaths in Scotland, an average of 7,500 per annum, were due to tuberculosis but there were also outbreaks of bubonic plague, typhus and smallpox. The outbreak of plague, the first in Scotland for two centuries, occurred in August 1900 in the dockside area of Glasgow, south of the river, and lasted until November, causing a dozen deaths. Another outbreak occurred the following year in the same district and the examination of rats killed or found dead near a Glasgow hotel confirmed that they were the carriers. A few further cases occurred during the next ten years, all in Leith or Glasgow. Typhus was far more prevalent in the black houses of the Western Isles than in the slums of Glasgow and Edinburgh, but there was a serious outbreak in Aberdeen during the winter of 1904, with over twenty deaths, about half of them children.

The Vaccination (Scotland) Act of 1863 had made the vaccination of infants against smallpox compulsory and this led to a marked decline in the incidence of the disease during the last twenty years of Queen Victoria's reign. There were serious epidemics in 1901, when almost two thousand cases, many of them in Glasgow, were reported, and in 1904, when there were over two thousand cases, but thereafter the number of reported cases fell rapidly. In 1907 there were only eight and although that year's Vaccination (Amendment) Act allowed parents exemption on conscientious grounds, the succeeding years brought only moderate increases and in 1914 there were none. A sign of changing times was manifest in an observation by the Local Government Board, which had been designated under the Public Health (Scotland) Act of 1897 as the central public health authority. In its report for 1904 the Board recorded its interest at hearing that a patient suffering from scarlet fever had been removed from the Inverness-shire Highlands to his home in the Lowlands, a distance of 165 miles, in thirteen hours by motor-car. 'It appears to us', continued the Board, 'that such rapid motor transport opens up a new possibility in hospital administration and isolation. We see no reason why motor ambulances should not be constructed, and we believe that this mode of conveyance would render the necessity of infectious hospitals in isolated districts less imperative for such diseases as could bear transport to a distance.'

The most daunting aspect of life for a working man and his family in Darkest Scotland was almost certainly the fear of unemployment. The completion of a contract, a recession in trade, a period of bad weather, a minor misdemeanour, an argument with a foreman, or merely the whim of an employer might result in dismissal. Like accident or death, the unemployment of the wage-earner could plunge the thriftiest and most law-abiding of families into the direst poverty. Most vulnerable of all were the unskilled, whose low wages left no margin for provision against such adversity.

A ten-year-old Scots boy suffered a misfortune which might have befallen any Victorian or Edwardian worker. The eldest of nine children, he had been born in 1856 in a one-roomed cottage in the mining village of Laighbrannock, near Holyton, in Lanarkshire. His father, a ship's carpenter, soon afterwards moved to Glasgow to work in Napier's shipyard but an accident in the yard, followed by a strike, made it essential for the boy to find work as a messenger. In 1866 there was a lock-out in the Clyde shipyards and the family's only income was 1s. 6d. strike pay and the 4s. 6d. earned by the boy. One by one the meagre sticks of furniture were sold to buy food, a younger boy died of fever and the mother, in an advanced stage of pregnancy, fell ill. One winter morning, after spending the night tending an ailing brother and rising early to help his mother about the house, the boy set out breakfastless for the baker's shop where he was employed. It was a few minutes past seven when he arrived to begin his twelve- or thirteen-hour day's work. 'I had to go upstairs to see the master', he wrote afterwards. 'I was kept waiting outside the door of the dining-room while he said grace—he was noted for religious zeal—and on being admitted found the master and his family seated round a large table. He was serving out bacon and eggs while his wife was pouring coffee from a glass infuser which at once—shamefaced and terrified as I was—attracted my attention. I had never before seen such a beautiful thing. The master read me a lecture before the assembled family on the sin of slothfulness, and added that though he would forgive me that once, if I sinned again by being late I should be instantly dismissed, and so sent me to begin work.'

Two mornings later the boy was again, for the same reasons, a few minutes late in arriving at the shop. This time the shop-woman informed him that the master had ordered his instant dismissal and, as a punishment, that he would forfeit the fortnight's wages due to him. The boy burst into tears and begged the shop-woman to intercede on his behalf with the master. 'The morning was wet', he wrote, 'and I had been drenched in getting to the shop and must have presented a pitiable sight as I stood at the counter in my wet patched clothes. She spoke with the master through a speaking tube, presumably to the breakfast room I remembered so well, but he was obdurate, and finally she, out of the goodness of her heart, gave me a piece of bread and advised me to look for another place. For a time I wandered about the streets in the rain, ashamed to go home where there was neither food nor fire and actually discussing whether the best thing was not to go and throw myself in the Clyde and be done with a life that had so little attraction. In the end I went back to the shop and saw the master and explained why I had been late. But it was all in vain. The wages were never paid. But the master continued to be a pillar of the Church and a leading light in the religious life of the city.'

The boy was James Keir Hardie. He next found work in a coal-mine at Newharthill, Lanarkshire, where his mother had moved with the children while her husband went back to sea. Keir Hardie became a 'trapper', squatting alone in the dark for ten hours a day to open and close a door regulating the flow of air in the mine. He was then promoted to become a pony-driver and when he was twelve years old survived an accident in which the cage was jammed in the shaft by a fall of rock, trapping the underground workers for some hours. Hardie's mother taught him to read and write, and he attended evening classes, becoming a temperance orator and lay preacher in the

Evangelical Union formed by the Rev. James Morrison, of Kilmarnock. Because of his ability as a speaker he was asked to lead a deputation of Hamilton miners protesting against the reduction of their wage to 2s. a day. The result was instant dismissal for Keir Hardie and for his two younger brothers, who worked in the same pit. The Hardie family was then boycotted throughout the Lanarkshire coalfield as an example to any other miner who might try to organise a protest against his wages or conditions of work. Keir Hardie next began to earn a modest living as a journalist and was elected national secretary of the Scottish Miners, with the task of building a federation for all Scottish mine-workers. In 1880 he and his wife, a temperance worker named Lillie Wilson, moved to a two-roomed cottage at Cumnock and began to organise a miners' union in Ayrshire. The following year the miners put in a claim for a 10% increase in their wages. The mine-owners refused the claim. There seemed no alternative but to strike, for if the union tamely accepted the refusal, it would forfeit the confidence of its members and lose the hope of attracting more miners to join. In his biography, *The Life of Keir Hardie*, published in 1921, William Stewart described the outcome.

'On the Saturday, at the end of the rows and on the quoitury grounds, the talk was: "Will there be a strike?" Nobody knew. On the Sunday coming home from the kirk the crack was the same: "Will there be a strike?" On Sunday night they laid out their pit clothes as usual, ready for work as usual, but for ten long weeks they had no use for pit clothes. On Monday, long before dawn, there was a stir on the Ayrshire roads.

'At two in the morning the Annbank brass band came playing through Trabboch village, and every miner, young and old, jumped out of bed and fell in behind. Away up towards Auchinleck they went marching, their numbers increasing with every mile of the road. On through Damconner and Cronberry and Lugar and Muirkirk, right on to Glenbuck by Aird's Moss where the Covenanter martyrs sleep, then down into Cumnock, at least five thousand strong. Never did magic muster such an army of the morning. . . . Over in the Kilmarnock district similar scenes were being enacted. The bands went marching from colliery to colliery and

'The rising sun ower Galston Muir
Wi' glorious light was glinting

110

upon processions of colliers on all the roads round about Galston village and Hurlford and Crookedholm and Riccanton, making, as by one common impulse towards Craigie Hill which had not witnessed such a mustering of determined men since the days of William Wallace.

''Ere nightfall a miracle had been accomplished. For the first time in its history there was a stoppage nearly complete in the Ayrshire mining industry'.

In the end the strike was successful and after the miners, with other working-class heads of families in the county constituencies, had been enfranchised by the Parliamentary Reform Act of 1884, Keir Hardie decided to stand for Parliament. His first attempt, at a by-election in March 1888 in Mid-Lanarkshire, ended in defeat but at the general election of 1892 he was returned as an independent member for West Ham South. Two other independent labour members were also elected, John Burns in Battersea and James Havelock Wilson, the seaman's leader, in Middlesbrough. From that time until his death in 1915, Keir Hardie was a familiar and controversial figure on the political scene in Scotland and at Westminster. He arrived at the House of Commons for the first time in a two-horse brake with a cornet-player on the box, not because he favoured such flamboyance but simply to please his excited West Ham supporters who had arranged the celebration.

Meanwhile, in August 1888 at a meeting in the Waterloo Rooms, Glasgow, a conference of workers agreed to form a Scottish Labour Party. Keir Hardie was elected its secretary, with R. B. Cunninghame Graham as president and J. Shaw Maxwell as chairman. Its programme included Scottish Home Rule, adult suffrage, the payment of Members of Parliament, the abolition of the House of Lords, free education, a system of national insurance, the state acquisition of the railways, and the establishment of a national banking system.

Delegates from the Scottish Labour Party and from the Fabian Society, the Social Democratic Federation and a few trade unions met under Keir Hardie's chairmanship in January 1893 at Bradford to form a new radical organisation for the whole of the United Kingdom. This was the Independent Labour Party. Among its early members was a 'Moray loon', James Ramsay MacDonald, who was then secretary of the Scottish Home Rule Association. Born at Lossiemouth in 1866, MacDonald had the traditional beginnings of many a poor Scottish lad, a long walk to school, spare-time farm work to earn a few pence, and the encouragement of a perceptive dominie.

On 27 February 1900 MacDonald was one of the Independent Labour Party delegates to an historic conference in the Memorial Hall, Farringdon Street, London. Here representatives of the Fabian Society, the Social Democratic Federation, the Independent Labour Party and sixty-five trade unions, from the Waiters' Union with 200 members to the Amalgamated Society of Engineers with 85,000, met to form the Labour Representation Committee. Its purpose was set out in an amendment carried by an overwhelming majority, 'That this conference is in favour of working-class opinion being represented in the House of Commons by men sympathetic with the aims and demands of the Labour movement and whose candidatures are promoted by one or other of the organised movements represented at this conference'.

Ramsay MacDonald was elected secretary of the new Labour Representation Committee. Six years later, almost to the day, the Committee met again in the Memorial Hall. At the general election the previous month it had put fifty candidates in the field and had secured the election of twenty-nine of them. 'A Labour Party now sits in the House of Commons', asserted the conference report, 'and our success at the polls has been regarded as the most significant event of the Election. We have won national recognition and for the time being the fate of our Movement has to be decided, not only on the platform, but also on the floor of the House of Commons.'

The new party was able to exert pressure on the Liberal government out of all proportion to its numbers, for in most matters it could also count on the support of the twenty-four Lib-Labs, of whom a dozen represented mining constituencies. This influence on the government was immediately apparent in the reversal of the Taff Vale Railway judgement by the Trade Disputes Act passed in 1906.

Impetus for the growth of the Labour Party came from the severe depression which occurred during 1904 and 1905, especially in ship-building and engineering. Glasgow, where the rate of unemployment in the ship-yards reached 16%, and Eastern Scotland, where the rate soared to 24%, were the worst affected areas. A Conservative measure, the Unemployed Workmen's Act of 1905, whose provisions extended to Scotland and Ireland, introduced some relief by enjoining councils in burghs of over 50,000 inhabitants to appoint distress committees.

Administration was in the hands of the Local Government Board, to which burghs of fewer than 50,000 inhabitants could apply for the extension of the Act's provisions. Within a few months Dumfries, Inverness, Kilmarnock and Pollokshaws had made application. The distress committees were empowered to provide 'temporary work on other assistance' for unemployed men whose cases were 'more suitable for treatment under this Act than under the Poor Law'. They could acquire land, establish farm colonies for agricultural work, provide temporary accommodation where needed, and assist a worker to move with his family to a place offering employment or even to emigrate. Among the schemes in Scotland were the purchase by the Glasgow Distress Committee of nearly six hundred acres of land at Cumbernauld, and by the Edinburgh Distress Committee of two hundred acres at Midcalder, for agricultural purposes. A firewood factory was opened in Edinburgh and the Aberdeen Distress Committee organised stone-breaking at the Dancing Cairns quarry during the winter of 1909, extended the embankment at the beach, and opened a factory to process waste paper. Such measures, valuable to those who were able to profit from them, no more than scratched the surface of the problem. During the last decade of the nineteenth century, over 50,000 Scots left their homeland to seek work elsewhere. During the first decade of the twentieth century, the number of Scottish emigrants increased to over 250,000. Despite the palliative measures, Scotland in the Edwardian era was no place to be poor, sick, aged or unemployed.

14

The Welfare State

The cold Christmas of 1908 found the Lord Provost of Glasgow, Sir Archbald McInnes Shaw, anxious about old age pensions. These were due to be introduced on 1 January 1909 at the rate of five shillings a week for everyone over seventy years of age, except for anyone who had 'failed to work according to his ability, opportunity and need', or who had received any Poor Law relief during the previous year, or who had been sentenced to imprisonment during the previous ten years, or who had other income totalling more than twelve shillings a week. Despite these prudent safeguards against the squandering of public funds, the Lord Provost voiced his earnest opinion that 'it was not those who had been thrifty who were going to be helped but practically those who had been thriftless'. This, he declared, was 'a very sad state of affairs'.

Sir Archibald was speaking at the annual meeting of the Glasgow Savings Bank on 23 December 1908 and he was proclaiming the absolute necessity that the people of Scotland should continue to be an independent race. He was quite favourable, he emphasised, to the new pension scheme but he thought that the people who had sensibly saved for their old age should be helped first, so that the thriftless should learn that thrift was the best thing for them, too. The trend in Scotland, he feared, was against thrift.

The Lord Provost's fears were widely shared. The Earl of Rosebery, the former Liberal Prime Minister, believed that the scheme was 'so prodigal of expenditure as likely to undermine the whole fabric of the Empire'. The Marquess of Landsdowne, Conservative leader in the House of Lords, echoed these sentiments. Old age pensions would, he was sure, 'weaken the moral fibre of the nation and diminish the self-respect of our people'.

By the end of the first year of operation about 75,000 old people in Scotland were drawing the state pension. The *Woman Worker*, one of the progressive political weeklies, set out the budget of a Glasgow widow who was receiving the full pension of five shillings a week. Rent, a pint of paraffin for her lamp and a stone of coal for her fire cost her a little over half the total. For her menu she bought one loaf at 2½d., 2 ozs. of tea, 1d., 2 lbs. of mutton, 1s., half a bag of flour, 1d., pepper, salt and vinegar, 1½d., beans, ½d., and onions, 1d. On Friday she paid a penny for a herring, and for her Sunday dinner, with a pennyworth of cheese, she spent 1¾d. on a pint of the dark bitter beer known as porter. This expenditure left a silver threepenny piece and a farthing each week to lavish on other luxuries.

Because he had prepared it, Asquith presented the 1908 Budget to Parliament although he had already succeeded Sir Henry Campbell-Bannerman as Prime Minister. He estimated the revenue for the coming year at a little under £158,000,000 and expenditure at a little under £153,000,000. With this surplus he was able to reduce the duty on sugar and to provide for the first quarter's old age pensions, estimated to need £1,200,000. It fell to Lloyd George, as Chancellor of the Exchequer, to defend the Budget in the Commons and to introduce the bill giving effect to the proposed pension scheme, so that he rather than Asquith became associated with old age pensions in the public mind. Echoing the fears of the Lord Provost of Glasgow and the Marquess of Lansdowne, Conservative members opposed the bill principally on the ground that the new pensions should have been self-financed by insurance contributions. Few members, however, were willing to be labelled in their constituencies as outright opponents of so philanthropic a measure and although there was more opposition in the Lords, the passage of the bill was not seriously hampered.

Old age pensions formed one element in a far-reaching programme of social and economic reform which laid the foundations of the modern welfare state. As Lord George Hamilton, that unusually liberal-minded Conservative Member of Parliament for Ealing, had suggested, Britain's task during the nineteenth century having been to accumulate vast wealth, her task during the twentieth century would be to ensure its more equitable distribution. A Children Act of 1908 codified and extended previous legislation for the protection of children. Juvenile courts were set up to hear charges against young offenders, with remand homes and reformatory schools, known as borstals because the first had been opened at Borstal, in Kent. Children were forbidden to beg in the streets or to enter the bars of public-houses. Alcoholic liquor was not to be given to a child under five and tobacco was not to be sold to a child under sixteen. It became an offence to leave a child under seven in a room with an unguarded fire. This important Children Act supplemented the measures being taken under the Education (Scotland) Act of 1908 to benefit children by widening the scope and improving the quality of Scottish education.

As President of the Board of Trade, Winston Churchill introduced two important measures. In 1909 a nation-wide network of labour exchanges was established at the suggestion of **William H. Beveridge**, a gifted young journalist who combined his work on the *Morning Post* with an intense interest in the problems of unemployment. The first Scottish labour exchanges were opened on 1 February 1910 in Aberdeen, Coatbridge, Dundee, Edinburgh, Glasgow, Greenock and Paisley. In the same parliamentary session Churchill introduced a Trade Boards Bill to offer some protection to the most severely exploited of Edwardian workers. These were the women and children in the 'sweated industries' such as dress-making, tailoring, lace-making, chain-making and the assembly of cardboard boxes. These tasks were usually performed at home or in small, dingy workshops, sometimes by whole families under contract to a middleman from whom they bought their raw materials and to whom they were forced to sell the finished articles at rates so low that only by slaving from dawn till dark were they able to earn even a subsistence wage. For making a pair of trousers the payment varied between 4d. and 9d., for a man's jacket from 4d. to 7d., and for making shirts the rate of payment was 8d. or 9d. a dozen. Matchbox-makers could ensure a weekly wage of five shillings only by working twelve hours a day. Because of the temporary and fluctuating nature of their employment, such workers had no trade union to protect them. Their case was taken up by a group of women led by a niece of Lord Kelvin, Margaret Ethel Gladstone, whom Ramsay MacDonald married in 1896. With him she visited the United States to see how the problem had been tackled there, and matters came to a head in 1906 when the Liberal *Daily News* staged an exhibition in London to proclaim the horrors of the sweated industries and to show upper-class women one result of their insistence on wearing clothes encrusted with yards of lace frills, braids, bows and embroidery, and hats adorned with miniature gardens of artificial flowers and fruits, all laboriously fashioned and assembled by hand. Winston Churchill set up trade boards to fix minimum wages in, at first, four trades: ready-made and wholesale tailoring, machine lace-making, chain-making and the assembly of paper and cardboard boxes.

Further legislation improved conditions for workers in other industries. An act in 1908 introduced, with slight modifications, an eight-hour day for coal-miners, whose average working day had been nine hours. When colliery owners in Scotland and South Wales retaliated by threatening to reduce wages in proportion, Churchill settled the dispute by persuading both sides to make concessions. A Shops Act in 1911, despite opposition from the retail shopkeepers who were traditionally staunch Liberal voters, gave shop-assistants the right to a weekly half-day holiday and to reasonable facilities for washing and eating.

The Liberal government ensured Labour and trade union support for this massive programme of reform by reversing the judgement of the House of Lords in the Taff Vale Railway case of 1901 and in the Osborne case of seven years later. A railwayman named W. V. Osborne objected to the Amalgamated Society of Railway Servants, of which he was a member, using part of its funds for political purposes, mainly to help in the payment of a salary of £200 to Labour Members of Parliament. Osborne brought an action to restrain the Society and although he was unsuccessful in a lower court, the Law Lords in December 1909 took the view that any political activity by a trade union was contrary to the law. One of them, Lord Shaw of Dunfermline, who had been the Liberal Member for Hawick, took an even sterner view. For a trade union member to be required to conform to the decisions and policies of the Labour Party, he stated, 'was not compatible either with the spirit of our Parliamentary constitution or with that independence and freedom which has hitherto been held to lie at the basis of the representative government of the United Kingdom'. Keir Hardie was not slow to assert that 'if the Labour Members were being paid by brewers or landowners, or railway directors or financiers to represent their interests in the House of Commons, no objection would have been taken. It is only because they are being paid to represent an interest which is dangerous to all other interests that the issue is being forced upon us'. More dependent upon Labour support after the 1910 general elections, the Liberal government reluctantly decided to reverse the Osborne judgement by a new Trade Union Act of 1913. This restored the right of the unions to impose a political levy on their members, provided that those unwilling to pay it should have the right to contract out of it without jeopardising their position as members. By this time the payment of a salary of £400 per year to all Members of Parliament made the political levy of less importance than it had previously been in sustaining working-class Members who had no other source of income.

The cornerstone of the Liberal reforms was the National Insurance Act of 1911. This was the joint effort of Lloyd George and Winston Churchill, with Asquith's steady stupport. Three years earlier Lloyd George had returned from a holiday in Germany enthusiastic over the state insurance scheme which had been introduced there by Bismarck. At about the same time Churchill was being encouraged by William Beveridge to add to the services offered by the new labour exchanges a state scheme of payments during unemployment. The National Insurance Act combined the two proposals. Part I, which applied to practically every employed person, provided that he or she should have a card on which the employer was to stick Inland Revenue stamps representing the weekly premium of 4d. deducted from the worker's wages (3d. for a woman) and 3d. contributed by the employer. To this would be added a state contribution of 2d., so giving, in Lloyd George's phrase, 'Ninepence for fourpence'. The services for which contributors became eligible included medical treatment and medicines, sickness benefit of 10s. per week (7s. 6d. for women) for a period of up to twenty-six weeks, with disablement benefit of 5s. for longer periods, and a maternity benefit of 30s. for insured women or the wives of insured men. Part II, which applied only to industries described as 'precarious', such as building, heavy engineering and shipbuilding, levied contributions of 2½d. from the worker, 2½d. from the employer and a smaller supplementary sum from the state. This entitled a worker to unemployment benefit of 7s. per week for a maximum period of fifteen weeks within any one year.

Lloyd George expounded the merits of the scheme in a series of lively meetings, one of which was held in the Music Hall, Aberdeen, on 29 November 1912. A few hours before the meeting was due to begin, three suffragettes with a stock of fireworks were discovered in a large packing-case at the back of the organ. They were promptly ejected, as was another young woman, who claimed to be a journalist but was suspected of even worse intent.

Although the National Insurance Act had been in force only for about four months, said Lloyd George, there were already remarkable examples of the benefits which it was bringing to working men in

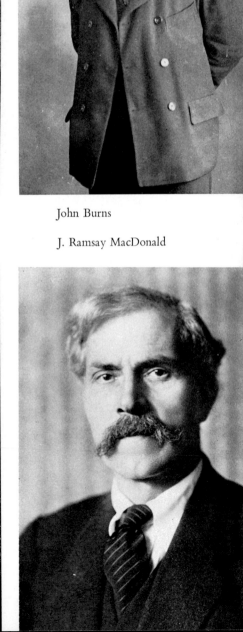

H. H. Asquith

John Burns

H. Campbell-Bannerman

J. Ramsay MacDonald

"Doon wi the Lords"

Punch cartoon, 2 October, 1907

distress. One labourer had paid only eight weeks' contributions, a total of 2s. 8d., when he was found to be suffering from tuberculosis and had to be taken to hospital. Now, declared Lloyd George, 'he is doing well. His health is improving but he has got to be kept there a further twelve weeks. What does it cost? Thirty-five shillings a week! Sanatoria have gone up in price since the days of the Good Samaritan (laughter). They only cost twopence in those days. They are now thirty-five shillings a week. It will cost twenty-one pounds. He has only paid two shillings and eightpence. He will get the best treatment that science can provide for him.

'That is one case. What did the Tories do there? The priest and the Levite of the Tory Party (laughter)—they were not satisfied with passing by and doing nothing. They attacked the Samaritan (loud cheers). They said he was a thief! (loud laughter). In a very short time they will be claiming both the mule and the oil, and they will swear to you that the inn was their idea (laughter).

'Here is another fellow', went on Lloyd George. 'The man is a blacksmith; he is only nineteen years of age. He paid fourteen weeks, four shillings and eightpence taken from his pocket, again by the descendant of the Welsh buccaneers. Seized by this terrible scourge, he had to leave his work on October 16, admitted to a London general hospital. They there discovered that he was suffering from tuberculosis of the spine and they recommended complete rest on his back for at least two years.

'Now what is the good of saying that to a poor fellow who was a blacksmith earning probably twenty-five or thirty shillings a week? You say to him, "You have got to rest for two years under the best hygienic conditions obtainable", but he says, "I have not got a penny and my last four shillings and eightpence was taken by a Welshman" (laughter). Now, what is to be done with him? The Insurance Act comes along. The moment he gets out of hospital—because they keep him there only a few weeks—they are going to make provision for him. He will be kept for two years under the best conditions that scientific invention can discover. It will cost two hundred pounds. It will all be found, and he will be cured, and this is the Act they have been calumniating all over the country!'

Although the broad mass of workers in the industrial centres of the United Kingdom welcomed the new act, there was vociferous opposition to it from some sections of the community. Domestic servants, encouraged by their employers, staged protest meetings at which they lamented the intervention of the chill hand of bureaucracy in their warm relations with the families they served. Farmers, traditionally generous in time of adversity to farm-servants whose work, comportment and morals were otherwise satisfactory, derided the prospect of 'licking Lloyd George's stamps for him'. One protester who openly defied the law was Robert Paterson, who farmed at Lendrum, near Turriff, in Aberdeenshire. Paterson steadfastly refused to stamp his employees' insurance cards and in 1913 a sheriff's warrant was issued for the impounding of a white dairy cow to be sold to pay the arrears. People came 'frae twal' mile roun'' to see 'fit wad happen neist' when the cow was put up for auction in Turriff. But the auctioneer found himself surrounded by a hostile crowd and the proceedings developed into a riot, so that the sale had to be abandoned. Even when the cow was later auctioned in Aberdeen, she was bought by some of Paterson's sympathisers and returned to her owner. The affair was a nine days' wonder and earned national fame for the central figure in the controversy, the 'Turra' Coo'.

To pay for all these reforms, for the old age pensions, for the labour exchanges, for the coming national insurance schemes and for the increasing number of civil servants needed to administer them, Lloyd George had, as Chancellor of the Exchequer, the task of raising additional revenue. He had also to provide for the cost of building more battleships of the giant *Dreadnought* class to keep pace with Germany's new programme of naval expansion. His proposals came in the Budget which he introduced on 29 April 1909.

Much of the proposed taxation was severe but not exceptional. Income tax was to be increased from 1s. to 1s. 2d. in the pound on incomes above £3,000 a year. Unearned income was to be taxed at a higher rate than earned income, and a new super-tax beginning at 6d. in the pound was to be imposed on incomes above £5,000. Estate or 'death' duties were to be increased, as were the duties on tobacco and spirits, while to finance a road-building scheme a tax was imposed on motor vehicles and petrol. Finally came the most controversial proposals, the new and complicated land taxes, of which there were four. A tax of 20% was to be levied on the unearned increment in land values and another of 10% was to be levied on the increased value of land let on lease, calculated at the renewal of the lease. A tax of a halfpenny in the pound was to be paid by the owner on the value of undeveloped land, where the site was over £50 per acre, and a tax, known as the Mineral Rights Duty, was to be paid at the rate of a shilling in the pound on mineral royalties. 'This is a war Budget', Lloyd George proclaimed in his peroration. 'It is for raising money to wage implacable warfare against poverty and squalidness. I cannot help believing that before this generation has passed away, we shall have advanced a great step towards that good time when poverty, and the wretchedness and human degradation which have always followed in its camp, will be as remote to the people of this country as the wolves which once infested its forests.'

The 1909 Budget aroused the bitterest political strife that Britain had known since the passing of the Reform Act in 1832. The grumbles of Labour Members at the increase in duty on the working man's 'baccy' and the complaints of Scottish and Irish Members at the increased duty on whisky were drowned in the storm over the Land Taxes. Lloyd George deliberately widened the argument by emphasising the opposition of the House of Lords, so that he was able to present the issue as a struggle for political power between the People and the Peers. He already had ammunition to hand in the action of the Lords in rejecting several important measures passed by the Commons. These included in 1906 a Plural Voting Bill prohibiting an elector from voting in more than one constituency, and an Education Bill; in 1907 a Land Valuation (Scotland) Bill extending to smallholders in the Lowlands the help already given to crofters in the Highlands; and in 1908 a Licensing Bill to reduce the number of public-houses in a fixed proportion to the population of the district concerned. With these rejections as evidence of the Lords' dislike for Liberal measures, Lloyd George opened his public campaign on behalf of the Budget with a memorable speech in the hall of the *Edinburgh Castle*, in Limehouse, on 30 July 1909 before an audience of four thousand people. He began, a little disingenuously, with an attack on his Conservative and Unionist opponents for their reluctance to pay extra taxes to provide the extra Dreadnoughts they were demanding for the Navy.

'We started our four Dreadnoughts', he said. 'They cost eight millions of money. We promised them four more; they cost another eight millions. Somebody has got to pay, and these gentlemen say, "Perfectly true; somebody has got to pay, but we would rather that somebody were somebody else" (laughter). We started building; we wanted money to pay for the building; so we sent the hat round (laughter). We sent it round amongst the workmen (hear, hear), and the miners of Derbyshire (loud cheers), and Yorkshire, the weavers of High Peak (cheers), and the Scotchmen of Dumfries (cheers), who, like all their countrymen, know the value of money (laughter). They all brought in their coppers. We went round Belgravia, but there has been such a howl ever since that it has completely deafened us.'

Lloyd George went on to paint a similar picture of the opposition to old age pensions. 'It is rather a shame', he lamented, 'for a rich country like ours—probably the richest country in the world, if not the richest the world has ever seen—that it should allow those who have toiled all their days to end in penury and possibly starvation (hear, hear). It is rather hard that an old workman should have to find his way to the gates of the tomb, bleeding and footsore, through the brambles and thorns of poverty (cheers). We cut a new path through it (cheers), an easier one, a pleasanter one, through fields of waving corn. We are raising money to pay for the new road (cheers), aye, and to widen it so that two hundred thousand paupers shall be able to join in the march (cheers). There are many in the country blessed by Providence with great wealth, and if there are amongst them men who grudge out of their riches a fair contribution towards the less fortunate of their fellow countrymen, they are shabby rich men (cheers).'

Defending the new Land Taxes, Lloyd George quoted examples of rises in land values which, he argued, justified his proposals. 'Take the very well-known case of the Duke of Northumberland', he said, 'when a county council wanted to buy a small plot of land as a site for a school to train the children who in due course would become the men labouring on his property. The rent was quite an insignificant thing; his contribution to the rates—I forget—I think on the basis of 30s. per acre. What did he demand for it for a school? £900 an acre! Well, all we say is this—Mr. Buxton and I say—if it is worth £900, let him pay taxes on £900.'

'There are no end of these cases', continued Lloyd George. 'There was a case at Greenock the other day. The Admiralty wanted a torpedo range. Here was an opportunity for patriotism! (laughter). These are the men who want an efficient Navy to protect our shores, and the Admiralty state that one element in efficiency is straight shooting, and say, "We want a range for practice for torpedoes on the west of Scotland". There was a piece of land there. It was rated at something like £11 2s. a year. They went to the landlord and it was sold to the nation for £27,225. And these are the gentlemen who accuse us of robbery and spoliation!'

Dealing with the Mineral Rights Duty, Lloyd George described a visit he had made to a coal mine. 'We sank down into a pit half a mile deep. We then walked underneath the mountain and we did about three-quarters of a mile with rock and shale above us. The earth seemed to be straining, around us and above us, to crush us in. You could see the pit props bent and twisted and sundered until you saw their fibres split. Sometimes they give way and then there is mutilation and death. Often a spark ignites, the whole pit is deluged in fire, and the breath of life is scorched out of hundreds of breasts by the consuming fire. In the very next colliery to the one I descended, just three years ago, three hundred people lost their lives in that way; and yet when the Prime Minister and I knock at the door of these great landlords and say to them, "Here, you know these poor fellows who have been digging up royalties at the risk of their lives, some of them are old, they have survived the perils of their trade, they are broken, they can earn no more. Won't you give something towards keeping them out of the workhouse?" They scowl at you, and we say, "Only a ha'penny, just a copper". They say, "You thieves!" and they turn their dogs on to us, and every day you can hear their bark. If this is an indication of the view taken by these great landlords of their responsibility to the people who, at the risk of life, create their wealth, then I say their day of reckoning is at hand!'

Lloyd George ended with a general defence, punctuated at almost every sentence by loud cheers from his audience. 'We are placing the burdens on the broad shoulders. Why should I put burdens on the people? I am one of the children of the people. I was brought up amongst them, I know their trials, and God forbid that I should add one grain of trouble to the anxiety which they bear with such patience and fortitude. When the Prime Minister did me the honour of inviting me to take charge of the National Exchequer at a time of great difficulty, I made up my mind, in framing the Budget which was in front of me, that at any rate no cupboard should be bared, no lot should be harder to bear. By that test I challenge them to judge the Budget!'

On 10 September 1909 Lord Rosebery spoke of the Budget at a meeting organised in the City Hall, Glasgow, by a committee of businessmen. Pointing out that he had 'long ceased to be in communion with the Liberal Party', Lord Rosebery declared that it was his duty to show why he believed that it was not in the best interests of the nation for the Budget to become law. 'I know it will be said', he admitted, 'that as I am well off, I have no right to speak on such a question, that it is only the cry of a wounded taxpayer that you will hear. Well, if you carry that proposition to its logical conclusion, and if you had the Budget only discussed by those who had nothing, it would be a most one-sided discussion.'

Lord Rosebery feared that the Budget would open the way for the nationalisation of land. 'I cannot forget', he said, 'that Mr. Lloyd George himself, the Chancellor of the Exchequer, speaking in October 1906—and he was already a highly-placed Minister—said, "Nationalisation of the land—that must come, but it must come by easy stages". This is the first easy stage. The other day the Land Nationalisation League held a meeting in which they were extremely jubilant over the Budget. Some Members of Parliament—all that were reported—have said that the private ownership of land was criminal and so forth, and Mr. Keir Hardie wrote—and he is a man whose words are valuable in these days—he wrote simply but pregnantly: "These are encouraging times for land nationalisers." '

As evidence of this intention, went on Lord Rosebery, he would cite the views of Mr. Alexander Ure, Liberal Member for Linlithgow, who had been Solicitor-General and was the newly appointed Lord Advocate. 'We all like him. We do not all quite agree with him, but nobody can help liking him. We like him for the engaging quality of frankness which is not always to be found in Ministers. Some Ministers try to keep their cat in their bag altogether; some let you see sometimes the tip of his ear and sometimes the end of his tail, but no bag has ever been constructed large enough to hold the cat of Mr. Ure. While other Ministers are thinking, Mr. Ure is speaking. Now, what are his reasons—and these are what I take the businessmen of Glasgow to attend to—what are his reasons for placing land in a special category as regards taxation? The main one is rather cynical—its immobility and visibility, which prevent the owner from evading or deceiving the tax collector. That is a strange argument. Your Budget is such that everyone will seek to evade it. Land, again, must be honest, so it must bear the full weight of the Government tax.'

Lord Rosebery argued that down the centuries the landowning class had rendered great service to the state. 'They have been centres of employment and bounty', he asserted. 'I do not say there have not been exceptions to this, as in every class, but, as a rule, I think you will endorse what I am saying—that they have been centres of bounty and employment and civilisation. From land have come most great servants of the State. They have conducted the arduous rural administration of the country without emolument and without pay—a fact which fills every foreign visitor with admiration and envy. And then suddenly a new Government comes in and tells them they are pariahs and may go about their business!'

As for the dukes, whom Lloyd George delighted in deriding, said Lord Rosebery, 'Well, I have not much experience of dukes, naturally, but I have always found them a poor but honest class.'

Next Lord Rosebery warned his audience of the bureaucracy which the Liberal government was erecting and of the Socialism which would spring from it. The government had created 'a whole new staff of well-paid officials under their Small-holdings Act, their Factory Inspection Act, their Old Age Pensions Act, their Housing and Town Planning Act'. The super-tax was to be administered by the Commissioners, from whom there was to be no appeal, except to themselves. And, added Lord Rosebery: 'This sort of tyranny is not Liberalism; it is Socialism.'

At the end of his two-hour speech, Lord Rosebery foretold the dire consequences which would follow in the wake of the Budget if it were allowed to pass unamended. 'I think my friends are moving upon the path that leads to Socialism. How far they are advanced upon that path I will not say, but on that path I at any rate cannot follow them an inch (loud cheers). Any form of Protection is an evil, but Socialism is the end of all, the negation of faith, of family, of prosperity, of the monarchy, of empire. (loud cheers).'

These speeches of Lloyd George and Lord Rosebery were, perhaps, the highlights in the Budget controversy, but meetings on a smaller scale were held in all parts of Britain to support or denounce its provisions. The Central Banffshire Farmers' Club met at Keith and protested unanimously against the increase in the duty on spirits, as this would adversely affect the interests of farmers who grew barley and who depended on cheap supplies of draff for winter feeding. The Spey, Avon and Fiddichside Farmers' Club assembled at Craigellachie under the chairmanship of Sir John Macpherson-Grant, of Ballindalloch, and heard him declare that 'they all knew for what reasons they had met and they also understood that they were going to make no mention of politics. It was entirely a matter affecting their own pockets.' Local newspapers, like their readers, took sides in the controversy. 'The Budget is a class and political one with a venegeance', insisted the *Northern Scot* on 1 May 1909. 'It is difficult, for example, to see why Scotland and Ireland should be so hard hit in connection with the heavy increase on the gallon of whisky, while nothing corresponding thereto has been placed upon the Englishman's beer.' But the *Perthshire Courier*, steadfast, in the Liberal cause, paid tribute to the meteoric rise of Lloyd George and recalled his assertion that 'When it is a question of deer and pheasants, you find the land measured out by the square mile. When it is a question of human beings, it is doled out by the square yard.'

Meanwhile in the Commons the passage of the Budget and the Finance Bill was occupying seventy days of debate and 554 divisions. It was finally passed on 4 November 1909 by 379 votes to 149. By this time there were clear indications that the Lords intended to take the unprecedented step of rejecting the Bill. The prospect delighted Lloyd George, because it offered the opportunity of attacking the powers of the Lords.

'Let them realise what they are doing', he said in a speech in Newcastle-upon-Tyne on 9 October 1909. 'They are forcing a Revolution. The Peers may decree a Revolution, but the People will direct it. If they begin, issues will be raised that they little dream of. Questions will be asked that are now whispered in humble voice, and answers will be demanded with authority. It will be asked why five hundred ordinary men, chosen accidentally from among the unemployed, should override the judgement—the deliberate judgement—of millions of people who are engaged in the industry which makes the wealth of the country. It will be asked who ordained a few should have the land of Britain as a perquisite? Who made ten thousand people owners of the soil, and the rest of us trespassers in the land of our birth? Where did that Table of the Law come from? Whose finger inscribed it?'

In Edinburgh a few weeks later he touched on a sore point with characteristic irony. 'In England every Peer is a Peer of Parliament', he said. 'In Scotland he is not. I don't know why a Scottish Peer is supposed to be inferior to an English Peer. I should not have thought that it was possible!'

The King, ageing and unwell, was anxious at the prospect of a head-on collision between Commons and Lords, with all the constitutional problems this would pose. In early October, at Balmoral, he conferred both with Lord Cawdor, one of the principal

Conservative opponents of the Bill, and then with the Prime Minister in efforts to find a compromise. Later in the month, at Buckingham Palace, he urged Balfour and Lord Lansdowne, Leader of the Conservative Party in the House of Lords, not to press their opposition to the point of rejection. The King's intervention was all to no avail. On 28 November the Lords voted by 350 to 75 to reject the Finance Bill. Asquith thereupon asked the King to dissolve Parliament and called a general election to be held in January 1910. Opening the campaign at the Albert Hall, he placed the main issue before the electors, 'that the will of the people, as deliberately expressed by their elected representatives, must, within the lifetime of a single Parliament, be made to prevail'.

Other speakers were less sedate. The Duke of Beaufort had expressed a desire 'to see Lloyd George and Winston Churchill in the middle of twenty couple of dog hounds'. Lloyd George echoed the canine theme at Wolverhampton when speaking of the qualifications needed by Peers of the Realm. 'No testimonials are required', he pointed out. 'There are no credentials. They do not even need a medical certificate. They need not be sound either in body or in mind. They only require a certificate of birth, just to prove that they are the first of the litter. You would not choose a spaniel on these principles!'

Although Irish Home Rule and tariff reform loomed large in the election campaign, the Liberals took their cue from Lloyd George and concentrated on abusing the House of Lords, singling out the dukes as special targets. One Liberal leaflet, headed 'The Dukes—Poor but Honest', reproduced a list from the *Daily Mail* showing each duke's estate and income. Buccleuch, with 460,000 acres and an income of £331,000 a year including £10,000 from Granton Harbour, was apparently the wealthiest of the twenty-seven, though there was no estimate of the income Westminster derived from his London properties. Other Scottish dukes on the list were: Richmond (286,000 acres and £80,000 a year), Hamilton (157,000 acres and £140,000), Argyll (175,000 acres and £51,000), Atholl (202,000 acres and £42,000), Montrose (103,000 acres and £25,000), Roxburghe (60,000 acres and £51,000), Sutherland (1,358,000 acres and £142,000), and Fife, a son-in-law of the King (249,000 acres and £74,000). Another leaflet, 'The Tears of the Peers', recorded that the Duke of Buccleuch had refused to make a donation to a Dumfriesshire football club 'owing', he said, 'to the large prospective increase in taxation proposed by the Budget'. The pensions of old retainers on his Drumlanrig estate had also been reduced from 14s. weekly to 7s. 6d. when they began to draw the state old age pension of 5s.

One poster published by the Liberal Party during the campaign uncannily foreshadowed the affair of the Turra' Coo. It showed a railway train, emblazoned '1909 Budget', speeding towards a white cow which wears a ducal coronet and stands in the middle of the track. 'George Stephenson', ran the caption, 'was once asked if it would not be awkward if a cow were to place itself on the line in front of a train. "Yes," promptly replied the great man, "it would indeed be awkward—for the coo." '

The first Scottish result to be declared was in Perth, where the Liberal candidate, Alexander F. Whyte, polled 2,841 votes and his Conservative opponent 2,103. The Liberal majority of 738 was lower than that in the 1906 election, when it had been 1,008, though higher than in the 'khaki election' of 1900. 'You have lighted a beacon which will shine brightly across broad Scotland,' said Mr. Whyte at the victory gathering in the Drill Hall, 'and no doubt some of those beams will find their way into the less enlightened corners of England.'

The election result was not entirely satisfactory for the government. The Conservatives and Unionists gained 116 seats to stand at 273 but the government, with 275 seats, could count on the support of 40 Labour Members and, to a less reliable extent, on that of 70 Irish Nationalists, leaving a dozen Independent Nationalists who opposed the Liberals. Although thus seriously weakened, the government survived its first uneasy months in office and on 29 April 1910, just a year after Lloyd George had introduced it, the 'People's Budget' of 1909 was passed by the Lords. A Bill to reduce the powers of the House of Lords had already been drafted and a copy sent to the King, who was on holiday in Biarritz. He had to face the virtual certainty that he would be asked by the Prime Minister to create the number of new peers necessary to carry the legislation in the Lords. He had also expressed the view that a second general election ought to be held to endorse the government's proposed reforms. These embodied three main changes, that the Lords should have no power to reject bills certified by the Speaker as money bills; that other bills passed by the Commons in three successive sessions should become law two years after their introduction, even if rejected by the Lords; and that the duration of a Parliament should be reduced from seven to five years.

As soon as the Lords had passed the Budget, Parliament rose and the Prime Minister embarked in the Admiralty yacht *Enchantress* for a cruise to Portugal and Spain. As the ship neared Gibraltar a wireless message informed Asquith that the King had been taken gravely ill and in the early hours of 7 May a further message, this time from the new King George V, announced the death of Edward VII. 'I went up on deck,' wrote Asquith later, 'and I remember well that the first sight that met my eyes in the twilight before dawn was Halley's comet blazing in the sky.'

By common consent, the party leaders felt that the new monarch should not have the burden of a serious constitutional controversy placed on his shoulders so soon after his accession. One way of gaining a respite was to organise a conference of the two parties to determine whether a compromise might be possible. Asquith, after conferring with the King, wrote to Balfour, who agreed with the suggestion. The first meeting was held on 17 June 1910, the government being represented by Asquith, Lloyd George, Lord Crewe and Augustine Birrell, and the Opposition by Balfour, Lord Lansdowne. Austen Chamberlain and Lord Cawdor. Eleven further meetings were held before the end of July but gradually the old differences revived and by November it was plain that no compromise would be found. On 16 November, after much heart-searching and with much conflicting advice from his two joint private secretaries, the King gave Asquith a secret undertaking that if the Liberals were returned at another general election and if the Lords then obstructed the Parliament Bill, he would create enough new Liberal peers to carry the Bill. Having secured that undertaking, Asquith appealed to the electorate in a lightning campaign again fought on the three issues of Parliamentary reform, Irish Home Rule and tariff reform, against a background of political bitterness and social discontent. Lloyd George remained the chief villain in Conservative eyes, his ambitions being caricatured in the story told of an elderly aristocrat who had been seriously ill in the early summer of 1910. While his daughter was reading the newspapers to him one day during his convalescence, mention came of King George.

'King George? King George?' asked the noble invalid irritably. 'Surely you mean King Edward?'

'No, father', replied his daughter gently. 'While you have been ill, King Edward has died and now we are ruled by King George.'

'Good God,' breathed the nobleman, sinking into a relapse, 'not that Welsh solicitor!'

Polling in the second election of 1910 took place in early December. Again the Perth constituency was the first in Scotland to declare its result. Again Alexander F. Whyte had defeated his Conservative opponent, this time Colonel Telfer Smollett, by a sound majority, 2,852 votes to 1,878. In the country as a whole there was practically no change. The Liberals lost three seats and the Conservatives one, so that both the parties had 272 Members in the new House, with 42 Labour Members and 82 Irish Nationalists. Having had his policy thus endorsed for the second time in a year, Asquith introduced the Parliament Bill in the Commons on 21 February. When it reached the Lords it was not rejected but drastically amended to reduce its impact on their powers. Asquith had meanwhile drawn up a list of about 250 names of men whom he would recommend for peerages. They included many Scots, among them James M. Barrie; Sir Samuel Chisholm, Lord Provost of Glasgow; Sir James Donaldson, Vice-Chancellor and Principal of St. Andrew's University; Lord Haddo; Sir Harry H. Johnston, the explorer and anthropologist; Sir Thomas Lipton; and Professor Gilbert Murray. Other celebrities included Thomas Hardy; Bertrand Russell; Sir Robert Baden-Powell; and Anthony Hope Hawkins, the creator of Ruritania.

Deep divisions now appeared in the Conservative and Unionist ranks. Balfour and Lord Lansdowne advised the Lords to accept the reform by abstaining from voting against it, Lord Curzon went further and organised his friends to vote in favour of it, but Lord Halsbury, who had been Lord Chancellor for ten years until 1905, rallied the Bill's opponents to 'die in the last ditch' rather than allow it to pass. But both 'hedgers' and 'ditchers' were united in their contempt for Asquith, Lloyd George and Winston Churchill. There was an ugly scene in the Commons on 24 July, when the Prime Minister stood at the despatch-box unable to speak a complete sentence, while the Conservatives and Unionists shrieked abuse at him. Balfour took no part in the uproar but after an hour the Speaker suspended the sitting, 'a state of grave disorder having arisen'.

Tempers ran almost as high on 10 August 1911, when the final division was taken in the Lords. Sir Almeric Fitzroy, Clerk of the Privy Council, later described the scene in his *Memoirs*: 'I never saw the House of Lords so full as on this, the hottest day in the annals of

British meteorology: the thermometer reached 97 degrees in the shade!' Lord Lansdowne, recorded Sir Almeric, spoke 'with the greatest tact, polish, dignity and address'. From Lord Halsbury, however, came a 'blunt appeal to blind passion, couched in terms of turgid rhetoric and senile violence'. But 'a few judicious remarks from the Archbishop of York restored the issue before the House to its true perspective'. The vote came at half-past ten. It was 'not without its comic features', Sir Almeric recalled, 'as two noble Lords, one on either side, were very drunk and voted in that state. One was so bad that for a long time he was kept under supervision in a committee-room, and Lord Ilkeston, who graduated in medicine, was summoned to see him. On his appearance, however, the patient shouted, "Take the -------- away—he wants to get two guineas out of me!" He was allowed to go into the division lobby'. Ten minutes later the tellers announced the figures. The government had won by 131 votes to 114. With the eighty-one Liberals had voted the two archbishops, eleven bishops and thirty-seven Unionist peers led by Lord Curzon. The opposition had included two bishops. 'At eleven o'clock', wrote the King in his diary, 'Bigge returned from the House of Lords with the good news that the Parliament Bill had passed with a majority of 17. So the Halsburyites were thank God beaten! It is indeed a great relief to me and I am spared any further humiliation by a creation of peers.'

The passage of the Parliament Act did not solve the problems of Irish Home Rule or tariff reform but it cleared the way for the Liberals to proceed with their welfare legislation. One important new feature of this was introduced by Lloyd George and passed by the Commons on the same day that the Lords agreed to the reduction of their powers. It was a motion proposing that Members of the House of Commons should be paid a salary of £400 a year. Its acceptance marked the end of the upper- and middle-class monopoly of parliamentary membership. The ten years since the accession of King Edward VII had brought a fundamental change in the balance of political power in Britain.

15

Brine and Blue Water

Long before Edward VII began his brief reign, Scottish iron-masters and ship-builders had earned a world-wide reputation for their inventiveness and skill. In 1784 a French scientist visiting the Carron ironworks, where the fearsome carronades were made, described the scene in words which would have been equally appropriate a century or more later.

'Amongst these warlike machines, these terrible death-dealing instruments, huge cranes, every kind of windlass, lever and tackle for moving heavy loads, were fixed in suitable places', wrote Faujas de Saint-Fond in his *Voyage en Angleterre, en Ecosse et aux Iles Hébrides*. 'Their creaking, the piercing noise of the pulleys, the continuous sound of hammering, the ceaseless energy of the men keeping all this machinery in motion presented a sight as interesting as it was new.'

Scotland had been richly endowed for developing the heavy industries from which Victorian Britain derived so much of its wealth. Local deposits of iron ore and coal provided the raw materials and the power for John Roebuck, a Yorkshireman who had originally crossed the Border to take a degree in medicine at Edinburgh, to found the Carron ironworks in 1759. The presence of navigable waterways in the Clyde and the Forth ensured that when steel replaced wood as the material for ships, and steam replaced sail as their motive power, Scotland was uniquely placed to profit from the changes. Scottish ports linked her industries to the world's markets while Scottish sea-captains and ships' engineers were renowned across the Seven Seas. 'The Clyde ship-builders', asserted *Shipbuilding Industry* in 1905, 'have been associated with practically every scientific advance in naval architecture for the last century. Through all the transitions—wood to iron, iron to steel, paddle to single screw, single screw to twin screw, twin screw to multiple screw, turbine engines—Clyde ship-builders have been to the front with exemplar ships.' The *Scottish Bankers' Magazine* expressed the same view in 1909.

'In point of equipment', it claimed, 'the Clyde ship-building yards are the finest in the world, and their chiefs are the Gamaliels at whose feet all other ship-builders and engineers of the world sit and learn. All the Cunarders were built at Glasgow; and with perhaps one exception the other great steamship companies patronise the Clyde, while the Admiralty is a constant and most lucrative stand-by.'

One of the most important features of marine engineering during the Edwardian period was the development of the steam turbine by the Hon. Charles A. Parsons and its application to ship propulsion. His tiny steam-yacht *Turbinia*, constructed in 1894, had created a sensation at the naval review held in Spithead three years later to celebrate the Diamond Jubilee of Queen Victoria. The *Turbinia* had raced down the lines of ships at over 34 knots, proving as economical in fuel as she was speedy through the water. Further successes in the torpedo-boat destroyer *Viper* and the cruiser *Amethyst* demonstrated that the Parsons turbines were suitable even for large passenger liners. The first of these was the triple-screw *Virginian*, built at Glasgow in 1904 by Alexander Stephen and Sons Ltd. for the Allan Line's trans-atlantic service. The Cunard Steamship Co. followed quickly with the triple-screw liner *Carmania*, launched at the Clydebank yard of John Brown and Co. in February 1905. She was followed from the same yard in 1907 by the Cunarder *Lusitania*, whose second voyage broke the existing transatlantic record with a time of 4 days, 19 hours, 52 minutes from Cobh to Sandy Hook, and 4 days, 22 hours, 53 minutes for the homeward run, an all-round average speed of well over 23 knots. Another famous Edwardian Cunarder built at John Brown's yard was the *Aquitania*, launched on 23 April 1913 and out-standing not only in size but also for her speed, comfort and economy. She was built to carry 597 first-class, 614 second-class and 2,052 third-class passengers but she had completed only three round voyages, the first beginning on 13 May 1914, before she was requisitioned for war service.

John Brown and Co. also built warships, among them the battleship *Tiger*, the battle-cruisers *Inflexible* and *Repulse*, and the dreadnought *Barham*. Other famous warships, including *Agamemnon*, *Benbow*, *Berwick* and *Conqueror*, came from Beardmore and Co., who had taken over the Govan yards of Napier and Sons in 1900. From the Fairfield Shipbuilding and Engineering Co., of Govan, came *Indomitable*, which made a record warship crossing of the Atlantic in 1908, *Valiant*, *Renown* and *Commonwealth*, the largest battleship afloat when she was launched by the Marchioness of Linlithgow in May 1904. The number of men employed in these large yards averaged five or six thousand, and the Clyde ship-building industry as a whole gave employment to some seventy or eighty thousand men and boys. The Clyde, indeed, was building a greater tonnage of shipping than the whole of the United States, and almost as much as France and Germany together.

The Parsons turbine also played an important part in the holiday pastime which generations of Clydesiders have enjoyed, 'a trip doon the watter'. In 1901 a syndicate was formed by the Parsons Marine Steam Turbine Co., William Denny and Brothers, of Dumbarton, and Captain John Williamson, a Glasgow steamship proprietor, for the purpose of building a turbine-driven steamer for the Fairlie and Campbeltown service. The ship was launched by Mrs. Parsons in May 1901 and named *King Edward*. After minor modifications she made her official trial run on 28 June from Craigendoran, calling at Dunoon, Rothesay, Largs, Fairlie, Lochranza and Campbeltown. During the voyage she won an impromptu race down Kilbrannan Sound against another Denny-built vessel, the Caledonian Steam Packet Company's paddle-steamer *Duchess of Hamilton*. The *King Edward* ran a daily service between Prince's Pier, Greenock, and Campbeltown, and she also made popular evening cruises from Greenock during the summer months, so that Glaswegians could leave by train at six o'clock, enjoy two hours afloat, with music played by a professional orchestra, and arrive back in Glasgow by half-past ten.

The success of the *King Edward* encouraged the members of the syndicate to form a new company, Turbine Steamers Ltd., to build a sister-ship, slightly larger and faster. This was the *Queen Alexandra*, launched from the Leven ship-yard in April 1902. The two spruce new ships, with their modern method of propulsion, their smooth, speedy runs, and their smart black-and-white livery and familiar star-and-crescent pennants, were prime favourites on the Clyde. They were also historic vessels in that their success prompted the large shipping companies to introduce turbine-driven liners to the oceans of the world. A disastrous fire damaged *Queen Alexandra* while she lay at her coaling berth in the Albert Harbour, Greenock, in mid-September 1911, so that she had to be replaced by a new *Queen Alexandra*, launched in April 1912. Among other companies which ran steamship services on the Clyde during the early years of the

The Royal Yacht *Victoria and Albert*.

S.S. *Carmania*.

H.M.S. *Dreadnought*.

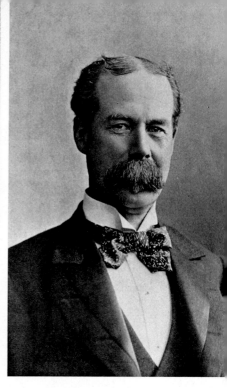

Lord Rosebery

Sir Thomas Lipton

A. J. Balfour

Sir Hector Macdonald

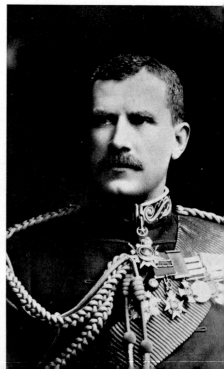

century were the Caledonian Steam Packet Co., whose paddle-steamers *Duchess of Montrose* and *Duchess of Fife*, and turbine ship *Duchess of Argyll*, were all Edwardian-built; the Glasgow and South Western Railway Co., whose paddle-steamer *Mars* and turbine ship *Atalanta* were Edwardians; and the North British Railway Co., whose fleet included the paddle-steamer *Marmion*, built in 1906.

The Edwardian years saw the heyday of the Clyde steamers. Many a Clydeside boy prided himself on being able to identify, across the misty miles of the Firth, the pale grey hull and tall red funnels of the Glasgow and South Western Railway Company's *Glen Sannox* or the fine yellow funnels of a Caledonian Steam Packet Company's stately *Duchess* or *Marchioness*. The steamers were at their brightest and busiest each year during early July, when the yacht clubs organised their Clyde Fortnight of races and regattas. The crowds aboard the steamers could wave and cheer as the graceful cutter-yachts winged their way across the shining water. One was the famous *Britannia*, which had been built for the Prince of Wales in 1893 by D. and W. Henderson, of Meadowside, Partick, to the design of George Lennox Watson. Almost identical, except that she was two feet shorter on the water-line, was *Valkyrie II*, built by Henderson's at the same time for Lord Dunraven. During her first appearance, in the Clyde Fortnight on 1893, *Britannia* won the Royal Largs and Royal Northern club races, while *Valkyrie II* won those of the Royal West of Scotland, Mudhook and Clyde Corinthian clubs. The following year the Southampton-built *Satanita* rammed and sank *Valkyrie II* at the start of the Mudhook Club's race, and *Britannia* won all eight of the major races. Unfortunately the German Kaiser arrived at Cowes in 1896 with a new Yacht, *Meteor II*, a larger version of *Britannia* by the same Scottish designer. It was not so much the fact that *Meteor II* proved consistently faster than *Britannia* as the undisguised delight of the bumptious Kaiser at this evidence of German superiority in seamanship that exasperated his uncle, the Prince of Wales. The following year the Prince decided to abandon the sport and sold *Britannia* to John Lawson-Johnston, the originator of Bovril, who continued to race her. The Prince of Wales re-purchased the yacht after his accession to the throne and although he took no further part in serious yacht racing, he remained an enthusiastic yachtsman. The Kaiser's yacht was seen in the Clyde in June 1901, when she participated in a series of races organised in Rothesay Bay during the Glasgow Exhibition.

The most renowned of all Edwardian yachtsmen was Sir Thomas Lipton. He had been born in Crown Street, Glasgow, in 1850, the son of Irish Protestants who had left Monaghan during the potato famine and settled in Glasgow, opening a grocer's shop. After three years at St. Andrew's School, Parish Green, paid for by a weekly fee of sixpence to the headmaster, Lipton became a message-boy before signing as a cabin-boy aboard the paddle-steamers which G. and J. Burns operated between Glasgow and Belfast. This experience gave him a taste for the sea which he never lost. In 1865, with eight dollars in his pocket, he emigrated to the United States to spend four adventurous years at odd jobs in the Carolinas, Louisiana and finally New York. Then he returned to Glasgow with a rocking-chair for his mother, a barrel of flour for his father, and five hundred dollars. He was soon applying the new-fangled advertising methods he had seen in the United States to extending his father's business, steadily adding shop after shop as his profits increased. He was a supreme showman, missing no opportunity of publicising himself and his groceries. He ordered mammoth cheeses from the United States, inserted sovereigns and half-sovereigns in them, and sold portions as 'lucky dips' at Christmas. He offered entertainment such as magic-lantern shows to children waiting in his shops while their mothers were buying their groceries. He dressed sandwichmen as Indians to parade through the city streets to advertise his blend of Indian and Ceylon teas. A bachelor, a teetotaller and a non-smoker, Lipton devoted himself entirely to his business and by the turn of the century he was a millionaire. When he was knighted in 1898, Keir Hardie wrote of him in the *Labour Leader*, the official organ of the Independent Labour Party: 'I have always had a soft spot for Thomas Lipton. As a small boy in Glasgow doing the shopping for my mother, I was ready to walk an extra two miles to see his pictures.'

That same year Lipton decided to try to regain for Britain the *America's* Cup, the historic yachting trophy which had been won at Cowes nearly fifty years earlier by the *America*. Off Sandy Hook the following year, amid great excitement, his *Shamrock* failed in three races against the American *Columbia*. Lipton's graceful acceptance of defeat endeared him to Americans and there was warm approval on both sides of the Atlantic when he announced his intention of making another attempt in 1901. The King visited him on board his new yacht, *Shamrock II*, in Southampton Water and narrowly escaped serious injury when a sudden gust of wind brought the mast crashing to the deck. 'I wish Sir T. Lipton would give up all idea of trying to win the American cup with his present yacht', the King wrote to Lady Londonderry. 'He can have no earthly chance and she is an unlucky vessel. He is merely wasting his money.' Although *Shamrock II* came very close to defeating *Columbia*, the outcome was as the King had expected. Still not discouraged, Lipton made a third attempt in 1903 with *Shamrock III*. His departure for New York was signalled by a cartoon in *Punch* showing him as a Norseman, with the caption 'Last of the Vi-kings and first of the Tea-kings', and by a telegram from the King: 'As you are just about to leave for America, let me wish you a prosperous journey and all possible good luck for the great race in August. Edward R.I.' But *Shamrock III* fared worse against *Reliance* than her predecessors against *Columbia*, and it was eleven years before Lipton made plans for yet another attempt with *Shamrock IV*. He was almost half-way across the Atlantic in his steam-yacht *Erin* when he learned from a wireless message that Britain and Germany were at war. Despite his austere origins, Sir Thomas Lipton fitted well into the circle of wealthy and flamboyant merchant princes whose company King Edward VII found so congenial. The Glasgow grocer differed from most of the others in leading a temperate life. Money was the key to almost every door in Edwardian Britain but Lipton was extraordinary in that he used the key so sparingly and to open only the most innocuous of doors.

The sea was Lipton's playground. For many other Scots it provided a hard livelihood. Until well past the middle of the nineteenth century Scottish fishermen used open, undecked boats and lines baited with mussels, so that the hazards of fishing were considerable and the catches were small. By the 1890s inshore fishermen were using larger, decked craft, trawling by sailing-smack was improving catches, and the first steam-trawlers were at sea. The *Toiler*, a wooden paddle-steamer fitted out during 1882, was Aberdeen's first steam-trawler but with the arrival of steam-drifters fishermen were able to make longer voyages and total landings became much larger, doubling between 1899 and 1909, and increasing still further until 1914. Much of the herring landed in Aberdeen was cured and exported to Germany and the Baltic, so that the years before the First World War brought a measure of prosperity to Scottish fishermen.

For herring there were three seasons in the year. From January to March the steam-drifters went north to Wick and Stornoway, and to the Firth of Forth. During the summer months they fished off the east coast, Peterhead and Fraserburgh, in Orkney, Shetland and the Isle of Man. From the beginning of October until the end of November they moved south for the English fishing off Lowestoft and Yarmouth. With the fishermen went the redoubtable fisher-lassies recruited by the fish-curers during December on payment of the recognised 'arles' of a gold sovereign. The lassies took their bedding, pots, pans and dishes with them, for they were accommodated in wooden huts or chandlers' store-houses and had to fend for themselves. As soon as the drifter landed its gleaming mass of herring on the quayside, the curer bought a load which was taken by horse and cart to be tipped into the pharlands, the long, deep wooden troughs at which the gibbers stood. These were the lassies who gutted each fish and flung the different grades into their respective tubs, separating the 'full' or unspawned herring from the 'spent', those that had already spawned. The fish was then packed in barrels, layer by layer, thick with salt which turned to brine, so that more fish and more salt had to be added each day for at least a week. The coopers then drained off the brine, added the last layers of salted fish and hammered home the bung to make the barrel ready for shipment. The fisher-lassies helped at every stage of the process, working in oilskins, sou'-westers and wellington boots, their fingers bound with cotton rags to protect them from the sharp gutting-knives, the salt and the rough boards of the barrels. During the northern summer the fisher-lassies worked an eighteen-hour day, except that Sunday was generally recognised as a day of rest. Fishing ceased at the end of August, the lassies drew their pay and went home for a few weeks' respite before setting out for Lowestoft or Yarmouth at the end of September. There they were usually able to find lodging in cheap boarding-houses, comparative luxury after the wooden huts of Shetland and Orkney. The autumn darkness was lit by oil-lamps smoking over the pharlands, and a lassie had to be alert and nimble-fingered to avoid cutting her hands badly as she worked at the gutting. A week or two before Christmas, with their pay in their purses and presents bought for the bairns in Lowestoft and Yarmouth shops, the fisher-lassies boarded the special trains for Aberdeen and the North-east, to be home for Christmas and Hogmanay.

One fishing community where life was even harsher than in Shetland or Orkney was that on the island of St. Kilda, fifty miles to the west of Harris. For many years steamers carrying tourists had paid occasional visits to St. Kilda during the summer months. The islanders gained their livelihood by fishing and primitive farming, but every household had a hand-loom so that wool could be spun, dyed and woven into blankets and clothing. All the islanders read the Gaelic Bible, observed the Sabbath strictly, enjoyed a simple diet of milk, porridge, potatoes, mutton and fish, and seemed content with their way of life. There were no games or music on the island and even whistling was forbidden. In 1900, when the medical officer of health for Harris, Dr. Duncan Fletcher, visited St. Kilda, he was agreeably surprised at the clean and tidy houses, the 'advanced state of sanitation', and the general appearance of the islanders.

The main hazard of life on St. Kilda was simply the uncertainty of communication with the outside world in time of distress, whether from illness or shortage of supplies, especially between October and May, when the tourist steamers were not operating. In 1906 James G. Weir, Liberal member for Ross and Cromarty, suggested that the islanders should be provided with a telephone cable or a wireless telegraph station, but the Postmaster-General considered that the cost of either would be prohibitive. Attempts were made over the next few years to persuade the Commissioners of Northern Lighthouses to allow a wireless link from St. Kilda to their station on the Flannans, but before this scheme could be put into effect, a sudden crisis occurred. In May 1912 the trawler *Strathmore* made a call at St. Kilda and returned to Aberdeen with the news that a hard winter had left the islanders on the verge of starvation. The Admiralty despatched H.M.S. *Achilles* to their aid, Sir Thomas Lipton provided groceries, and the *Daily Mirror* also rushed stores and reporters. This emergency, despite a subsequent suspicion that it had been a little exaggerated, led to renewed pleas for wireless equipment to be sent to St. Kilda, but before it could be installed another crisis occurred, this time an outbreak of influenza. The Hull trawler *Mercury* called at the island in May 1913 to find that a steamer which had brought mail and stores to the islanders a few days previously had also made them a present of some influenza bacilli. Only one old man, reported the *Mercury*, was able to rise from his bed. Once again the Admiralty despatched a warship, H.M.S. *Active*, a doctor and two nurses arrived by steamer, and the *Daily Mirror* again scooped the news. Within a month St. Kilda had its wireless equipment and by the end of July the first messages had been transmitted, one to King George V and the other to J. M. Hogge, the Liberal member for Edinburgh East, who had taken a particular interest in the welfare of the islanders.

At the end of June 1904, a young Scottish naval officer was appointed as a watch-keeping lieutenant to H.M.S. *Northampton*, lying at Campbeltown. In accordance with King's Regulations and Admiralty Instructions, he attired himself in frock-coat and sword, and leaving his home in Edinburgh, where his father was Professor of Anatomy at the University, he presented himself on board his new ship, a barque-rigged, two-funnelled steam-and-sail cruiser five years older than he was. Within a couple of hours the newcomer was ordered, as officer of the day, to 'Furl sails', an undertaking for which he needed the expert advice of the chief bosun's mate. Eventually, as the young lieutenant afterwards recorded, the sailors scrambled aloft 'like a lot of ploughboys' and the unruly canvas was tamed. He never again saw H.M.S. *Northampton* use her sails at sea.

The lieutenant whose days in sail ended so inauspiciously later earned fame as Admiral of the Fleet Viscount Cunningham of Hyndhope but his dilemma in 1904 reflected the state of the Royal Navy at the beginning of the Edwardian era. For a century Britain had rested on the laurels won for her by Nelson and his wooden ships off Cape Trafalgar. No other power had emerged to challenge British supremacy at sea and every aspect of the Senior Service had become permeated by a deadening complacency. Conditions on board ship, methods of instruction and of enforcing discipline, even rates of pay still resembled those of the Navy which Nelson had known. Promotion of officers was largely determined by seniority, commanders-in-chief spent little time, except for the desultory annual manoeuvres, in handling fleets or even squadrons in simulated war conditions, and there was a dangerous lack of urgency in their study of the strategic and tactical implications of new inventions and improvements in marine engineering, ship construction and naval weapons. Only in its victualling allowances, which were generous, had the Navy real cause for satisfaction.

As long as there was no serious challenge to Britain's command of the seas, the condition of the Navy was not a dangerous weakness. Despite its shortcomings it was the strongest navy in the world, and it was well able to cope with its normal tasks of escorting expeditionary forces to recalcitrant colonies or showing the flag in foreign ports. But after the accession of Kaiser William II and the resignation of the veteran Chancellor Bismarck, Germany made plans for naval expansion which were clearly intended as a challenge to Britain. The Kiel Canal, opened in 1895, had enabled German warships to move without interference quickly and securely from the Baltic to the North Sea. A German Navy League, patriotically financed by Krupps, attracted a quarter of a million members in three years, and Navy laws passed in 1898 and 1900 provided for a programme of warship building on an unprecedented scale. Britain lived by her overseas trade. She fed herself on cheap imported food and she fed her industries on imported raw materials. She paid for these essential commodities by selling her manufactured goods in the markets of the world. Any rival able to destroy Britain's command of the ocean trade routes could thus strangle her commerce, confiscate her empire and reduce her to penury. One man, more than any other, deserves the credit for perceiving these dangers and preparing the Royal Navy to avert them.

John Arbuthnot Fisher was born in 1841 in Ceylon, the son of Captain William Fisher of the 78th Highlanders, the Ross-shire Buffs. His father's choice of regiment was purely fortuitous and Fisher was of English Midland stock, despite later rumours that his mother had been a dusky Cingalese beauty. She was, in fact, the daughter of a London wine merchant. Fisher had the good fortune to be a god-child of Lady Wilmot-Horton, wife of the Governor of Ceylon, and through her influence he was accepted in 1854 as a naval cadet. His rise was meteoric. He saw service in the Baltic during the Crimean War, saved his captain's life during the China War of 1860 and commanded H.M.S. *Inflexible* at the bombardment of Alexandria in 1882. After holding a series of important appointments both at sea and ashore, he hoisted his flag in 1899 in H.M.S. *Renown* as Commander-in-Chief, Mediterranean. Thenceforth he dominated the British naval scene. At the end of his three-year commission he became Second Sea Lord of the Admiralty and in 1903 was appointed First Sea Lord, serving until his retirement in January 1910, following a long and bitter quarrel with Admiral Lord Charles Beresford.

Strengthened by his friendship with the King, Fisher dragged the Navy willy-nilly into the twentieth century. His ruthless authority and inexhaustible energy made him many enemies in the higher ranks of the Service, but his devotion to the needs of the lower deck made every sailor his friend. The preparation of the Navy to meet the German threat, and the Navy's triumph when battle at last was joined, were Fisher's achievements. Winston Churchill, who was First Lord of the Admiralty from 23 October 1911 to May 1915, was best able to assess the work of the fiery little admiral, for Fisher returned as First Sea Lord in October 1914 and the two men served in uneasy harness until May 1915, when both resigned over the Dardanelles campaign. 'His great reforms', wrote Churchill in *The World Crisis*, 'sustained the power of the Royal Navy at the most critical period in its history. He gave the Navy the kind of shock which the British Army received at the time of the South African War. After a long period of serene and unchallenged complacency, the mutter of distant thunder could be heard. It was Fisher who hoisted the storm-signal and beat all hands to quarters. He forced every department of the Naval Service to review its position and question its own existence. He shook them and beat them and cajoled them out of slumber into intense activity. But the Navy was not a pleasant place while this was going on.'

One of Fisher's most spectacular and controversial achievements was the introduction of a new class of battleship taking its name from the first, H.M.S. *Dreadnought*. Laid down in October 1905 and at sea just a year later, *Dreadnought*, with her ten 12-inch guns, her speed of 21 knots and many radical changes in general design, made every other battleship in the world obsolescent. For Britain this was a dangerous development in that at a stroke her naval rivals, notably Germany, were on almost equal terms, able to replace their old battleships by new giants of the *Dreadnought* type. Germany proved the point at once by laying down the *Nassau* in July 1907. If Britain was to maintain her naval superiority, she would have to out-build Germany in the new battleships.

Unhappily for Fisher's plans for a large building programme, Lloyd George and Winston Churchill were pressing in the Cabinet for more revenue to be allocated to the projected social reforms. 'A fully equipped duke costs as much to keep as two dreadnoughts,' joked Lloyd George, 'and dukes are just as great a terror but they last longer.' He wanted to dispense with both extravagances. By 1908 Britain had seven dreadnoughts while Germany had none yet in active commission, but in April the Reichstag passed a Navy Law embodying a programme of four new battleships a year for three years. This prompted Fisher to demand that the Liberal government's programme of four battleships a year should be doubled. He conducted a vigorous and unscrupulous campaign, leaking accounts of Cabinet discussions to his friend J. L. Garvin, editor of the *Observer*, and curdling the blood of patriotic Britons with statistical projections overestimating Germany's potential naval strength and underestimating Britain's. 'Insist on the Eight, the whole Eight and nothing but the Eight, with more to follow, and break any man or faction that now stands in the way,' urged the *Observer*. 'We want Eight—we won't wait!' ran the popular jingle.

Eventually Asquith hit upon an adroit compromise. Four dreadnoughts would be built under the 1909 Navy Estimates, and contingency plans would be prepared for the building of four more if they should be required. A resounding Conservative victory in a by-election at Croydon, endorsed by the Conservative capture of the Liberal seat in another at Glasgow Central on 2 March 1909, provided the stimulus to set the contingency plans in motion. Fisher's shining vision of a Blue Water Navy had made too strong an appeal to the public imagination and Lloyd George had to provide for increased naval expenditure in his 1909 Budget. 'The unswerving intention of four years has *now* culminated in *two* complete Fleets in Home Waters, *each of which* is incomparably superior to the whole German fleet mobilised for war', wrote Fisher triumphantly to Viscount Esher, another of his cronies. To Churchill he suggested, with jovial irony, that the four extra dreadnoughts should be named *Winston, Churchill, Lloyd* and *George*. Churchill's sense of humour was equal to the occasion. 'The Admiralty had demanded six ships,' he wrote in *The World Crisis*, 'the economists offered four and we finally compromised on eight.'

One aspect of Jackie Fisher's reforms had special repercussions in Scotland. This was the development of naval bases more effectively located for operations against German fleets than the English Channel ports which had served so well when Britain's quarrels had been with France. If the North Sea was to be the new naval battleground, bases on the east coast were necessary. The Admiralty had already, in 1903, bought land at Rosyth to build a naval dockyard but the project had been shelved. Although the Forth could provide anchorage for about twenty battleships above the Forth Bridge and almost as many below, Fisher was afraid that the bridge might be destroyed by explosives and part of the fleet penned in the Firth. The risk had to be accepted, however, and construction of the base began in 1909, although it was still not complete by the outbreak of war.

Fisher expressed a preference for the Cromarty Firth, which had unlimited anchorage and was guarded by the massive headlands of the Sutors. There were objections that it was a hundred miles farther away from the German bases and from the Fife collieries which could supply the Navy's coal, but with the steady change to oil-firing the latter consideration became less important. The 1911 Navy Estimates included £8,000 for the erection of oil-tanks at Invergordon, and Winston Churchill, as First Lord, paid a visit to Cromarty in the Admiralty yacht *Enchantress* in September 1912 to inspect progress on the base. At least one Scottish sailor, Captain R. E. Wemyss of H.M.S. *Orion*, found the Cromarty Firth a congenial station. 'Today,' he recorded in his diary on 26 September 1913, 'I have been to some famous golf links at Tain, not far from here, and it was one of the most beautiful days I have ever seen. The clearness of the atmosphere was most remarkable and the colouring of the mountains most gorgeous, which I fancy seldom happens under these conditions. Golspie Bay, Dunock Firth in the foreground, low ground behind which, gradually rising and ending in mountains in the background, with everything most clearly and even sharply delineated, made up a really magnificent and beautiful view. We have athletic sports for the men today and tomorrow, and so far I am glad to say *Orion* is as usual coming well to the fore; all this is very good for the men and helps to provide exercise and recreation for them, neither of which they get much of.'

Although Scapa Flow had already been used occasionally during exercises by the Home Fleet and the Channel Fleet, and in 1905 the Chief Hydrographer had made a survey in H.M.S. *Triton*, no further action had been taken. There were few facilities of any kind and the only defence was provided by 12-pounder guns manned by Territorials to cover the harbour entrance. But the traditional British naval strategy of blockading an enemy's ports had been nullified by the development of the mine, the submarine and the fast torpedo-boat, so that by 1912 the Admiralty had prepared fresh war plans entailing a distant blockade of Germany by closing the outlets from the North Sea. The Straits of Dover could be dominated from the Channel ports but for the northern outlet a base at Scapa was essential.

After the assassination of the heir to the Austro-Hungarian Empire, the Archduke Franz Ferdinand, in Sarajevo on 28 June 1914 and the worsening quarrel between Austria and Serbia, the First Sea Lord, Prince Louis of Battenberg, took the decision that the Fleet, assembled for the summer manoeuvres, should not be dispersed. On 26 July 1914 he issued a notice to the Press announcing that: 'Orders have been given to the First Fleet, which is concentrated at Portland, not to disperse for manoeuvre leave at present. All vessels of the

Second Fleet are remaining at their home ports in proximity to their balance crews.' On the day that Austria declared war on Serbia, Tuesday, 28 July 1914, the Admiralty signalled to the Commander-in-Chief, Sir George Callaghan: 'Tomorrow, Wednesday, the First Fleet is to leave Portland for Scapa Flow. Destination is to be kept secret except to flag and commanding officers. As you are required at the Admiralty, Vice-Admiral 2nd Battle Squadron is to take command. Course from Portland is to be shaped to southward, then a middle Channel course to the Straits of Dover. The Squadrons are to pass through the Straits without lights during the night and to pass outside the shoals on their way north. *Agamemnon* is to remain at Portland, where the Second Fleet will assemble.'

Appropriately, it was a Scottish vice-admiral, Sir George Warrender, of Lochend, East Lothian, who as acting Commander-in-Chief led the Fleet to its northern battle station. In accordance with the Admiralty's order, the darkened ships passed through the Straits of Dover during the night of 29 July and on the morning of 31 July anchored under grey skies and a light drizzle in Scapa Flow. Two days later Vice-Admiral Sir John Jellicoe, appointed to supersede the elderly Callaghan, travelled north by train and left Wick for Scapa in the light cruiser H.M.S. *Boadicea*. At one bell in the forenoon watch of 4 August 1914 he hoisted his flag in H.M.S. *Iron Duke* as Commander-in-Chief of the Grand Fleet. That night Britain declared war on Germany.

The mobilisation of the remaining naval reservists and the recruitment of new seamen proceeded steadily as the weeks went by, and the Scottish fishing industry was drained of many of its crews. There were, reported *the Northern Scot*, 'remarkable scenes at Buckie' on 14 October 1914, when the townsfolk gave a rousing farewell to local men leaving to join the Royal Navy. 'The sending-off of the largest contingent of recruits from any single town on the Moray Firth was made the occasion at Buckie on Wednesday of a remarkable demonstration of public feeling', ran the account. 'Over 120 recruits for the Moray Firth Company of the Naval Brigade assembled in the Cluny Square under Lieutenant McLeod, preparatory to marching to the G.N.S.R. station to entrain for the Crystal Palace. In presence of a crowd estimated at about 5,000 the men were photographed. A packet of cigarettes was presented to each man by the Town Council, after which the men formed fours and headed by the town band marched to the station by way of Low Street. The men were conveyed by special train, which left at 3.30 p.m., and as the train moved slowly out of the station, a thunderous roar of cheering rent the air. The scene was the most remarkable of its kind ever witnessed in the town.'

16

Soldiers of the King

The last months of Queen Victoria's life were saddened by the news from South Africa. For the second time in twenty years Britain was at war with the Boers of the Transvaal, to whom those of the Orange Free State were allied. The ostensible causes of the Boer War, or the South African War as it was usually known to the Edwardians, lay in the grievances of the Uitlanders. These were the 'foreigners', most of them British, who had flocked to the Transvaal after the discovery of gold on the Rand in 1886. Although heavily taxed and forced by Transvaal government monopolies to pay excessive prices for dynamite and for railway freightage, the Uitlanders were virtually denied the franchise by the government's insistence on a fourteen-year residential qualification for the right to vote. Even their request for Johannesburg to be granted municipal status had been rejected.

The Uitlanders' dissatisfaction with the Boer government was encouraged by Cecil Rhodes, the bold and unscrupulous English diamond millionaire who was also Prime Minister of Cape Colony. His burning ambition was to extend British power over the whole of southern Africa and, as a symbol of that power, to build a railway from the Cape to Cairo, running its entire length through British territory. Rhodes's plan entailed the absorption into the British Empire of the Transvaal, the South African Republic, whose president was the seventy-year-old Paul Kruger, sombre, truculent and xenophobic. He, like many of his people, bitterly resented the influx of thousands of mercenary, irreligious foreigners with scant regard for the strait-laced, God-fearing farmers to whom the country belonged, if the claims of its original Bantu inhabitants were discounted. Unfortunately for the Boers, their republic would have faced bankruptcy without the revenue from the goldfields. With that revenue it had prospects of becoming immensely rich, populous and powerful. It would thus become a far more formidable barrier to

Rhodes's plan than it had been as a poor, pastoral burgher community.

Among Rhodes's protégés in his British South Africa Company was a Scottish doctor named Leander Starr Jameson. Born in Edinburgh in 1853, Jameson had emigrated to South Africa as a young man and had been a member of the expedition which Rhodes had despatched in 1890 to occupy Mashonaland. With the support and encouragement of Rhodes, Dr. Jameson planned to invade the Transvaal with a force of five hundred Company police and free-booting horsemen. The invasion was to coincide with an Uitlander uprising in Johannesburg, so that Kruger would be overthrown and the Transvaal would fall, if not to Rhodes, at least to Britain.

The Jameson Raid was a fiasco. The Uitlanders were willing to grumble over their grievances but unwilling to exchange their profitable subservience to the Boers for domination by the British South Africa Company or colonial status under the British Crown. Instead of rising to greet Dr. Jameson as their liberator, they preferred to negotiate yet again with Kruger. The Boers shadowed every movement of the raiders from the moment they crossed into the Transvaal from Pitsani, in Bechuanaland, on 29 December 1895 until they surrendered to the Boer commandos four days later at Krugersdorp, thirty miles short of Johannesburg. Rhodes thereupon resigned his premiership while Jameson, with a dozen of his followers, was handed over by Kruger for the British government to bring to trial. 'Dr. Jim', lionised by London society and the British popular Press, and generally regarded in Britain as a worthy successor to Drake and Raleigh, Livingstone and Mungo Park, was sentenced in May 1896 to fifteen months imprisonment for offences under the Foreign Enlistment Act. He was released a few months later on the ground of ill-health but recovered to return to South Africa to become a director of the British South Africa Company, Prime Minister of Cape Colony from 1904 to 1908, a Privy Councillor in 1907 and a baronet in 1911.

The Jameson Raid had wide repercussions. The angry Kaiser caused deep resentment in Britain by sending an ill-judged telegram to President Kruger, congratulating him on rounding up the raiders so effectively 'without appealing to the help of friendly powers'. Opponents of the Colonial Secretary, Joseph Chamberlain, accused him of complicity in the planning of the raid, but a select committee of the House of Commons picked delicately at the evidence and discovered nothing to his discredit. Since Chamberlain himself presided over the committee, this was a tactful conclusion. Whatever the truth may have been about Chamberlain's involvement with Cecil Rhodes and Dr. Jameson, there is no doubt about his determination to create a southern African federation under British control, incorporating Cape Colony and Natal with the Boer republics of the Transvaal and the Orange Free State. His instrument in achieving this ambition was Sir Alfred Milner, a forceful young Liberal Unionist diplomat who had served in the British administration in Egypt and shared Chamberlain's faith in Britain's imperial destiny. Milner was appointed in 1897 as Governor of Cape Colony and High Commissioner for South Africa. In an atmosphere of growing distrust and antagonism, Milner and Kruger drew their countries inexorably down the road to war. Both have been blamed for its outbreak but the conflict was not only between two men of opposing views and between two countries of competing interests, it was the culmination of almost a century of hostility, a clash of two incompatible moral and political philosophies.

The breaking point came in October 1899. Kruger had been amassing arms while making minor concessions to the Uitlanders. Because the British forces in South Africa numbered only about 12,000 men, the government decided to reinforce them by a further 10,000, mainly from India. Kruger complained that these troop movements menaced his country's independence and asked for them to be rescinded. The British government rejected Kruger's demand. The grass on the veldt was springing green and fresh. The Boer horsemen, wearing their farming clothes but with rifle and bandoliers slung from their shoulders and saddle-bags filled with biltong, were riding their shaggy ponies to join their commandos. Early in the morning of 12 October 1899 they crossed the frontiers into British South Africa and laid siege to Mafeking, Kimberley and Ladysmith. During one week of mid-December the commandos inflicted three sharp defeats on British forces. General Gatacre's attack on Stormberg Junction, on the railway running south into Cape Colony, was repulsed with heavy losses on 10 December. Five days later the Commander-in-Chief, General Redvers Buller, moving to relieve Ladysmith, was repulsed at Colenso with the loss of ten guns and over a thousand men killed or wounded. Some of the heaviest casualties occurred in the cavalry brigade commanded by a young Scottish officer of the Life Guards, the Earl of Dundonald.

The most shattering defeat of Black Week, however, was suffered by General Lord Methuen, who had begun his army career thirty-five years earlier as a lieutenant in the Scots Guards. Commanding the First Division, which included the 1st Battalion of his own regiment and was reinforced by the redoubtable Highland Brigade, Methuen was marching to relieve Kimberley. He had already won three actions against the Boers, being wounded in the third, the crossing of the Modder River. On 10 December he set out on the last lap, confident that one more thrust would bring him to the beleaguered town.

The Highland Brigade which had reinforced Methuen's division comprised the 2nd Battalion Royal Highlanders, the 1st Battalion Highland Light Infantry, the 2nd Battalion Seaforth Highlanders, and the 1st Battalion Argyll and Sutherland Highlanders. It was commanded by a remarkable Scottish officer, Major-General 'Andy' Wauchope, of Niddrie. In 1859, as a boy of thirteen, Wauchope had become a naval cadet but after three years requested his discharge so that he could join the army. He was commissioned as an ensign in the 42nd Highlanders, the Black Watch, and saw service with Sir Garnet Wolseley in the Ashanti campaign and at the battle of Tel-el-Kebir in 1882 against the Egyptian nationalists. His courage and leadership proved him an outstanding officer and in 1889, while still serving, he was invited by the Midlothian Liberal Unionist Association to stand as the parliamentary candidate against Mr. Gladstone, whose majority at the 1885 general election had been 4,631. Making the main issue the question of Irish Home Rule, which he opposed, Colonel Wauchope conducted a vigorous but courteous campaign and on 12 July 1892, in an 84% poll, he reduced Gladstone's majority to the astonishingly low figure of 690. He was thus renowned not only as a soldier but also as a formidable politician.

The only obstacle between Methuen's camp on the Modder River and the town of Kimberley twenty miles away was a range of low hills, the highest of which, Magersfontein, was two hundred feet. Methuen planned to take it by a dawn assault following a heavy bombardment of the Boer positions on its summit. He chose the Highland Brigade to lead the attack, with the 1st Battalion Gordon Highlanders in support. The bombardment, by the standards of Victorian artillery, was long and destructive. There was later some misgiving in Britain that it had taken place on a Sunday afternoon and was believed to have killed a large number of Boers at their prayers. Methuen, confident that it had achieved its purpose, gave his orders and soon after midnight Wauchope set out, the Black Watch leading. Three hours march through the darkness and in drenching rain brought the Highland battalions in a solid phalanx of four thousand men to the foot of Magersfontein. A stretch of scrub thickly scattered with mimosa bushes delayed the advance a little but at four o'clock Wauchope gave the command to his Highlanders to deploy into extended line for the last few hundred yards. As they began to move away, the ground seemed to erupt in front of them. From thousands of Boer rifles came a hail of fire, pouring at point-blank range into the confused and stumbling Highland ranks. Wauchope was among the first to fall, his body riddled with bullets.

Despite the gallant efforts of the Scots—Piet Cronje, the Boer general, afterwards wrote of their 'sublime courage'—they could make no progress at any part of their three-mile front. The Boers, secure in their trenches behind barbed wire entanglements, kept up a controlled and accurate fire which pinned the Highlanders down, unable to advance but unwilling to retreat. During the forenoon the Gordons were ordered into action but they, too, could not reach the Boer trenches. Captain Ernest Towse gained a Victoria Cross for carrying his wounded commander, Lieutenant-Colonel G. T. F. Downman, out of range.

Towards the end of the scorching day, the Boer artillery opened up and the remnants of the Highland Brigade fell back. By nightfall the battle of Magersfontein was over. The Boers, by the simple stratagem of digging their trenches well below the summit of the hill had avoided the effects of Methuen's preliminary bombardment and tempted Wauchope into a trap. British losses amounted to almost a thousand killed, wounded or missing, three-quarters of them Highlanders. Four of the five Highland battalions lost their commanding officers and almost sixty officers were killed. A week later Andy Wauchope was buried in a private cemetery at Matjesfontein to the pipers' lament of *Lochaber no More*.

The disasters of Black Week spurred the British government to action. The veteran Field-Marshal Lord Roberts of Kandahar, whose only son had won a posthumous Victoria Cross in trying to save the guns at Colenso, was appointed Commander-in-Chief in South Africa, with General Lord Kitchener of Khartum as his chief of staff. Another celebrated officer was given the task of re-forming and invigorating the Highland Brigade. He was Brigadier-General Hector Macdonald, a Ross-shire crofter's son who had risen by skill, courage and determination to national fame as 'Fighting Mac'.

Born in 1853 at Rootfield, near Dingwall, Macdonald had enlisted at seventeen in the 92nd Regiment, the Gordon Highlanders. He spoke all his life of the kindness and sympathy he met in that famous regiment from the first day, when a friendly corporal escorted him up to Castle Hill barracks, in Aberdeen. Promotion came steadily and as a colour sergeant in 1879 Macdonald fought so bravely at the battle of Charashiah, during the Afghanistan campaign, that General Roberts offered the young Gordon Highlander the choice of a Victoria Cross or a commission. Macdonald chose the latter. He took part in Roberts's historic march from Kabul to Kandahar and in 1881 was captured by the Boers in the disastrous defeat at Majuba Hill. When they freed him, the Boer general returned Macdonald's sword, saying that 'a brave man and his sword should not be separated'. Having spent several years in Egypt and the Sudan, where he trained a battalion of Sudanese mercenaries, he was given command of a native brigade in Kitchener's expedition in 1898 to re-conquer the Sudan. At a crucial stage in the battle of Omdurman, Macdonald's brigade withstood an attack by four times its number of Sudanese dervishes. A young subaltern who had taken part in a charge by the 21st Lancers at an earlier stage in the battle later recorded, in his book *The River War*, that Macdonald's position 'was one of extreme peril. The attack in his front was weakening every minute, but the far more formidable attack on his right rear grew stronger and nearer in inverse ratio. Both attacks must be met. The moment was critical; the danger near. All depended on Macdonald, and that officer, who by valour and conduct in war had won his way from the rank of a private soldier to the command of a brigade, and will doubtless obtain still higher employment, was equal to the emergency.' Macdonald's brigade held, the dervishes were annihilated, and Omdurman was transformed into a resounding victory. The young subaltern was also to obtain higher employment in later years. His name was Winston S. Churchill.

Macdonald came home to be promoted full colonel and to be fêted in London and Scotland. Five hundred guests attended a banquet in his honour at the Hotel Cecil, where the Duke of Atholl presented him with a commemorative sword, a gift from the Highland Associations of London. Dingwall, on a public holiday, made Colonel Macdonald a freeman of the burgh. There were more cheering crowds and a lively procession in Inverness and a civic luncheon in Glasgow. At a Gordon Highlanders' dinner in London the Prince of Wales remarked to Macdonald that it was strange they had not met previously. 'But, sir,' replied Macdonald, 'we have. When you were in India, I was posted as a sentry outside your tent.'

By early February 1900 Roberts, Kitchener and Fighting Mac were in the Modder River camp. In a ten-day campaign before the end of the month the Boers had been defeated at Paardeberg and General Cronje had surrendered, Kimberley had been relieved and the way was clear for Roberts to advance on Bloemfontein, capital of the Orange Free State. In May the seven-month siege of Mafeking was raised by a flying column of cavalry from General Sir Archibald Hunter's Tenth Division. The news of the relief of Mafeking was received in Britain as if it had been a tremendous victory over a foe who was threatening the very existence of the Empire. London streets were thronged for two nights and a day with cheering, singing, dancing crowds, and in towns throughout the country there were similar scenes. Traffic in Glasgow was brought to a standstill by a procession of ship-yard workers with flags and banners and an effigy of President Kruger labelled 'To St. Helena'. Union Street, Aberdeen, was gaily decked in flags and bunting while hordes of children paraded in fancy dress and the Lord Provost sent a telegram of congratulations to Baden-Powell in Mafeking. Kirkwall had a fireworks display, Crieff burned Kruger in effigy in James Square, at Kirkintilloch there was dancing in the streets all night, and in Buckie the police commissioners, their duty nobly done, the foe defeated, the Empire saved, awarded themselves a celebratory banquet. On 5 June 1900 Roberts entered Pretoria, the Transvaal capital, and three months later President Kruger sought refuge in Portuguese East Africa to await a ship to take him to exile in the Netherlands. Early in December Roberts came home, leaving Kitchener to complete the rounding up of the Boer commandos.

Fighting Mac also returned home, to be knighted by the King in May 1901 and then to visit Australia and New Zealand, where he was warmly welcomed, especially by emigrants of Scottish descent who regarded him as the living embodiment of the Highlander's historic qualities of courage, determination and manly bearing. His next appointment was to command the garrison in Ceylon. It was monotonous, routine duty far different from the eventful soldiering that Fighting Mac had enjoyed for thirty years. In February 1903 whispers of a scandal involving Macdonald reached the ears of the

Governor of Ceylon, Sir Joseph West Ridgeway. Macdonald countered the Governor's enquiries by asking for leave to return to London to consult the Commander-in-Chief, his old mentor, Roberts of Kandahar. Roberts discussed the matter with the King, who granted Macdonald a private audience. Nothing of what passed at these interviews has yet been revealed but on 20 March 1903 Macdonald left England for Paris, en route for Marseilles and Ceylon. The Governor had meanwhile announced in his Legislative Council that grave charges, not indictable under Ceylon laws, had been made against Macdonald, adding: 'He has decided to return to Ceylon and meet the charges, and I have been authorised to convene a court martial for this purpose.'

On 25 March 1903 the European edition of the *New York Herald* headlined a *Daily Express* report from Colombo 'Grave charge lies on Sir H. Macdonald'. Alongside a grim-faced portrait, the report began: 'Charges of a grave character, involving the moral conduct of the gallant and popular general, Sir Hector Macdonald, commander of the troops in Ceylon, have been made public here. The offences alleged were not amenable to the law in Ceylon, but were such that the Governor had no choice but to summon Sir Hector Macdonald from Kandy to Colombo to answer the charge.' A shorter *Daily Express* report from London concluded that 'the purport of the charges cannot be entered into here, but it may be stated that, while they do not constitute an offence under the laws of Ceylon, they are criminally punishable at home'. Having seen the newspaper reports after breakfast in his hotel, Fighting Mac went to his room and put a bullet through his head.

The news was received in Scotland with incredulity and consternation, as if Macdonald's death had been a national calamity. When his body was brought from Paris, Scots waited with wreaths to carpet the railway coach in which the coffin was placed and as the train drew out of King's Cross Station, pipers played *The Flowers of the Forest*. At the insistence of Lady Macdonald, the funeral, private and unannounced, took place immediately after the train arrived in Waverley Station, the small cortège making its way through the empty streets of Edinburgh in the grey, rain-swept dawn to the Dean cemetery. But in the days that followed, the cemetery was thronged by quiet crowds come to pay their last respects to the memory of Fighting Mac. Four years later, with subscriptions from Scots all over the world, Dingwall erected a splendid granite memorial in his honour.

With the departure of Roberts from South Africa in December 1900 there seemed little left for Kitchener to do except round up the remaining Boers and impose his peace terms upon them. The task was less simple than it seemed. The Boers, no more than twelve to fifteen thousand in all, adopted guerilla tactics, moving swiftly in small commandos to attack the British lines of communication, blowing up railway tracks, cutting telegraph lines, capturing or destroying supply wagons and isolating the over-stretched British forces. Relying on their knowledge of veldt-craft and the help of a friendly population, the Boers were able to outwit troops many times their number. Kitchener introduced ruthless measures to counter this guerilla warfare. He built long chains of blockhouses linked by barbed wire fences, burned Boer farms suspected of harbouring the 'rebels', and herded women, children and the aged into what were termed 'concentration camps'. Conditions in these camps, more from inefficiency than intent, were appalling. Most families were crowded into canvas tents offering little protection against the weather, with inadequate sanitation and meagre rations of poor quality food. Mortality, especially among children, was high. Quoting War Office statistics, the *Morning Leader* recorded in October 1901 that the annual death rate had risen that winter from 109 per thousand in June to 264 per thousand in September. This overall figure disguised the fact that in the camps in Cape Colony and Natal mortality was no more than normal, while in the Transvaal and Orange Free State camps it was disastrously higher. 'At this rate,' declared Lloyd George, 'within a few years there will not be a child alive in the veldt.'

From the beginning of the South African War, the young Welshman had been one of its most vociferous opponents, but there were many others, especially in Scotland and Ireland, who were disturbed both by origins of the war and by the manner in which it was being fought. One of them was the Liberal leader, Sir Henry Campbell-Bannerman, who spoke of Kitchener as using 'the methods of barbarism' to defeat the Boers. The popular newspapers labelled anyone who expressed such opinions as a 'Pro-Boer' and a series of meetings addressed by Lloyd George in different parts of the country provided the occasion for remarkable demonstrations of patriotism, loyalty and lawlessness. The first of these 'Lloyd George Nights', as they were called in music-hall jargon, was held in Glasgow on 6 March 1900. 'The travelling troupe of "Stop-the-War" propagandists reached Glasgow last evening', reported the *Glasgow Herald*, extending the metaphor, 'and gave a performance in the City Hall. It was not very impressive, but what else could be expected with a ridiculous programme and a platform composed of "wild Irish" and gentlemen of "agin-everything" persuasion?'

Bailie John Ferguson chaired the meeting and Lloyd George was supported on the platform by Henry J. Wilson, Liberal Member for Holmfirth, Yorkshire, Keir Hardie, whose Independent Labour Party had already expressed its opposition to the war as one of aggression and conquest, and Cronright Schreiner, the husband of Olive Schreiner, authoress of *The Story of an African Farm*. More than half the audience was estimated to consist of Irishmen, who happily applauded every anti-Unionist sentiment, but there was a constant barrage of heckling from a large contingent of patriots, who waved loyal banners and sang *God Save the Queen* and *Rule, Britannia!* Lloyd George was the most successful in making himself heard above the din, the theme of his speech being his assertion that 'the Gordon Highlanders and the Black Watch had died to cut down wages and to increase the dividends of the gold-mine shareholders'.

After Keir Hardie had proposed the votes of thanks, the platform party prudently started *Auld Lang Syne*, in which all could join. Then, while the Pro-Boers struggled home through jostling, abusive crowds, the loyalists assembled noisily in Candleriggs and marched to Queen Square to sing *Rule, Britannia!* once more round the Queen's statue. 'It may be possible in some benighted English towns', commented the *Glasgow Herald* smugly, 'to convince a carefully-picked audience that Mr. Lloyd George's account of the negotiations is composed of the essential facts, and that Mr. Henry Wilson is honestly seeking for information when he parrots the question, "What are we fighting for?" We are not so ignorant here.'

Cronright Schreiner had an equally hostile reception when he spoke against the war at the Trades Hall, in Aberdeen, on 20 May 1900. Angry Aberdonians broke windows in the hall, fought with police trying to protect the meeting, sang the national anthem and *Soldiers of the Queen*, and were finally dispersed only after a detachment of sixty Gordon Highlanders had been summoned to reinforce the police.

Birmingham, the centre from which Joseph Chamberlain drew his support, was even less hospitable when Lloyd George tried to speak at a huge meeting in the Town Hall on 18 December 1901. Not a word of his speech could be heard as the Chamberlainites stormed the building, breaking over a thousand window-panes and attacking with democratic impartiality the police, the platform party and the representatives of the Press. 'Rather lively for a peace meeting!' shouted Lloyd George to one of the reporters. After being barricaded in a darkened committee room for two hours at the insistence of the distraught Chief Constable, Lloyd George eventually escaped with his life by marching out with a file of policemen, himself dressed in a policeman's uniform.

Although Lord Salisbury's government had still almost two years to run, he decided in September 1900 to take advantage of the patriotic fervour engendered by the war to call a general election. The result was a clear endorsement of his policy and even Lloyd George was able to scrape home in the Caernarvon Boroughs by only 296 votes in a total poll of 4,528. In Scotland the result was notable in that the Conservatives and Unionists won more seats than their opponents, 38 to 34, taking all seven Glasgow seats and even Orkney and Shetland. The fifteen candidates of the Labour Representation Committee were decimated, only Keir Hardie and Richard Bell being successful.

Eventually and inevitably the war came untidily to an end. The Boer leaders, with thirty delegates from each of the two republics, met at Vereeniging on 15 May 1902 and agreed proposals to put to the British. There followed nine days of negotiations in Pretoria and on 31 May 1902 peace was signed in the dining-room of the house where Kitchener had established his headquarters. Its name, derived from the South African owner's happy memories of a holiday visit to the Borders, was Melrose House.

Scottish casualties during the war had been, by Edwardian standards, very heavy. The Royal Scots Greys had suffered 40 killed and 109 wounded, the Scots Guards 49 killed and 141 wounded, the Royal Scots Fusiliers, the King's Own Scottish Borderers, and the Cameronians (Scottish Rifles) comparable numbers. Worse hit were the regiments of the Highland Brigade caught in the trap at Magersfontein. The Royal Highlanders, the Black Watch, suffered 133 killed and 366 wounded, the Highland Light Infantry 34 killed and 170 wounded, the Seaforth Highlanders 132 killed and 299 wounded, and the Argyll and Sutherland Highlanders 89 killed and 222 wounded. The Gordon Highlanders, in support at Magersfontein, lost 132 killed and 384 wounded, but far outstripped all other regiments except the much larger Royal Artillery in the number of decorations they gained. Six Gordons won the Victoria Cross, ten the Distinguished Service Order, and thirty-two the Distinguished Conduct Medal.

All over Scotland, cities, burghs, villages and crofts welcomed the soldiers returning from the war. Lovat's Scouts arrived in Inverness by special train on 20 August 1902. They were, reported the *Northern Scot*, 'a very serviceable looking body of men; all wearing new khaki outfits and apparently none the worse of their spell of trekking in Cape Colony'. Headed by the band of the Cameron Highlanders, the khaki-clad veterans paraded to the Town Hall to be greeted by the provost, magistrates and town council, with speeches, toasts and 'an excellent repast'.

Four years later, in November 1906, Lord Rosebery unveiled the memorial to the Royal Scots Greys in Princes Street, Edinburgh, with a speech as eloquent and moving as President Lincoln's famous address at Gettysburg. 'Honour to the brave who will return no more', said Lord Rosebery. 'We shall not see their faces again. In the service of their Sovereign and their country they have undergone the sharpness of death, and sleep their eternal sleep, thousands of miles away in the green solitudes of Africa. Their places, their comrades, their saddles, will know them no more, for they will never return to us as we knew them. But in a nobler and a higher sense, have they not returned to us today? They return to us with a memory of high duty faithfully performed; they return to us with the inspiration of their example. Peace, then, to their dust; honour to their memory. Scotland for ever!'

The South African War taught the British Army some salutary lessons. For more than two and a half years the Boer republics, with a citizen army totalling only about fifty thousand, had defied the military might of the British Empire and had eventually required an army of 450,000 men and an expenditure of £150,000,000 to subdue them. Relief in Britain at the outcome of the war did not disguise the fact that the Army needed radical reform. Public disquiet prompted the government to appoint the Earl of Elgin, a Scottish diplomat who had been Viceroy of India, to head a royal commission 'to inquire into the military preparations for the War in South Africa and into the supply of men, ammunition, equipment and transport by sea and in campaign, and into the military operations up to the occupation of Pretoria'.

The Elgin commission's report recommended fundamental

changes in the structure of command and after Hugh Arnold-Forster became Secretary for War in 1903, he prepared to put the recommendations into effect, beginning with the institution of the Army Council, a replica of the Board of Admiralty. But although a staunch Conservative, Arnold-Forster found himself thwarted by those who were even stauncher. 'I find I am dealing with at least six armies', he complained in the House of Commons on 28 March 1905. 'I am dealing with the Army in India, the Indian Army, the Army at home, the Militia, the Volunteers, and the great army of those who have left the colours and are now entrenched in the clubs of this city.'

Arnold-Forster's term as Secretary for War ended prematurely with Balfour's resignation on 4 December 1905. In his place the new Liberal prime minister, Sir Henry Campbell-Bannerman, appointed a small, rotund, chubby-faced Scottish lawyer who, even in that ministry of many talents, was outstandingly talented. He was Richard Burdon Haldane, of Cloan, in Perthshire. He proved, without gainsay, to be the greatest Secretary of State for War that Britain has ever had.

The Duke of Wellington is reputed to have considered his army as 'the scum of the earth'. Lord Roberts described his soldiers as 'heroes on the battlefield and gentlemen everywhere'. The typical Edwardian soldier found himself, no doubt, somewhere between these two extremes. Privates in regiments of the line still received the traditional Queen's shilling as their daily rate of pay, though guardsmen, sappers in the Royal Engineers and gunners in the Royal Horse Artillery were paid a few pence above the basic rate. Rations were comparatively generous but marriage allowances were meagre, and a wife with children to rear was faced with real hardship if she was not on the official married establishment, limited to only a small percentage of those men who were below sergeant's rank. The pay of an infantry second lieutenant, at 5s. 3d. per day, normally did not cover even his mess bill, so that without some private means it was practically impossible for a young man to live in the style expected of an Edwardian officer and gentleman. Even Winston Churchill, the grandson of a duke, found difficulty in making both ends meet as a subaltern of Hussars, and had to turn to journalism to supplement his army pay.

Educational standards were low and much of the ordinary soldier's spare time was spent in the regimental wet canteen or sleazy public-houses and music-halls. The prejudice characterised in

Rudyard Kipling's celebrated poem *Tommy*, one of the *Barrack-Room Ballads* published in 1892, was not entirely unjustified, especially as Tommy's pay was unlikely to provide much profit for a publican with expensive premises to keep:

'I went into a public-'ouse to get a pint o' beer,
    The publican 'e up an' sez, 'We serve no red-coats here'.
The girls be'ind the bar they laughed an' giggled fit to die,
    I outs into the street again an' to myself sez I:
        O it's Tommy this, an' Tommy that, an' 'Tommy, go away';
        But it's 'Thank you, Mister Atkins', when the band begins to
play . . .

'I went into a theatre as sober as could be,
    They gave a drunk civilian room, but 'adn't none for me;
They sent me to the gallery or round the music-'alls,
    But when it comes to fightin', Lord! they'll shove me in the stalls!
        For it's Tommy this, an' Tommy that, an' 'Tommy, wait outside';
        But it's 'Special train for Atkins' when the trooper's on the
tide . . .

Local loyalties were strong and a soldier's pride in his regiment was sometimes carried to excess. On 2 January 1904 *The Northern Scot* reported that when the Scottish express from Euston had arrived at Crewe the previous Tuesday, 'the officials were confronted with a horrible spectacle. Trickling down over a compartment was a quantity of blood, and on the door being opened a number of soldiers were found lying in all directions. The floor of the compartment was covered with blood, while the carriage seats and windows were also bespattered. One of the soldiers was bleeding profusely from terrible cuts and gashes, and when taken out of the carriage was in a critical condition through loss of blood. His name is Private David Smith of the 1st Argyll and Sutherland Highlanders, and he was at once removed to Crewe Railway Accident Hospital. The officials ascertained that the soldiers, about a dozen in number, belonged to the Gordon Highlanders and the Argyll and Sutherland Highlanders, and during the journey from London they quarrelled as to the merits of their respective regiments. A terrible fight ensued, and it is supposed that weapons were brought into action. Both of Smith's arms were shockingly mutilated. The men have all been through the South African War. The train is one of those which do not stop between Euston and Crewe or between Crewe and Carlisle. The men were en route for Scotland. The injured man has a ticket for Cumberland', concluded the report, a little inconsequentially.

Although the twentieth century was still so young when Richard Haldane became Secretary of State for War, the office had already tested and a little tarnished the reputations of two Edwardian occupants, St. John Brodrick and Hugh Arnold-Forster. 'We shall now see how Schopenhauer gets on in the kailyard', chuckled Campbell-Bannerman when Haldane had accepted the appointment. Haldane later described how, with Sir Edward Grey and Sir Henry Fowler, the new Chancellor of the Duchy of Lancaster, he made his way to the War Office from Buckingham Palace, where they had received their seals of office from the King. 'It was a day of the blackest fog that I remember', he wrote in his *Autobiography*. 'When the ceremony was over we set off with our Seals to our respective offices. I had a hired brougham, and Grey and Fowler left in it with me. We stuck in the darkness of the Mall. I got out to see where we were and could not find the carriage again. Fowler got back to the Palace. Grey, after a long wandering round and round, eventually reached the Foreign Office. By trudging through the mud and feeling among the horses' heads I at last got to the War Office, then in Pall Mall. Fortunately I had kept hold of my Seals. I was a little exhausted when I arrived. I handed the Seals to the Permanent Under-Secretary to take charge of, and asked the tall ex-Guards soldier in attendance for a glass of water. "Certainly, sir: Irish or Scotch?" '

The following day the generals on the Army Council gathered for their first interview with the new Secretary of State. They said that they would like him to give them some idea of the reforms which he intended proposing to Parliament. 'My reply', recorded Haldane, 'was that I was as a young and blushing virgin just united to a bronzed warrior, and that it was not to be expected by the public that any result of the union should appear until at least nine months had passed.'

Haldane's forecast of the gestation period proved accurate, for in September 1906 he created a General Staff of seventy-two officers who were to meet regularly at the War Office under the Chief of Staff to study problems of strategy. Among its most notable members were three Scots, General Sir Ian Hamilton, who had been Kitchener's chief of staff in South Africa, Major-General Sir Douglas Haig, who was Director of Staff Duties from 1907 to 1909 and later became the British Commander-in-Chief on the Western Front, and Brigadier-General Sir William Robertson, who had risen from the ranks to become Assistant Director of Military Operations from 1901 to 1907, and was later the first ranker to become Field-Marshal.

The creation of the General Staff was the first in a series of sweeping reforms which Haldane then introduced, enlisting the support of his colleagues in the Cabinet by combining greater efficiency in the Army with a saving of money for the Treasury. He disbanded a number of units and transferred their men to other regiments or arms of the service, and he freed soldiers from coastal defence duty by handing over responsibility for this to the Admiralty. He introduced a balanced service engagement of seven years with the colours and five years in the reserve, and revived the system of linked battalions which Edward Cardwell had instituted during Mr. Gladstone's first administration, so that each of the Army's seventy-two battalions of line infantry on home service was linked with a battalion serving overseas, for the purposes of recruitment, elementary training and relief. The infantry regiments were grouped into six home divisions and the cavalry into four brigades. These, with their staffs and the necessary artillery and engineer units, together formed an expeditionary force of some 120,000 men, capable of being moved to a continental theatre of war within fifteen days.

Haldane had more difficulty with the reform of the reserve forces, because any changes in their traditional status and conditions of service more closely affected people in the counties who could exercise political influence. Nevertheless he succeeded in bringing order to the haphazard array of second-line units which had their origins in different periods of crisis during the previous two or three centuries. The old Militia was reconstituted as a Special Reserve but the Volunteers, dating mainly from the 1860s, when the French Emperor Napoleon III was pursuing belligerent policies, and the Yeomanry, mainly a creation of the eighteenth-century wars against France, were organised into a Territorial Force of fourteen infantry divisions and fourteen cavalry brigades, including one of each in the Lowlands and another in the Highlands. To provide officers for the Territorial Army, as it later became known, Haldane encouraged the formation of officers' training corps in public schools and universities. To provide a steady flow of local recruits he set up county associations, inviting the Lords-Lieutenant to serve as presidents, with county councillors and even trade union officials on the committees.

Tenuous as it seemed at first, this nation-wide network of county associations under the Army Council proved a most successful means of developing the reserve forces to a point where they could undertake the defence of the kingdom if the Expeditionary Force were ordered abroad, as well as form the nucleus for further expansion in time of war.

The King, with occasional misgivings, lent his support to Haldane's schemes, receiving the Lords-Lieutenant at Buckingham Palace in October 1907 so that he could invite their co-operation. The Territorial Force was formally inaugurated on 1 April 1908 and by the end of the following year it embodied 9,700 officers, 480 officer cadets in training corps, and 262,000 men. These supported a Regular Army of 165,000 officers and men, with 134,000 Army Reserves and 75,000 Special Reserves. By continental standards this was, in the Kaiser's immortal phrase, 'a contemptible little army', but it proved not without merit when tested in action.

Scottish regiments played a full part in this historic programme of reform and when war came in August 1914, Haldane's arrangements for the mobilisation and movement of both regular and reserve forces proved equal to the demands made on them. The Royal Scots Greys were stationed at York and mobilisation of the regiment's reserves was completed by 8 August 1914. A week later the regiment left by train for Southampton, where they embarked on 16 August for Le Havre as part of the 5th Cavalry Brigade commanded by Sir Philip Chetwode. The Brigade crossed into Belgium on 21 August, with orders to take up its position at the extreme right of the British line. Within a few days the Scots Greys were in action alongside the 12th Lancers and the 20th Hussars in the retreat from Mons. The 1st Battalion Gordon Highlanders was at Plymouth, five hundred miles from its depot at Aberdeen, when mobilisation orders were received on 4 August. Two days later the first reservists, numbering over two hundred, arrived from Aberdeen and on 7 August came a further three hundred. Thus reinforced, the battalion landed at Boulogne a week later and on 23 August, as part of General Hubert Hamilton's Third Division, it was deep in the fighting at Mons.

The Territorials were not far behind. The first unit to leave Britain for service abroad was the 7th Middlesex, which sailed for Gibraltar on 4 September, but the first to enter the actual theatre of war was the London Scottish. They sailed for France on 16 September and by the end of October were in action at Messines, the first major battle for the Territorials. John Buchan, in his *History of the War*, described the welcome which the British Expeditionary Force, and especially the Scottish regiments, received as they disembarked in France. At Boulogne, wrote Buchan, 'the landing of the troops awakened wild enthusiasm. The geniality and fine physique of the men, and their gentleness to women and children; the cavalryman's care of his horses; above all the Highlanders, who are the heroes of nursery tales in France, went to the hearts of the people. The old alliance with Scotland was remembered, the days when Buchan and Douglas led the chivalry of France. The badges and numbers of the men were begged for keepsakes, and homely delicacies were pressed upon them in return. Many a Highlander was of the opinion which Alan Breck expressed to David Balfour, "They're a real bonny folk, the French nation".'

By this time Haldane was no longer at the War Office. In March 1911 the Earl of Crewe, the Liberal leader in the House of Lords, became seriously ill, and Asquith persuaded Haldane to accept a viscountcy and to go to lead in the Lords while still remaining as Secretary for War. He did so but in June 1912 succeeded the Earl of Loreburn as Lord Chancellor, while Colonel J. E. B. Seely, Member for the Abercromby division of Liverpool, took his place at the War Office. By this time the true value of Haldane's work for the Army could be assessed and appreciated, not only by his Liberal colleagues but by the Conservative and Unionist Opposition, and in the country at large. To this story there is, however, a sequel, so gross and vicious as to be almost incredible.

Among his other attributes, Haldane was a philosopher of note. While at Edinburgh University he had spent five months in Göttingen under the eminent German philosopher Hermann Lötze and for the rest of his life he remained an admirer of many aspects of German life and culture. As well as spending holidays in Germany, Haldane paid important diplomatic visits and he had German friends in all walks of life, from the Kaiser and the Imperial Chancellor to Fraülein Schlote, who taught him German in 1874 and whom he visited for the last time almost fifty years later. On one occasion he remarked casually that Professor Lötze's classroom was his 'spiritual home'.

The outbreak of war against Germany in August 1914 was the signal for a surge of anti-German feeling as irrational as it was widespread. Harmless shopkeepers whose families had been settled in the East End of London for generations but whose names were German in origin had their shops attacked and looted by angry mobs. In Elgin a suspected German spy was arrested while pencilling names and figures in a notebook, only to be eventually identified as a deaf and dumb Irishman collecting subscriptions for an institution for the similarly handicapped. Lord Northcliffe, proprietor of *The Times* and the *Daily Mail*, and Sir Max Aitken, with the *Daily Express*, launched a scurrilous campaign against Haldane, alleging that he was pro-German and that he had wished to delay the despatch of the British Expeditionary Force to France. His casual remark about Professor Lötze was twisted to suggest that he considered Germany to be his spiritual home. The megalomania of Northcliffe and the egotism of Aitken were matched by the pusillanimity of Asquith and the cowardice of Balfour and Bonar Law. None of them raised a finger to protect Haldane, who throughout the vendetta conducted himself with quiet courage and dignity. In the end Northcliffe and Aitken got their way. Haldane was sacrificed when the Conservative leaders refused to join the Liberals in a coalition government if he were given any post in it.

There is an epilogue to this sequel. Winston Churchill, forced out of the Admiralty at the same time, wrote to Haldane expressing his disgust at the 'vile Press campaign'. The day after the coalition government was formed, King George V received Haldane in audience and conferred upon him the Order of Merit. Finally, when victory at last was won, Field-Marshal Earl Haig of Bemersyde, Commander-in-Chief of the British Armies on the Western Front, presented Haldane with a copy of his printed Despatches. He inscribed it: 'To Viscount Haldane of Cloan—the greatest Secretary of State for War England has ever had. In grateful remembrance of his successful efforts in organising the Military Forces for a War on the Continent, notwithstanding much opposition from the Army Council and the half-hearted support of his Parliamentary friends. Haig, F.M.'

17

The End of an Era

The English have a fondness for attaching labels to the names of their monarchs. Some of these sobriquets have long endured. The king who paid Danegeld to buy off the Viking invaders is fated to go through history as Ethelred the Unready. Another Saxon king, dead these thousand years but notable still for his saintliness, is known to this day as Edward the Confessor. Few laurels can have faded so quickly as those bestowed by the popular Press on Edward VII. Typical was the comment of the *Elgin Courant and Courier* on 10 May 1910. 'King Edward', it recorded, 'has been called "The Peacemaker", a title that, like Mercy, becomes the throned monarch better than his crown. How much he contributed to the maintenance of peace in the world will not be known in our time, but it is now recognised that the King's pacific influence was very great.'

On the same day, the *Perthshire Courier* was announcing, less cautiously, that 'May has been transformed from the month of mirth to the month of mourning by the sudden demise of King Edward the Peacemaker'. He had earned the title, it was argued, because he had left Britain, strong, secure and at peace. Yet within three years of his death the kingdom was riven by internal disputes, verging in one vital sector on civil war, and within two more years the whole Empire was enmeshed in the costliest conflict it had ever known.

'The Rising Tide of Popular Unrest' was the headline to a sombre leader in the *News of the World* on 24 September 1911. 'Almost every day that passes', it began 'adds some new and exciting factor to the growing story of popular unrest. There is hardly a European state from which the symptoms are absent. Everywhere the people are discontented. Everywhere there is a more or less coherent demand, a more or less irresistible demand for better social conditions. For, analyse the unrest as you will, that is what it always comes to in the end. Here and there the unrest may seem to be tinged with political motives. But the politics are more apparent than real. What the people want is some share in that inheritance of comfort and prosperity which their industry helps to create, and which never was more abundant, or indeed more blatant, than at the present day.'

The leader went on to quote as examples of this widespread unrest the violent clashes between workers and police in France, culminating in a railway strike which had to be crushed by the mobilisation of army reservists; a general strike in northern Spain, which led to a week of pitched battles in the streets of Barcelona; poverty in Germany, where soup kitchens had to be opened to feed the poor in the imperial capital; political strife in Austria, suppressed only by ruthless police action; and violence in Portugal, where King Carlos I and his Crown Prince had been assassinated in 1908 and the son who succeeded him as Manoel II had been driven into exile two years later by republican revolutionaries.

Britain was not safe from the rising tide of unrest, although it was generally less violent in character. Following the industrial recession of 1908 and 1909 unemployment fell slightly but wage rates showed hardly any improvement, so that in 1910 many workers were still earning less in real terms than they had earned in 1900. The ostentatious display of wealth and extravagance which had characterised the reign of Edward VII had left the lower classes resentful and dissatisfied. The year of the King's death introduced three years of civil strife on an unprecedented scale.

The long and melancholy catalogue begins early in 1910 with strikes of Northumberland miners, North-Eastern Railway employees, Glasgow thread-workers, Nottingham miners and Clyde dockyard workers. In November a miners' strike for an agreed minimum wage in the South Wales coalfields became so bitter that the Home Secretary, Winston Churchill, had to despatch General Nevil Macready, of the Gordon Highlanders, with troops and several hundred constables of the Metropolitan Police to restore order. After the use, in Macready's words, of 'a little gentle persuasion with the bayonet', the strikers were eventually brought under control and forced back to work, although not until one had been killed and many injured in what *The Times* described as 'an orgy of naked anarchy'.

Anarchy was again in the news headlines the following month when a gang of Russian immigrants, suspected of being anarchists and revolutionaries, planned to rob a jeweller's shop in Houndsditch. They were surprised by the police and shot their way out, killing three policemen before escaping into the darkness. They were quickly run to earth in a house in Sidney Street, in the East End, but resisted all attempts to arrest them. Winston Churchill ordered a detachment of Scots Guards to help the police in surrounding the house and there was even talk of bringing up artillery but before this could be done, the anarchists set fire to the house. Two charred corpses were found in the ruins but of the alleged ringleader, popularly known as Peter the Painter, no trace was ever found.

The 'Siege of Sidney Street' provided a tragi-comic, if macabre, introduction to the troubles of 1911. The early months were fairly quiet but a few days before the coronation of King George V on 22 June seamen striking at Southampton for a minimum wage and better living conditions sparked off a series of strikes which spread like wildfire to seamen, dockers, vanmen and carters in provincial ports throughout the country. Detachments of the Metropolitan Police, the Birmingham Police and, from their depot at York, the Royal Scots Greys had to be sent to Manchester, where there was fighting in the streets. George R. Askwith, a Board of Trade official, had hardly settled this strike by persuading shipping companies and port employers to make concessions, when the London dockers came out on strike again for a minimum wage of 8d. an hour for day work and 1s. an hour for overtime. The vanmen and carters joined them, asking for their working week to be reduced to sixty hours. Churchill was for sending troops to break the strike, which threatened to paralyse London, but Askwith and Ben Tillett, the dockers' leader, dissuaded him. Eventually, with substantial concessions from the employers, the strike was brought to an end. Within a few days it was the turn of the railwaymen. This time Lloyd George brought the companies and the unions together in agreeing to accept the recommendations of a special commission of inquiry. The year ended with a strike of dockers, vanmen and carters in Dundee.

Early in 1912 Scottish miners joined with those in Northumberland, Durham and South Wales in striking for a minimum wage of 5s. per day for men and 2s. for boys. Glasgow was crippled by a general strike in January and there was more trouble in the London docks in May. The contagion spread even to small communities far from the restless industrial centres. In September 'operative plumbers' in Elgin went on strike for an extra halfpenny to raise their wages from 7½d. to 8d. an hour. Refusing the increase, the master plumbers pointed out that the operative plumbers were the best paid of all the workers in the building trade and that they had been enjoying the hourly rate of 7½d. for years, while the masons' wages had reached that level only a few weeks previously. Moreover, threatened the master plumbers, there were plenty of new men ready to work at the established rate of pay as soon as the strike was over. The catalogue of conflict seemed endless. During 1908 some four hundred industrial disputes had been reported to the Labour Department of the Board of Trade. During 1911 the number rose to nine hundred but in 1913 no fewer than 1,800 disputes were reported. They were growing in extent as well as in number. During 1909 the total of working days lost through strikes and lock-outs had amounted to just over 2,500,000. During 1912 the total exceeded 38,000,000.

As well as the internal strife which troubled the last years of the Edwardian period, there were imperial problems for the Liberal government to solve. Although the Liberals were traditionally reluctant Empire-builders, they had come to recognise the importance of the Empire as a commercial asset and as an outlet for emigration. Provided that it could be administered as economically as possible and that the white dominions could be persuaded to shoulder their own responsibilities, the Liberals were content to accept the maintenance of the Empire as part of their duty.

As Colonial Secretary, the Earl of Elgin presided over a colonial conference held in London in 1907. The Transvaal prime minister, General Louis Botha, who had been the Boer Commander-in-Chief for the greater part of the South African War, made a particularly favourable impression, so that Campbell-Bannerman was encouraged to proceed with the creation of a Union of South Africa from the two British colonies, Natal and Cape Colony, and the two former Boer republics, the Transvaal and the Orange Free State. The Union was not finally achieved until after Campbell-Bannerman's death, but on 23 August 1909, when General Botha wrote to congratulate Asquith on the passing of the South Africa Act, he spoke warmly of the late prime minister. 'My greatest regret', wrote Botha, 'is that one noble figure is missing—one man who should have lived to see the fruits of his work, the late Sir Henry Campbell-Bannerman.'

Meanwhile India, also under Scottish guidance, was taking the first steps on the long road to self-government and independence. In 1905 the Viceroy, Lord Curzon, quarrelled with the Commander-in-Chief in India, Lord Kitchener, mainly on the question of their status in relation to each other and to the Indian Army. Curzon offered his resignation which, to his surprise, Balfour accepted. In his place Balfour appointed as Viceroy the Earl of Minto, who had begun his career as an ensign in the Scots Guards and had been, from 1898 to 1904, Governor-General of Canada. Although a Liberal Unionist, Lord Minto worked successfully, if sometimes a little uneasily, with John Morley, the Liberal Member for the Montrose Burghs, whom Campbell-Bannerman appointed as Secretary of State for India in the new Liberal administration. Together Morley and Minto introduced a far-reaching programme of administrative and legislative reform. For the first time the Viceroy was empowered to appoint an Indian to serve on his Executive Council, hitherto exclusively British. Two Indians were also appointed to the Secretary of State's Advisory Council. At the same time the provincial legislatures were enlarged by the introduction of members elected on a limited franchise. These, with the nominated members, provided the first Indian majorities in the provincial councils. The Morley-Minto reforms fell short of satisfying the radical Indian nationalists but they were sufficient to pacify the moderates and to enlist widespread support in India for the British cause when the First World War broke out.

Although Egypt was *de jure* a khedivate of the Ottoman Empire, it was *de facto* a British protectorate, occupied since 1882 by the British army and ruled not by its native Khedive, Abbas Hilmi, but by His Britannic Majesty's Agent and Consul General, the Earl of Cromer. Viceroy in all but title, Lord Cromer had as his principal assistant a Counsellor, Charles Mansfeldt de Cardonnel Findlay, who owed part of his exotic name to his mother but whose father and family were Scottish, of Boturich Castle, Dunbartonshire. Under Cromer's long administration Egypt had flourished and it was said that when ill-health forced him to retire in 1907, twelve million people were living in prosperity under Cromer's rule where six million had starved under the Khedive's rule twenty-five years earlier. Despite this material progress, there was a strong undercurrent of nationalist feeling, especially among educated Egyptians, with whom the British had little social contact. There was a marked upsurge in this Egyptian nationalism as a result of an incident at Denshawai, near Tanta, in the Nile Delta.

On 13 June 1906 five British officers, pigeon-shooting at Denshawai, were accused by the villagers of shooting at domestic pigeons and of setting fire to a threshing-floor. In the ensuing scuffle four Egyptians were wounded by a gun fired accidentally, a British officer then died of concussion and heat-stroke while hurrying to a near-by army camp for assistance, and another Egyptian, who had been succouring him, was beaten to death by British soldiers who wrongly accused him of attacking the dying officer. Lord Cromer was about to take his annual summer leave in England, so Mansfeldt Findlay, left in charge of the Agency, had the responsibility of administering justice. He appointed a special tribunal of three British and two Egyptian officials. Of the fifty-two villagers brought before it, four were sentenced to death, nine to terms of imprisonment and eight to be flogged. The hangings and floggings were carried out at the village itself with studied brutality intended to impress upon the Egyptians the futility of resistance to British domination. Despite Findlay's confident assertion that 'the conduct of the villagers is looked upon as casting discredit on the whole Egyptian people', Campbell-Bannerman and Sir Edward Grey were startled at the severity of the sentences. As these were to be carried out on the day after the trial ended, just fifteen days after the fracas at Denshawai, they had no time to consult the Cabinet. With only two telegrams from Findlay on which to base their judgement, they decided not to interfere. 'When the full facts were before me,' Sir Edward Grey wrote later, 'I felt that what had been done was open to question.'

Eventually to prove far more serious than these imperial problems in Ireland, South Africa, India and Egypt was the European legacy which the Liberal governments of Campbell-Bannerman and Asquith inherited from their Conservative and Unionist predecessors. The Crimean War had taught British governments the folly of becoming involved in continental quarrels, but the South African War had shown the converse danger of having no friends or allies in time of trial. Not only had Germany and the Netherlands expressed vociferous sympathy with the Boers and condemnation of Britain's policy in South Africa, but there had also been similar sentiments in France and Belgium, while volunteers from Scandinavia had actually fought in Kruger's commandos.

The strength of the Royal Navy had deterred Germany and any other Pro-Boer power from sending aid to Kruger but a different factor had prevented Russia from taking advantage of Britain's preoccupation in South Africa to make the long-feared move against India and to threaten the British position in the Far East. This factor, the growing rivalry between Russia and Japan, persuaded Lord

Lansdowne, at the Foreign Office, that an alliance with Japan would ease some of Britain's difficulties. On 30 January 1902 the two governments agreed that if either country found itself at war with a third power, the other would remain neutral. If either country were at war with two other powers, the other would support its ally. For Japan the new alliance ensured that if she quarrelled with Russia, Britain would deter Russia's ally, France, from entering the war and lending naval support against Japan. For Britain the alliance reduced the possibility of a Japanese attack on Australia, while enabling her to withdraw naval units from the Pacific to reinforce the Home and Mediterranean fleets. The alliance was the signal for a surge of pro-Japanese sentiment in Britain. It became customary to think of the Japanese as a sturdy and rugged island race, depending on the sea for their survival, clever, industrious and loyal, much, indeed, like the British themselves.

Meanwhile France and Russia had in 1894 concluded a secret treaty which became an open alliance the following year. The alliance was bizarre in that it linked the thirty-year-old bourgeois republic with the centuries-old autocracy but it was the logical outcome of their common distrust of Germany, of Russia's ambitions in the Balkans, where France had few interests, and of France's ambitions in Africa, where Russia had none. It is recorded that when the French fleet paid a courtesy visit to the Russian naval base at Kronstadt in 1891, the Tsar Alexander III winced as the bands broke into the stirring revolutionary strains of the *Marseillaise*, but he found more acceptable the large French loans which were helping to finance the Russian industrial revolution.

The prospect of a war in the Far East between Russia and Japan left France in a dangerous predicament, for she might find herself, as Russia's ally, embroiled in a conflict with Japan's ally, Britain, in Europe and Africa. The obvious solution was to seek an understanding, if not an alliance, with Britain. King Edward VII is popularly credited with engineering this Anglo-French understanding, the *Entente Cordiale*, and the title of 'the Peacemaker' was certainly bestowed upon him with that achievement in mind. In fact the initiative came from the French and the King's contribution was simply to smooth the way for it, notably during his state visit to Paris in May 1903. As, accompanied by President Loubet, he drove along the Champs Elysées to the British Embassy, the King was greeted coolly by the crowds and there were occasional shouts of

'Vivent les Boers!' But his warmth and friendliness, his careful courtesy and his obvious delight in meeting old friends at the Théâtre Français and the Longchamps race-course quickly won the hearts of the Parisians, so that the visit was transformed into a glittering success. A year later, after the French president had paid a return visit to London, the two governments finally reached agreement on almost all the matters that divided them. Britain acknowledged France as the dominant power in Morocco while France recognised that Egypt was a British protectorate in all but name. There were also arrangements concerning French fishing rights in Newfoundland waters, frontiers in West Africa, the condominium of the New Hebrides, spheres of influence in Siam and other minor matters.

The third stage in Britain's foreign policy during the Edwardian period came in 1907 when, as a logical consequence of the *Entente Cordiale* with France, an understanding was reached with Russia. By this time Campbell-Bannerman was prime minister and Sir Edward Grey had replaced Lord Lansdowne at the Foreign Office. The Anglo-Russian convention, signed on 31 August 1907, was unpopular among British radicals, for whom Tsarist Russia was the epitome of autocracy, bolstered by a ruthless police, a corrupt bureaucracy and a sycophantic church. But Grey saw the convention as a safeguard for India and as a final deterrent to German belligerence.

Not unnaturally, Germany saw the Triple Entente in a different light. On her eastern Frontiers was the Russian Colossus, recovering from the disastrous defeat at the hands of the Japanese and from the effects of the abortive 1905 revolution, and likely to become militarily more powerful as French capital steadily developed Russian industrial potential. On Germany's western frontier was France, the old enemy, eager for revenge for her defeat in 1871 and intent on the recovery of the lost provinces of Alsace and Lorraine, perhaps even on setting her republican tricolour once again along the Rhine. Across the North Sea, and with her warships in every ocean of the world, was Great Britain, determined to hold her Empire inviolate and so to deny Germany her rightful 'place in the sun'. To counter these three giants, Germany had two uncertain allies, the ramshackle Austro-Hungarian Empire, likely to disintegrate in the stress of war, and Italy, poor and backward, hostile to Austria-Hungary and likely to sell her support to the highest bidder.

Three times between 1905 and 1911 international crises threatened to bring the two power blocs into conflict with each other. The first, over French control of Morocco, was provoked when the Kaiser visited Tangier in his steam-yacht *Hohenzollern* and encouraged the Sultan of Morocco to resist further French demands. The United States intervened to advise an international conference at Algeciras, where the representatives of thirteen interested powers virtually conceded France's claims. The next came in 1908 in the Balkans, when Austria-Hungary formally annexed the Turkish Slav provinces of Bosnia and Herzegovina, which she had been occupying for thirty years. Serbia, enraged at the annexation, which cut her off from the Adriatic sea-board, could not prevent it because Russia, although posing as the protector of the Balkan Slavs, was unwilling to press her support of Serbia to the point of war against Austria-Hungary and Germany. The third crisis came again in Morocco in 1911, when the Kaiser despatched a warship, the *Panther*, to 'protect German interests' in Agadir when the French occupied Fez, the most important city in Morocco. The possibility that Germany might try to establish a naval base at Agadir, and thus to threaten British sea routes to South America and southern Africa, prompted Lloyd George to express the British government's attitude in a speech at a bankers' dinner at the Mansion House on 21 July 1911. He emphasised the importance to Britain of her overseas trade and of world peace to enable her to conduct it.

'But', he continued, 'if a situation were to be forced upon us in which peace could only be preserved by the surrender of the great and beneficient position Britain has won by centuries of heroism and achievement, by allowing Britain to be treated, where her interests were vitally affected, as if she were of no account in the Cabinet of Nations, then I say emphatically that peace at that price would be a humiliation intolerable for a great country like ours to endure.'

The Kaiser fumed and blustered and complained but eventually climbed down. The French sweetened the pill by ceding to Germany some territory in their West African colony of the Congo.

The fourth international crisis led to war. When the Archduke Franz Ferdinand was assassinated, Austria-Hungary, determined not to lose her hold over the Slav minorities who chafed under her rule, seized upon the event as an excuse to crush Serbia, the nursery of Slav nationalism. Russia, having long claimed the right to protect the Slavs in the Balkans, saw an opportunity to counter Austro-Hungarian influence in south-eastern Europe and perhaps also to destroy the Ottoman Empire, so that she might seize control of the Bosphorus

and the Dardanelles, the Straits through which Russian shipping had
-to pass to reach the warm seas of the world.

Germany appealed to Russia not to enter the conflict between
Austria-Hungary and Serbia but the Russian reply was to order
mobilisation. This placed Germany in a dilemma. She could not rely
on French neutrality and if she waited until Russian mobilisation was
complete, she faced the prospect of war on two fronts. Her only
alternatives were to stand aside and see her ally, Austria-Hungary,
defeated and dismembered by Russia and Serbia, or to strike first at
France and then at Russia to gain a quick victory. In order to defeat
France within the few weeks before Russia could attack in the East,
the German High Command believed that a passage for the German
armies through Belgium was essential. If Belgium agreed to this
course, her integrity would be respected after hostilities were ended.
If not, she must accept the consequences, invasion and occupation.

In Britain the Cabinet was divided. Lloyd George; John Burns,
the President of the Board of Trade; and Lord Morley, Lord President
of the Council, opposed intervention in what they considered to be a
European quarrel. Their views were widely shared. On 1 August,
under the headline 'Why we must not Fight', the Liberal *Daily News*
declared that 'if we crush Germany in the dust and make Russia the
dictator of Europe and Asia, it will be the greatest disaster that has
ever befallen western culture and civilisation'. For Lloyd George, the
argument was settled by the German ultimatum to Belgium. As an
independent kingdom Belgium was barely eighty years old but its
neutrality had been guaranteed by the five Great Powers in a treaty
signed in London in 1839. This was the treaty which Bethmann-
Hollweg, the German Imperial Chancellor, scornfully described to
the British ambassador in Berlin as 'a scrap of paper'. Morley and
Burns remained adamantly opposed to intervention, the former
because he abhorred the prospect of enhancing Russian hegemony in
the Balkans and French power in Africa, and the latter because he
abhorred the whole prospect of war. They found support among the
leaders of the Labour Party. During the afternoon of Sunday, 2
August, a large anti-war demonstration was staged in Trafalgar
Square, at which Keir Hardie and R. B. Cunninghame Graham were
among the speakers. 'Do not,' said Cunninghame Graham, 'do not
let us commit this crime or be parties to the misery of millions who
have never done us harm!'

The following afternoon, 3 August 1914, Sir Edward Grey put the government's case in a rambling, repetitive speech to the House of Commons. He recalled Britain's unequivocal guarantee of the independence of Belgium and quoted the appeal King Albert of the Belgians had made to King George V for help in preserving the integrity of his country. For the Opposition, Bonar Law pledged the support of his party for whatever steps the government might think necessary for the honour and security of the country. John Redmond spoke of Ireland's determination to sink her differences and to participate in the defence of the United Kingdom. Then Ramsay MacDonald rose. Of Sir Edward Grey's speech he said: 'I think he is wrong. I think the government which he represents and for which he speaks is wrong. I think the verdict of history will be that they are wrong. We shall see.'

MacDonald went on to voice his doubts about the proposed policy. If the country's safety or its honour were at stake, he promised, the Labour Members would offer their support and even their lives to preserve it. 'But what', he asked, 'is the use of talking about coming to the aid of Belgium when, as a matter of fact, you are engaging in a whole European war which is not going to leave the map of Europe in the position it is in now?' Britain, he warned, was entering the conflict without knowing where it would lead. So far as Labour Members were concerned, he concluded: 'Whatever may be said about us, whatever attacks may be made upon us, we will take the action that we will take, of saying that this country ought to have remained neutral, because in the deepest parts of our hearts we believe that that was right, and that alone was consistent with the honour of the country and the traditions of the party now in office.'

Two days later the executive committee of the Labour Party met in the House of Commons and agreed, in effect, to support the government's war policy. Ramsay MacDonald thereupon resigned the party leadership and, with Keir Hardie and a few of the Independent Labour Party members, faced the hostility, ostracism and physical violence which objectors to the war were to suffer for the next five years.

Britain thus sent her sons to war in fulfilment of a seventy-five-year-old treaty. France marched for a very different reason, to break another treaty by liberating the occupied provinces of Alsace and Lorraine. Russia cared little for treaties or the integrity of small nations, as her oppression of Finland, Poland, Estonia, Latvia, Lithuania and the Ukraine had long borne witness. Her purpose was to dominate the Balkans and to secure unhindered passage for her ships from the Black Sea to the Mediterranean. Germany fought to break the circle of steel which she believed to threaten her and to obtain a fairer share of the African and Asian colonies. Austria-Hungary fought for survival as a Great Power, and if the price was to be the destruction of Serbia and the oppression of Czechs, Slovaks, Poles, Croats and a dozen other minorities, that price must be paid. These aims were logical enough, even in some respects desirable, but few were entirely honourable. Their cost, ten million lives and untold human misery, followed by years of poverty and finally a Second World War, seems in retrospect to have been excessive.

The day after Ramsay MacDonald's speech in the Commons, the Territorials in his home town of Lossiemouth received their orders to muster that evening in the Drill Hall, in Cooper Park, Elgin. The county of Moray was able to provide a full Territorial battalion of the Seaforth Highlanders. The next day the Elgin company paraded at seven o'clock for medical inspection and was then joined by the companies from neighbouring Garmouth and Fochabers. Later in the day pipers led the Territorials through crowded streets to the Highland Railway station, whence they left by train for 'an unknown destination'. Other troops were also on the move. Three battalions of Regulars who had been training in camp at Blair Atholl were ordered to their war depots, the Cameron Highlanders to Edinburgh Castle, the Cameronians to Glasgow, and the Argyll and Sutherland Highlanders to Fort George. All over Scotland men were on their way to war.

The Scotland they left behind them was not one land, but two. Across the Lowlands stretched a belt of busy industrial towns whose people were in many ways closer akin to the Anglo-Saxons of the south than to their own Celtic compatriots, the Highlanders of the north and west. The dichotomy between Highlands and Lowlands was parallelled by the disparity between rich and poor but these inequalities were slowly diminishing. There were many reasons for this. Among them may be instanced the spread of popular education, the development of trade unionism, especially among the unskilled, the increasing mobility provided by new modes of transport, and a growing distaste for the extravagance in high society. The Liberal government's social and economic legislation reflected the changing mood which characterised Edwardian Scotland. After centuries of division, Scotsmen were again forging for themselves a single nation.

Bibliography

There is much in print about England and Ireland during the Edwardian period but little directly concerned with Edwardian Scotland. Of the general histories, the most useful have been:

Scotland from 1603 to the Present Day by George S. Pryde (Thomas Nelson and Sons Ltd., 1962)

Scottish Social Welfare, 1864–1914, by Thomas Ferguson (E. and S. Livingstone Ltd., 1958)

The following have also been helpful:

Memories and Reflections, 1852–1927, by the Earl of Oxford and Asquith (Little, Brown and Co., Boston, 1928)

The Autobiography of Margot Asquith (Thornton Butterworth Ltd., 1920)

General Wauchope by William Baird (Oliphant, Anderson and Ferrier, 1900)

History of the War by John Buchan (Thomas Nelson and Sons, Ltd., 1914–1919)

Arthur James Balfour by Blanche E. C. Dugdale (Hutchinson and Co., 1939)

Twenty-Five Years, 1892–1916 by Viscount Grey of Fallodon (Hodder and Stoughton, 1925)

Richard Burdon Haldane: An Autobiography (Doubleday, Doran and Co., New York, 1929)

J. Ramsay MacDonald by Mary Agnes Hamilton (Jonathan Cape Ltd., 1929)

Oscar Slater: the Great Suspect by Peter Hunt (Carroll and Nicholson, 1951)

An Edwardian Youth by L. E. Jones (Macmillan and Co., 1956)

Barrack-Room Ballads and Other Verses by Rudyard Kipling (Methuen and Co., 1892)

The Days I Knew by Lillie Langtry (Hutchinson and Co., 1922)

Roamin' in the Gloamin' by Sir Harry Lauder (Hutchinson and Co., 1922)

Sir Henry Campbell-Bannerman by T. P. O'Connor, M.P. (Hodder and Stoughton, 1908)

Tempestuous Journey: Lloyd George, his Life and Times by Frank Owen (Hutchinson and Co., 1954)

King Edward VII as a Sportsman by Alfred E. T. Watson (Longmans, Green and Co., 1911)

The Outline of History by H. G. Wells (Cassell and Co., 1920)

The Life and Letters of Lord Wester Wemyss by Lady Wester Wemyss (Eyre and Spottiswoode, 1935)

Thorough Guide Series: Scotland by M. J. B. Baddeley (Dulau and Co., 1901, and Thomas Nelson and Co., 1915)

Black's Shilling Guide to Scotland by Adam and Charles Black, 1906

Daily Mail Year Book for 1911
Who's Who, 1910
British Political Facts, 1900–1960 by David Butler and Jennie Freeman (Macmillan and
    Co., 1963)

The main contemporary sources which have been used are acknowledged in
the text. Charles Shearer, Esq., J.P., has kindly permitted the use of unpublished
papers of his grandfather, Charles Innes Shearer, lately Provost of Buckie.

Acknowledgement is also due to the Editors of the following newspapers
from which quotations have been made:

Aberdeen Free Press	*Daily Express*
Elgin Courant and Courier	the *glasgow Herald*
Illustrated London News	*News of the World*
the *Northern Scot*	the *Observer*
the *Perthshire Courier*	*The Times*

The Edwardian picture postcards, from the author's collection, are reproduced with acknowledgement to their artists and publishers. Other illustrations
are by courtesy of:

the National Motor Museum, the South African Information Service, and
Messrs. Robson Lowe Ltd.

Index